ECONOMICS *and* THE COMMON LAW

CASES AND ANALYSIS

Allan C. DeSerpa
Arizona State University

THOMSON
SOUTH-WESTERN

Australia · Canada · Mexico · Singapore · Spain · United Kingdom · United States

THOMSON
SOUTH-WESTERN

Economics and the Common Law: Cases and Analysis

Allan C. DeSerpa

VP/Editorial Director:
Jack W. Calhoun

VP/Editor-in-Chief:
Dave Shaut

Executive Editor:
Peter Adams

Developmental Editor:
Sarah K. Dorger

Sr. Marketing Manager:
Jennifer Garamy

Production Editor:
Cliff Kallemeyn

Sr. Technology Project Manager:
Peggy Buskey

Media Editor:
Pam Wallace

Sr. Manufacturing Coordinator:
Sandee Milewski

Art Director:
Mike Stratton

Production House:
Litten Editing and Production, Inc.

Compositor:
Cadmus Communications

Printer:
Malloy Lithographing
Ann Arbor, MI

Printed in the United States of America

1 2 3 4 5 07 06 05 04

ISBN: 0-324-28977-4

Library of Congress Control Number: 2004113659

For more information contact South-Western, 5191 Natorp Boulevard, Mason, Ohio 45040.
Or you can visit our Internet site at: http://www.swlearning.com.

DEDICATION

Luke Allan Rounds

(June 28, 2004)

I wish you a long, joyful, and peaceful life, filled with knowledge, love, and a spirit of adventure.

BRIEF CONTENTS

CONTENTS

PREFACE

The publication of this book coincides with my 25th anniversary of teaching undergraduate economic analysis of law. Like many of my counterparts at other universities, I have no formal training in the law or a specialty field in law and economics. My interest in the economics of law continues to evolve from a general fascination with applied price theory and a particular interest in problems of externality, public goods, and the Coase theorem. At some risk of overgeneralization, I suggest that we economists invariably begin to teach with the theoretical and then proceed to application as an afterthought. Our students are conditioned to pick up their pens or pencils only when we put the graph on the board. In offering this book of cases, I am not advocating a de-emphasis of theory. Quite the contrary, I believe that fundamental theory and abstract modeling merits more attention than it currently receives.

The book revolves around 45 cases that have been carefully selected to meet three criteria: (1) to be an interesting story, (2) to cover important economic themes, and (3) to have social and/or historical significance. The story grabs student attention, the economic themes link sometimes highly abstract theory with reality, and the social significance enhances the general education experience. As much as possible, the background material for each case is designed to provide some general educational benefits in addition to laying the foundation for the case itself. *Transatlantic v. United States* (Chapter 8) centers upon the 1956 Suez Crisis, prefaced by a brief history of the canal back to King Darius I. *Hymowitz v. Eli Lilly* (Chapter 10) chronicles the economic saga of a miracle drug (diethylstilbestrol) with catastrophic side effects. *Union Oil v. Oppen* (Chapter 11) focuses on the Santa Barbara oil spill that brought environmental issues to social consciousness. Almost every case provides useful tidbits on a wide array of topics that includes whaling, coal mining, bald eagles, cedar rust, landmarks, raisins, sunflower seeds, railroad sparks, salmonella, perfume, and cigarettes. This material provides both useful paradigms for economic principles and diversions from the analytical rigor.

The overriding purpose of this text is to explore the intimate connections between economic theory and the law. More specifically, economic theory is used to explain why the common law has evolved as it has and to provide an intellectual basis for the actual outcomes of the cases. The links between microeconomics and case law can be established only through close attention to detail, with regard both to abstract theoretical logic and to factual circumstances. Economic logic is critical to interpreting and analyzing the facts, but it is just as important that the facts impart substance to the logic. In offering this selection of cases, I seek to fill a significant gap between traditional textbooks and casebooks. Textbooks (both theoretical and applied) tend to mention cases in passing, at best offering summaries of stylized facts. Casebooks typically refer to theoretical concepts without developing them in depth or detail.

The unique feature of this book is that the link between theory and reality is unrelenting. Each chapter provides a theoretical discussion of a specific economic theme (e.g., property rights, zoning, nuisance externality, public goods) or legal theme with strong economic overtones (e.g., contract formation, contract performance, penalties for breach, tort liability rules, product liability). The relevant theory is developed in the introduction and the individual cases are developed in a way that emphasizes how the subtleties of the theory connect with key facts of the case. The introductions provide reasonably self-contained presentations of important economic models and are intended to help instructors who want to integrate rigorous theory into the course without having to search for and package a cumbersome array of supplements. A major benefit to students is that the presentation of the pure theory is developed in the context of legal problems. Case summaries typically provide some background circumstances that led to the legal problem, along with key facts and the court opinion. A point-by-point analysis follows the case to make the theoretical connections with precision and detail. The point-by-point analysis is designed primarily to provide focus for class discussion or student research.

Though I am not shy about asserting my analytical conclusions, I try to avoid being dogmatic about them. In spite of my attempts to be ideologically neutral, there is a slight bias in the presentation. Much of modern law and economics is about the so-called efficiency hypothesis, which I present and develop in Chapter 1. Whether the law does or does not evolve toward efficiency is not something that can be expressed as pure truth. The question, "Is the law efficient?" is not amenable to a "yes" or "no" answer, but court opinions can be evaluated in terms of whether, by means of the precedents that they establish, they encourage or discourage socially constructive behavior. Largely for pedagogical purposes, my tendency is to overstate the argument in favor of efficiency. Students are encouraged to think deeply into the long-run effects of law upon behavior and to inquire as to why the law *is* efficient. If they still conclude that the law is *inefficient*, so be it.

For the undergraduate who plans to attend law school, the approach of this book provides a means of understanding the underlying economic issues present in many legal cases. It is designed to explain and use microeconomic theory to analyze the law in a way that is accessible to noneconomics majors. The approach emphasizes not the arcane properties of the models, but their direct relevance to real problems, and it conditions students to look for economic principles as they sort through the legal concepts and complex factual detail. While the material will (I hope) speak for itself, I will briefly explain how it has been developed and why it has proven to be successful.

I began teaching the law and economics course to undergraduates at Arizona State University in the spring semester of 1978. In the early years (1978–88), the course was popular because the subject matter was so interesting, but students had to struggle with excerpts of books and professional journal articles. I had virtually no background in case law, and economic theorists paid scant attention to it. Later, from 1988 to 1998, a few good texts had appeared—with some emphasis on case law, but still with major focus on theory. As noted above, that is the "economics way," and my curriculum was strongly influenced by my research activity in the theory of externality, public goods, and historical issues pertaining to Pigouvian economics and Coase's criticisms of it. Coase strongly advocates case analysis in economic research, and I began to integrate a substantial number of cases into the course.

At the time, I was fortunate to have Eva Shine (a third-year law student pursuing a joint degree in law and economics) doing an independent study course with me. As part of the project, Eva audited the undergraduate course and provided me with briefs (half-page or less) of cases that were both interesting and relevant. What I thought was that economics majors could read the briefs, "see" the economic models that were buried in the circumstances of the cases, and analyze them without having to sort through lengthy court opinions. To my dismay, students simply could not make what I believed to be simple connections between economic models and the underlying facts of the cases. Herein lies the crux of the matter, what distinguishes the "economics approach" to law from all other approaches. Connections between the models and the underlying facts of the cases are obvious to those of us who have spent a decade (or two or three) teaching and writing about applied price theory. Those connections are obvious *to us* because we are trained to reduce factual detail to *abstractions* that capture essential elements of a problem or situation. In the world of abstract modeling, the essential elements (see Chapter 4) of *Hadacheck v. Sebastian* (dust from the manufacture of bricks) are "identical to" those of *Spur v. Del Webb* (odor from cattle feed lot). That initial recognition of similarity of circumstances is generally not difficult, but the importance of the similarities needs development and reinforcement. Economic models provide the development and reinforcement, but that merely lays the foundation for the actual economic analysis of a case. The easiest cases are those whose circumstances fit the underlying models very closely. Beyond that comfort zone, the main difficulties lie in pinpointing *important conceptual differences* between the facts of actual cases and the models used to represent them. This is where the real learning experience takes place, and this is what had been missing from my courses.

The fact that it took the better part of 20 years for me to recognize this deficiency explains why I am a teacher instead of a practitioner. The good news is that I have (or at least think I have) blundered upon something important about connecting law and economics. My students' inability to make theoretical connections produced an amazing side effect—they turned to reading the actual court opinions! When they began to uncover the subtle details, I began studying the opinions along with them. We uncovered a number of what I now call "twins"—cases with divergent outcomes despite virtually identical facts. These cases provide the "laboratory experiments" that are so often missing in economics, and we would use economic theory to explain the divergent outcomes. As I began to compile more case material, enrollment grew from about 30 students per semester to current levels of over 60, with some turned away for lack of capacity. This casebook is the fruit of my experience with these students, and most of the material has survived five or six years of classroom application.

A significant number of students who take this course apply it directly and immediately. Many of the very fine honors theses that I mentor have their roots in this course. Some of them find employment with consulting firms. Many of these firms are directly involved with litigation consulting, but those with a more general clientele have a strong appreciation for the ability to relate abstract thought to practical problems. Those who attend law school do very well. I regularly receive comments from students about how helpful my course was in preparing them for law school. They invariably mention two factors: improvement of thought processes and exposure to cases that get covered in their first-year courses.

Writing a book is an economic undertaking, fraught with scarcity, choice, and compromise. Perhaps the most important trade-off was between developing the substance of the economic models and maintaining the flow of the overriding messages. Emphasizing the theoretical detail detracts from the essential purpose of connecting stories and models. That detail can be reinforced with handouts, supplementary readings, and class discussions.

SUPPLEMENTAL MATERIALS

PowerPoint Slides

I have created PowerPoint slides that can be requested through your local South-Western sales representative (locate your rep at http://www.swlearning.com).

The Economics Web Site

The South-Western/Thomson Learning Economics Web site (http://economics.swlearning.com) includes free access to Newsedge, which culls and organizes the most recent news and economic information. The Economics Web site also provides links to resources and information useful to instructors and students.

The e-con @pps Web Site

The purchase of this new textbook* includes access to South-Western's Economic Applications (e-con @pps) Web site (http://econapps.swlearning.com). The e-con @pps Web site includes a suite of regularly updated Web features for economics students and instructors: EconDebate Online, EconNews Online, EconData Online, and EconLinks Online. These resources can help students to deepen their understanding of economic concepts by analyzing current news stories, policy debates, and economic data. They are also useful for instructors in developing assignments, case studies, and examples based on real-world issues.

- EconDebate Online provides current coverage of economics policy debates, including a primer on the issues, links to background information, and commentaries.
- EconNews Online summarizes recent economics news stories and offers questions for further discussion.
- EconData Online presents current and historical economic data with accompanying commentary, analysis, and exercises.
- EconLinks Online offers a navigation partner for exploring economics on the Web, with a list of key topic links.

The West Legal Studies Web Site

The West Legal Studies in Business Web site at http://www.westbuslaw.com provides case updates and a case search feature for instructors and students wanting additional examples of cases relevant to chapter topics.

* Students buying a used book can purchase access to the site at http://econapps.swlearning.com.

ACKNOWLEDGEMENTS

I am heavily indebted to my good friend, Jeanne Lucas, and to my loving wife, Sylvia, for reading and commenting on the "general interest" appeal of early drafts and final copy. Their eyes may have glazed on occasion, but their approval of the main course has been unwavering and remains sincerely appreciated. I am similarly grateful to Nils Frei, who pored over the manuscript with the metaphorical "fine-toothed comb," and to Susan Van Etten for her fine work in accessing and securing copyrights for the illustrations.

Much of what I have learned about law and economics has come from discussions with my colleagues. Roger Faith helped me to become a better economist and a better man. Roger was never too busy to listen, and we miss him more than words can convey. Thanks also to Todd Sandler, Ryan Amacher, Chuck Knoeber, Kent Hill, Nancy Roberts, Janet Smith, and Steve Happel.

I have benefited immeasurably from the commitment, dedication, and enthusiasm of the editors at South-Western Publishing. Peter Adams jump-started this project during a visit to my office and has provided unwavering encouragement. Sarah Dorger, my Developmental Editor, did all the work and gave me all the credit. Peter and Sarah are not just my business associates; they have adopted my dream and become my good friends.

I have also benefited from the many thoughtful comments and valuable insights provided by the reviewers of three iterations of the manuscript:

Richard Boylan, University of Alabama
Thomas Carroll, University of Nevada, Las Vegas
Henry Demmert, Santa Clara University
John Dobra, University of Nevada, Reno
David Friedman, Santa Clara University
Joseph Jadlow, Oklahoma State University
Peter Klein, University of Georgia
Lawrence Martin, Michigan State University
David B. Mustard, University of Georgia
Georgiy Nikitin, Boston University
Edward Sattler, Bradley University
John Sell, College of Wooster
Sarah Stafford, College of William and Mary
Charles W. Upton, Kent State University

They have tried to educate me about law, economics, and the juxtaposition of the two. To the extent that they have been only partially successful, I retain full responsibility for the errors and misconceptions that remain. In my defense, finding the "answers" is not an easy task.

Finally, we teachers often remark that we learn from our students. At times, we might question the sincerity of that sentiment, but this is not such a time. I have been blessed with so many inspiring students, whose respectful attention, thoughtful questions, insightful answers, passionate interest, sincere appreciation, fulfilling achievements, and thrilling successes have contributed invaluably to the quality of my work and to my motivation to undertake and to complete this project. Thank you all for your innumerable kindnesses:

Evie Boone
David Ahlstrom
Jamie Hogue
Carolynne Muller
Howard Andari
Eva Shine
Takis Makridis
Mary Echeverria
May Lu
Gina Moshiri
Rachel Rivera-Coe
Mary Wyman
Ryan Knapp
Amy Leung
Michael Komenda
Scott Ripley
Kelly Oetinger
James Ray
Jennifer Lehman
Natalie Hyser
Jason Barnes
Sarah Allgood
Sherri Colson
Eric Bryant
Dylan Cunningham
Jon-Paul Holyoak
Michael Coccaro
John Hamman
Jeanah Lacey
Joseph Echeverria
Jason Foster
Nils Frei
Russell Gold
Michael Griffith
D. J. Harper
Elise Moore
Scott Price
Blake Lindemann
Mikelle Fretz
Galen Satterlee
Alison Stover
Kristen Stephenson
Kara Rohe
Anna Torraca
Seth Miller
Matt Hagenbush
Jacqueline Manning
Tom Eckert
Sam Reeve
Joseph Ashby
Jonathan Beekman
Christine Graham
Aaron Cain
Rene Schmidt
Lia Adams
Jennifer Svrlinga
Brennan Platt
Christine Sindlinger
Jennifer Broatch
Patrick Harless
Johanna Wallenius
Jeff McLellan
Riikka Leskela
Gabe Quihuis
Michael Orcutt
Danielle Alley
Scott Sifferman
Brian Looker
Chris Schnucker
Tim Miller
Colin Raymond
Jim Rough
Dimitrios Gakidis
Christine Dumas
Karen Liu
Sherri Schilling
Laura Beth Barnes
Stephanie Vaughn
Caroline Polansky
Denis Mrkva
Kristen Mortensen
Andrew Broderick
Daniel King
Greg Rowland
Leslie Witting
Peter Mikulek
Scott Callard
Jennifer Heirman
Suzana Prole
Claire Fuller
Jake Gable
Elizabeth Thomas-Hoffman
Nicole Manos
Mark Hill
Dan Rollman
Stephen Gross
Pamela Harris
Nicole Zuckerman

You are why I love what I do.

Allan DeSerpa
Arizona State University

CHAPTER 1

INTRODUCTION

The study of law and economics is concerned with how legal rules, regulations, and precedents interact with the market mechanism to influence the allocation of resources. This book of cases narrows the scope to its primary focus of inquiry, the common law fields of property, contract, and tort. In relation to the cases that we are about to analyze, the primary objectives are to explain, to predict, and to evaluate. The unifying framework for moving toward these objectives is the efficiency hypothesis. In that context, the economic analysis of a case—or more specifically, a set of cases with similar facts and circumstances—promotes a clearer understanding of why the law has evolved as it has. Inasmuch as the common law is continually evolving through legal precedent, a thorough understanding of prior outcomes paves the way to predicting future outcomes and to evaluating their potential impact upon societal welfare.

In relation to the vast economic arena, in which millions of producers, workers, and consumers interact on a daily basis, it is nothing short of miraculous that more disputes do not arise. Of those that do arise, only a fraction actually go to court, and most of those that end up in court involve rules of law and procedure that might be regarded as routine. The ones that are difficult and controversial comprise the great economic margins, where old principles are applied and refined. As applied to common law cases, economic analysis is a systematic examination of the environment and motivations that preceded the dispute and the potential effects of alternative legal remedies. Familiar principles (at least to students of economics) of rationality, choice, prices, and incentive structure are brought to bear on a range of unusual, if not truly bizarre, problems. It is here that legal and economic analyses bear striking similarities:

1. Whereas legal scholars search for precedent, economic scholars search for models and economic principles, but both are seeking a broader framework or context in which to cast the unusual problem into more familiar light.

2. Just as the law expects all citizens to act reasonably and responsibly, economic theory expects all "agents" to act rationally, with rationality broadly defined in relation to the full expected consequences of their actions.

3. The strongest link between law and economics is an eye toward the future. The law places a strong emphasis upon the "message" that the judicial outcomes send out to others who might have to make decisions in analogous circumstances in the future. In economics, that message translates into **incentive structure**.

Collectively, the application of economic principles, the emphasis upon individual rationality, and the nexus between law and incentive structures point toward an economic hypothesis about the common law. Reduced to bare bones, the economic objective of the common law is to create a set of incentives that encourage efficient behavior.

The Efficiency Hypothesis

In a classic article dealing with risk and uncertainty, Milton Friedman and Leonard Savage[1] offered an analogy about behavioral hypotheses in economics. The analogy pertained to expert billiard players, who acted *as if* they knew the complicated mathematical formulas that give the optimal direction and speed of each shot. Few billiard players have mathematical expertise (the assumption is false), but elementary physics provides better predictions and explanations of billiard shots than other alternatives.

The analogy is useful in lending perspective to the use of abstract assumptions (e.g., perfectly competitive markets) and simple hypotheses (e.g., utility or profit maximization) in economic models. It is also useful for drawing a clear distinction between positive and normative economics. No one is suggesting that billiard players actually use the formulas or that billiard players could improve their performance by learning and applying them. Rather, the hypothesis abstracts from reality by design in order to generate accurate prediction and explanation of how things *are* (positive economics) independently of how they *should be* (normative economics).

These principles of economic method have direct application to the common law. Economic models describe abstract scenarios in which individual agents pursue their separate interests, in ways that create inefficient theoretical outcomes. In essence, the model predicts that corrective action is warranted and suggests alternative means of structuring the law to promote improvements. The broad hypothesis is that the common law evolves in directions that are consistent with an explicit objective of efficiency: the law operates "as if" its essential purpose were to promote efficiency. This hypothesis sits apart from any notion that real jurists actually pursue economic objectives or that they should do so. It is amenable to empirical test, although of a much less rigorous form than ordinarily found even in the social sciences.

The direct analysis of actual cases provides a number of ways of subjecting the efficiency hypothesis to empirical test. Three of these are particularly prominent. The most obvious is to compare the judicial outcome with the theoretical outcome that is predicted from the model. Many cases produce strong parallels with simple economic models. A second approach is to consider cases in which matters of equity or ethics clash with those of efficiency, with an eye toward which theory (justice or efficiency) is the better predictor. A third is to isolate pairs or multiples of highly similar cases with divergent outcomes, identifying subtle margins where key differences drive the decision. All of these procedures have their flaws. The fit between case and model is never perfect, and notions of efficiency become more subjective as cases become more complex. Perhaps most vexatious is the fact that so many cases involve subtle tradeoffs between economic margins that are not comparable or quantifiable.

The issues of whether the common law is or ought to be efficient and the testability of the efficiency hypothesis are too grandiose to be resolved in a book of cases. However, they lie at the fore of every case. Above all, cases drawn from the pages of the real world are a refreshing supplement to abstract theorizing. Concepts like externalities, public goods, property rights, liability rules, corrective taxation, exclusivity, contract curves, adverse selection, and moral hazard become more meaningful as they arise in the context of unusual and intriguing circumstances. The general approach will be to stretch the arguments in support of the efficiency hypothesis, without suppressing the occasionally compelling counter-arguments.

Before progressing to the actual presentation of cases, it is important to clarify the meaning of "economic efficiency" as it applies to the common law. Modern economic theory draws much of its substance from two great nineteenth-century protagonists: Leon Walras and Alfred Marshall. Walras developed the fundamental principles of general equilibrium theory, which emphasizes the interdependence of all markets and the existence of sets of prices that connect initial positions, allocations of resources, production plans, and distribution of final outputs. Walras's student, Vilfredo Pareto, established the great nexus between competitive equilibrium and pure efficiency—positions such that no individual's well-being can be improved without harming that of another. Marshall developed the tools of partial equilibrium theory, with emphasis on descriptive modeling for the purpose of shedding light upon practical problems. It was Marshall's student, A. C. Pigou, who developed the concept of **externality** in an effort to determine the appropriate role of government in a largely free enterprise economy.

General Equilibrium Theory

Before treading into this relatively difficult subject, it is important to acknowledge that many practitioners of the economic analysis of law have little or no use for **general equilibrium theory**. Indeed, what began as a highly abstract component of the marginal revolution of the 1870s has evolved into an apparent black hole of formidable mathematics.

In spite of its intimidating veneer, general equilibrium theory offers a wealth of insight about how laws and prices interact. Perhaps more importantly, it offers insight about economic thought with regard to these matters. William Jaffe, who translated Walras's magnum opus into English, had this to say about the *Elements of Pure Economics*:

> [T]his book . . . directly inspired Vilfredo Pareto, Enrico Barone, Knut Wicksell, Irving Fisher, Henry Ludwell Moore and Joseph Schumpeter during Walras's own lifetime. The number of economists and econometricians it inspired, directly or indirectly, since Walras's day is legion. . . . The fame of the *Elements* was not suddenly acquired, but has grown slowly, almost imperceptibly since . . . the early 1870s. The Walrasian theory did not make its appearance as a "flash of light illuminating a dark and confused landscape," but rather as a penetrating pencil of esoteric rays serviceable only to specialists to whom it gradually revealed a clear design of organic unity inherent in socio-economic phenomena.[2]

The simplest version of the general equilibrium (henceforth, GE) story involves no production. Rational consumers have endowments of goods and exchange them at prices that are set by an imaginary auctioneer in response to offers to buy and sell. The main event, or first theorem of GE theory, establishes the existence of a **Walrasian equilibrium**—a set of relative prices that induces simultaneous equality of demand and supply of all goods. Endowments are assigned arbitrarily, but all exchangeable commodities have definite owners. Even in this simplest of all economies, private property and the right to contract are fundamental. Along with the existence of market clearing prices, the second theorem establishes that final allocations are efficient. In particular, all consumers are better off (in the sense that they prefer their final choices to their initial positions) and, more importantly, further unambiguous improvements are not possible. In the vernacular, the Walrasian equilibrium allocation is also a **Pareto**

optimal allocation. This is the formal version and rigorous proof of Adam Smith's renowned "invisible hand."

It is important to dwell on the forces that actually drive this result. Superficially, the prices link endowments and preferences to final allocations, but there are three dominant forces at work. The first is that all consumers choose goods in response to prices over which they have no control, as individuals. The second is that the prices are formed as the collective result of individual choices. These two get the most attention in the theoretical literature, but the third is of prime importance for understanding the role of the law: the process embodies a very specific set of rules. The set of rules is usually stated as one: no exchanges take place at terms other than those set by equilibrium prices. For this terse rule to operate, potential traders submit binding offers in response to prices that are contingent upon acceptance of offers. When the auctioneer finds the appropriate set of prices, exchange occurs. There is no explicit role for government because nothing ever goes wrong, but nothing ever goes wrong because the auctioneer is a cop as well as an economic intermediary.

The substance of the story remains unchanged as firms and production possibilities are introduced into the model. A more generic term (agents) is substituted for consumers, agents are endowed with resources, and ultimately resources are exchanged for final goods. This procedure places a greater burden on the imagination, but a plausible story can be constructed. Would-be consumers offer inputs in exchange for a claim on final outputs. Firms offer claims on final outputs in return for the use of inputs. Once the correct set of prices is established, production occurs and firms deliver goods to the auctioneer, who distributes them in accordance with the specifications of the auction. As more complexity is introduced, the literal story becomes less believable, and the potential for mistakes expands exponentially.

When the price mechanism fails, the state intervenes; if the auctioneer and the government perform their jobs correctly, the system functions efficiently. The interaction of market and government yields a set of prices and taxes that determines—and is determined by—allocations of resources. That is, individual economic responses to prices and taxes add up to the choices made by an economic society, and those choices collectively determine the prices and taxes. In mathematical vernacular, prices (including taxes) and allocations map into each other. There is more than a grain of truth to be found in this scenario, and even the most adamant critics of general equilibrium theory are influenced by it.

The real world version of GE theory makes informal allowances for dynamics, uncertainty, and information flows. The simple tools of prices and taxes give way to complexities of contracts and regulations. It is particularly useful to think of taxes as metaphors for the regulation of economic problems that are too complex to be corrected by such a simple instrument as a tax. The dynamic version of the GE story is that people respond rationally to two broad sources of incentives: the market and the law. Reasonably well-informed agents know that prices and regulations continually adjust to economic conditions and, accordingly, their choices make allowances for expectations about the future. In particular, they expect market prices to adjust to changing conditions of supply and demand, and they expect the taxes to do the same. Movement of prices and taxes are predictable because they are responses to rules (mathematical conditions) that are embodied in the operation of the system. To pursue one hypothetical example: the discovery that some people like to smoke cigarettes encourages others to produce them; producers learn about the properties of cigarettes and plan to exploit the addictive properties, knowing that the government will ultimately tax and regulate them; to the extent that the plan embodies deception and intent to addict, producers understand the risk of potential lawsuits.

The principles governing the operation of the market are established in the "initial position," even though the actual prices are generated as history unfolds. The same is true of the common law. Prices (terms of exchange) and taxes (laws and regulations) develop interactively in response to changing conditions. In order for rational people to plan accordingly, the movement of the two must be essentially predictable. The mere fact that the common law is based on precedent and that precedents are set with an eye to the future underscores predictability. By design, GE theory is too general and abstract to provide tools for explaining the specifics of how the law adapts to economic conditions. It is just a sketchy plan for a system that operates efficiently with a minimum of governmental interference. However, a number of important inferences can be drawn about the application of the model in the context of a constitutional democracy:

> First, endowments include property, property rights, and a flexible set of rules. The government does not act like a monarch, establishing endowments arbitrarily. Rather, it acts as an extension of the collective preferences and morals of the economic agents. There is a huge difference between exogenous and arbitrary, just as between democratic and despotic.
>
> Second, the rules are flexible because the real version of the story transpires over space and time. Space encompasses differences in topography, geography, geology, etc. Time encompasses evolution of preferences and social mores, but most importantly, time gradually reveals information that was unknown in the initial position. It follows that (1) at any point in time, rules will vary according to key characteristics of property and circumstances and (2) over time, specific rules that apply to similar characteristics adapt to changes in preferences and information. At best, GE theory provides a consistent *plan* about movement of resources.
>
> Third, the government's corrective taxes and the auctioneer's prices are called out simultaneously in the initial position. The dynamic analogue is that, in principle, prices and taxes are anticipated. The market and the government operate cooperatively so that rational agents can form rational expectations. In reality, cooperation between market and regulatory forces is far from perfect; however, a noncooperative game between the auctioneer and the government is not what the framers of general equilibrium theory had in mind.
>
> Fourth, a corrective tax is a marginal adjustment that is not (expected to be) accompanied by radical redistributions of income or endowments. Although some groups are inevitably harmed by regulations, Pareto improvement remains a useful ideal. Regulations that have massive redistributive effects or force minorities to bear disproportionate burdens are contrary to the spirit of the model.

That final point merits strong emphasis. Constitutional protections of individual rights are designed to prevent governments from engaging in activities that are offensive to the GE blueprint. What is missing is additional detail describing the externalities and public goods that governments are expected, in the initial position, to regulate. The great limitation of general equilibrium theory is its inability to deal with breakdowns with any specificity. Despite modern controversies, partial equilibrium analysis is more insightful with regard to specific details, so long as the principles of GE are not abandoned.

Corrective Taxation

It bears repeating that the term "corrective tax" is not to be taken literally as a legal policy prescription. Just as the invisible hand of market arrangements is more complex than a set of price-quantity points in two-dimensional graphs, the visible hand of government rules and regulations is more complex than a simple tax (or subsidy). As it shall be employed in this book, the term is a metaphor for rules and regulations designed to correct free market outcomes. In most instances, the regulations will have been imposed or modified in response to an economic problem that may loosely be categorized as an externality.

The theoretical prescription of taxing externalities evolved from the work of British economist Arthur C. Pigou.[3] Although Pigou did propose corrective taxes and subsidies, his concerns were more broadly focused on what he called "extraordinary encouragements and restraints." The term "externality" was not in vogue until the late 1950s. In theory, taxes correct for false or missing prices. The most common textbook example is a tax to correct for the external cost of pollution. In practice, the law finds creative alternatives to the blunt instrument of taxation, but the outcomes frequently resemble what would result from taxation. The "before" and "after" positions are illustrated in Figure 1.1.

Under pristine conditions, a competitive equilibrium coincides with maximum economic surplus (gains from exchange), as measured by the area below the demand curve (D) and above the supply curve (S). In equilibrium (point A), the competitive price (P_1) induces a convergence of marginal benefits (accruing to buyers) and marginal cost (incurred by sellers). The output (Q_1) is ideal from the standpoint of those directly participating in the market. However, the presence of an externality implies a divergence between supply prices (marginal *private* cost) and marginal social cost (MSC). Whereas the theoretical supply curve is derived solely from the costs incurred by sellers, the MSC curve includes the additional costs incurred by others not directly involved in the market (e.g., the costs of pollution generated as a by-product of the production or consumption of the output). As a result, social surplus is maximized at an output of Q_2, not Q_1.

To correct for the misallocation of resources, the government imposes a **Pigouvian tax** equal to the divergence (BC) between private and social cost at the socially optimal output of Q_2. In relation to Q_1, this alternative position generates an increase of social surplus equal to the shaded welfare triangle AA′B. It is particularly important to note that the amount of the divergence (BC) in the neighborhood of the socially optimal output is different from what might exist (AA′) at output level Q_1. Indeed, even the appearance of an explicit movement from an inefficient unregulated position (A) to an efficient position (B) is misleading. In pure theory, no "A" is ever observed; rational agents go directly to "B" because the efficient tax is determined before the misallocations occur!

The economic appeal of corrective taxes is that they have the trappings of surrogate prices. To the extent that a government agency has knowledge of the external costs of pollution, a tax on pollution relays that information to producers and provides incentives

FIGURE 1.1 A Pigouvian tax (BC) internalizes a negative externality, causing industry output to be reduced from Q_1 to its efficient level of Q_2.

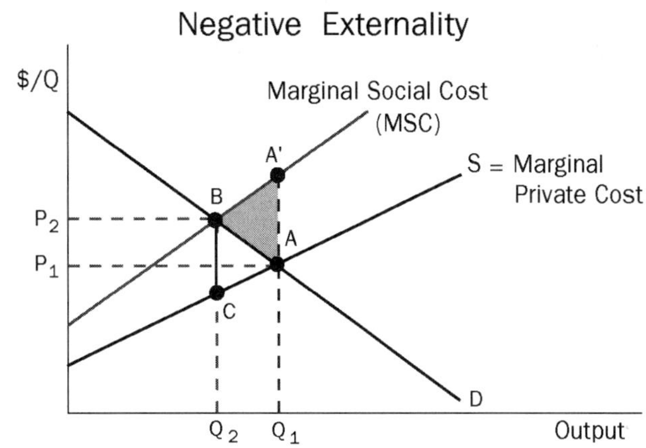

for the polluters to take those costs into consideration. In turn, the polluters rate to be better informed about the costs of reducing pollutants. In stark contrast with administered solutions, wherein pollution is banned or plant emissions are subject to rigid quotas, a tax tends to separate the inefficient polluters from the efficient polluters. Ironically, a tax on *output* would not have this effect—the correct focus of the tax would be the smoke, not the output. Unfortunately, "smoke" is not homogeneous, so the correct tax would have to distinguish between emission of sulphur, carbon monoxide, carbon dioxide, etc. Similar caveats would apply to where the emissions go and how long they remain in the atmosphere, with continual adjustments for changing economic conditions. Despite their theoretical appeal, corrective taxes tend to be administratively infeasible. Pigou himself suggested *subsidizing* the adoption of "smoke-preventing appliances!"

In short, taxes on outputs are very blunt instruments, but often they represent the only feasible way of taxing externalities. A notable exception was a tax imposed on CFCs in aerosol sprays, which ultimately led to the development of useful substitutes in both production and consumption. While taxes on alcoholic beverages and cigarettes are designed in theory to discourage undesirable side effects of drinking and smoking, they cannot distinguish between responsible and irresponsible use of the products themselves. One step removed from taxation of goods and services is the imposition of fines to enforce restrictions upon antisocial behavior. Fines for littering, speeding, and a host of misdemeanors resemble Pigouvian taxation in their effects of reducing the incidence of these activities. Similarly, the prospect of having to pay compensatory damages has important deterrent effects. Collectively, the system of taxes, fines, penalties, and liability rules comprises a significant part of the incentive structure that applies (at least in principle) to all individuals.

Arthur C. Pigou: *Individual suppliers consider the direct costs of production (payments for labor, capital, and materials), but not the external costs associated with side-effects like pollution. The divergence between private and social cost can be corrected by "extraordinary restraints" (e.g., a tax).*

Ronald H. Coase: *Social costs are reciprocal. If "transactions costs" are negligible, potential victims could bargain with culprits to achieve efficient results without government restraints. In fact, firms and markets exist to deal with complex problems like these.*

In order to understand the relevance of this model, it is important to view reality in relation to the two extremes. Externalities are regulated in a myriad of ways, depending on their specific characteristics and circumstances. Misallocations do occur, but rational agents generally have some expectation of regulation and take steps either to avoid being regulated or to minimize the adverse consequences of regulation. In contrast to the stark and highly "visible hand" of government, in which "wrongs" are corrected to "rights," an efficient system of laws maintains a steady course, with relatively infrequent and minor corrective action. Particularly in Chapters 2–4, we shall see that the law tends to reward (or, at least, not to penalize) those who "go directly to B" and to restrain overzealous governments from excessive regulation. These considerations, together with the difficulties inherent in the administration of regulations and corrective taxes, provide a useful transition to the major criticism of Pigouvian economics.

Property Rights, Transactions Costs, and Bargains

Traditional externality theory places exclusive emphasis upon one administrative form. The paradigms inevitably embody independent entities, with one person or group apparently imposing costs (or conferring benefits) upon another person or group. Whether the externality is one-on-one (rancher and farmer), one-upon-many (railway and farmers), or many-upon-many (polluters and pollutees), the source of the damage is unilateral. Indeed, there are physical and technological bases to draw such inferences. Crops do not crawl overland to expose themselves to the hooves of neighboring cattle, nor do they reach out and grab sparks from passing railroad trains. Wandering cattle are part of the technology of ranching and the flying sparks are part of the technology of railroad transportation, independently of the location of the crops.

The key word is "technology" and, in particular, the manner in which it is treated in economic theory. As a general practice, technology is presumed to have a character of its own, independently of institutions. For example, the production function—the relationship between the output of a particular commodity and the inputs used to produce it—would be the same in a communist or socialist economy as in a free enterprise system. Insofar as technology pertains to physics, engineering, and other purely scientific relationships, it is hard to quarrel with this view of the world. However, traditional economic theory adds one additional step—which can, in practice, turn out to be a gigantic leap.

That additional step is the presumption that "inputs" and "outputs" have well-defined market prices. It is largely in relation to this presumption that the sparks, the smoke, and the straying cattle become a special problem. These things become special problems because it is impossible in theory, and implausible in reality, for them to have market prices. That being the case, the only solution is for the government to create artificial tax prices.

Largely due to the work of Ronald Coase,[4] the traditional externality theory has softened considerably. Technology, as it is embodied in actual production relationships, adapts to property rights and, in turn, property rights evolve in subtle ways that tend to minimize "transactions costs." Indeed, Coase contended as early as 1937 that the primary reason for the existence of firms is to circumvent transactions costs, organizing production and distribution administratively where a price mechanism would be too cumbersome.[5] Essentially, without transactions costs, there would be little reason for firms to exist. It was not until 1960, however, that Coase applied his work to externality theory.

We begin with the observation that price (market) mechanism, although it functions very satisfactorily, does not work perfectly. In Coase's terms, the flaws in the price mechanism are the result of transactions costs. In other words: equilibrium prices are not automatically set by an auctioneer, exchanges do always take place at equilibrium prices, mistakes are made, etc. In fact, many transactions that are essentially shaped by market forces require the details to be worked out and specified in complex contractual terms. In context of that view of the market, the trials and tribulations of neighboring farmers and ranchers appear to be small.

The Coase Theorem

To drive home his point, Coase devised a story about cattle trampling neighboring wheat. If, he argued, we are to insist upon ignoring transactions costs in economic models, let us be consistent and ignore transactions costs between ranchers and farmers. Under that radical assumption, government intervention becomes unnecessary. In particular, a rule of liability (the most likely form of intervention) holding ranchers liable for damages would not be necessary to achieve efficient outcomes. The essence of the argument may be stated clearly in terms of Figure 1.2. Without transactions costs, technology alone determines obtainable combinations of wheat and cattle, for various combinations of inputs. Straying cattle is only one of a host of administrative variables that influence the tradeoff. Accordingly, the rancher and the farmer can always form a contract or make a bargain to get to a position that maximizes their combined profits.

That "bargain" between two independent firms generates the same set of decisions that would be implemented by a single integrated firm. Whether there are two firms or

FIGURE 1.2 Given any combination of resources, the efficiency frontier is the result of administrative choices implemented by the firm.

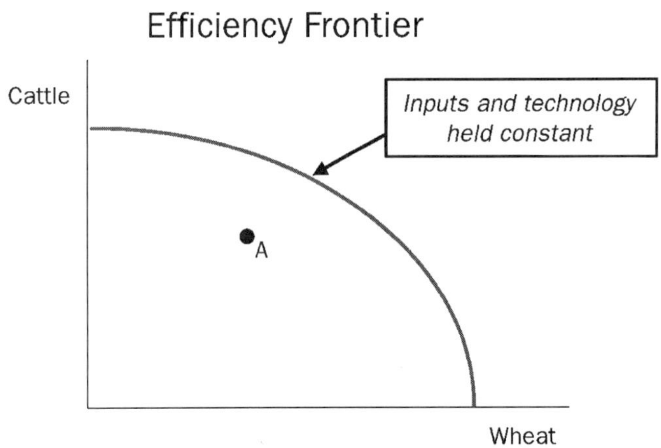

one firm is unimportant: firms are unnecessary if transactions costs are negligible! The end result of this line of reasoning has come to be known as the **Coase Theorem**, which may be loosely stated as follows: If property rights are clearly defined and transactions costs are negligible: (1) any initial definition of property rights leads to *an* efficient outcome; (2) ignoring wealth or income effects, any initial definition of rights leads to the *same* outcome. Part (1) is pretty straightforward. In simple terms, holding ranchers liable for damages internalizes the externality by forcing ranchers to act as though the costs imposed on farmers are their own. On the other hand, if ranchers are not liable for damages, the farmer can make a bargain with the rancher. Part (2) is more complex and more controversial. If economic activity commences before property rights are clearly defined, rights are clarified as economies develop. If the law has to take a position after both parties have incurred some initial investment, one party (or group) will gain at the expense of another. In context, holding ranchers liable for damages translates into distributional gains for farmers, and vice versa. That still would not affect the profit-maximizing outcomes unless the redistribution of wealth had an indirect effect upon prices.

Rather than exploring the more obscure controversies that have arisen in connection with the Coase Theorem, it will prove more productive to examine some of its implications for the economic analysis of law. By far the most important corollary is that, if transactions costs were literally negligible, there is little purpose in studying the connection between law and efficiency. Any set of laws would suffice. The converse is that the study of law and economics is inseparable from the study of transactions costs. Studying transactions costs requires a focus on a general set of things that have economic importance but are not readily quantifiable or amenable to mathematical models. The subject of when, where, and how far cattle stray into neighboring property is a perfect example, which underscores the beauty of Coase's paradigm. A clear definition of rights would involve addressing a multitude of contingencies, suggesting that rights are never fully defined and certainly not clearly specified before economic activity begins.

As we explore the connection between rights and efficiency, the ideas underlying the Coase Theorem provide a genuinely unique perspective. In relation to Figure 1.2, a position like point A would represent an inefficient outcome. The social cost could be measured in terms of foregone wheat and/or cattle, relative to production possibilities. However, there is nothing in the graph to suggest that ranchers are imposing costs upon farmers. Certainly, the independent farmer's cost schedules for wheat production would be less without the presence of the rancher—unless, of course, the law forces ranchers to compensate farmers for crop damage. In the latter case, the farmer is imposing costs upon the rancher. The correct interpretation is that neither firm is imposing costs upon the other; the costs are joint or reciprocal. The idea that social costs are reciprocal neutralizes the direction of causality. The resolution of disputes that arise in connection with property rights ceases to be a matter of distributive justice. Issues of liability cease to be matters of guilty culprits compensating passive victims.

If you are tempted to throw out all of Pigouvian externality theory, don't do it. The law of nuisance would tend to side with farmers because of the simple technology of ranching. Ranchers are in a better position to monitor the movement of cattle, and a system that required farmers to continually negotiate with ranchers would be absurd. Like Newtonian physics, Pigouvian economics tends to be accurate far more often than not. It will still prove helpful to think about tax prices and their effects upon incentives, even though using taxation as an administrative tool may not be the most effective choice.

Economic Theory and Method

Throughout this book, we will be employing a wide range of economic models and applying general principles of economic theory and method. Those models that get applied directly will be developed in some detail in the introduction to the individual chapters. For example, the models of common property resources and congestion externalities will be discussed in Chapter 3, the nuisance externality will be analyzed in Chapter 4, and the theory of public goods will precede the case analysis in Chapter 5. Similarly, some of the more stylized models that have evolved from economic analysis of specific legal problems will be developed in Chapters 7–12.

The purpose of all of these theoretical discussions is to make firm connections between theory and reality. Those of us who have spent half our lives teaching and writing about economic models tend to have little difficulty recognizing the principles when they manifest themselves in the real world. Everyone else needs to have the connections spelled out in more detail, with continual reminders. The plan of this book, which is to apply economic theory to case analysis, involves four essential steps:

1. Generalize from specific paradigms.
2. Identify theoretical problems and solutions.
3. Associate real stories with theoretical paradigms.
4. Compare actual outcomes with theoretical solutions.

For example, Coase's farmer and rancher provide the classic paradigm for a one-on-one externality, wherein negligible transactions costs beget efficient bargains when property rights are clear. In Chapter 2, we will see mining companies and homeowners treated as one-on-one externalities by the law. In Chapter 3, however, the same economic agents will fit an alternative paradigm in which mining companies collectively impact upon surface property owners.

Beyond the specific paradigms and models lies a wealth of analytical techniques that add up to partial equilibrium theory. Even a cursory development of these ideas lies outside the scope of a casebook in law and economics. Some liberties will be taken in applying certain general principles and concepts (e.g., risk preference, asymmetry of information, adverse selection, moral hazard, holdout problem, principal-agent problems, etc.) in context as they arise. A similar sort of benign neglect will be afforded to **cost-benefit analysis**. However, that pragmatic branch of economics will be neglected in its own section, largely because it can be an extremely important part of analyzing cases, particularly with reference to their efficiency implications.

Cost-Benefit Analysis

Cost-benefit analysis may be loosely defined as a systematic enumeration and evaluation of costs and benefits of nonmarket activities. Its application in economics dates back at least to the 1844 work of the French engineer, Jules Dupuit, who established the all-important link between subjective value and willingness to pay.[6] Cost-benefit analysis is commonly used by government agencies to assess the social value of public projects such as highways, dams, airports, and sports facilities. As applied to market activity, cost-benefit analysis may also be used to assess the extent of external costs and benefits—both in absolute terms and in relation to net gains accruing to buyers and sellers.

The usual purpose of cost-benefit analysis is to arrive at a "bottom line," to derive a monetary value as a means of assessing an overall net social benefit. Arriving at such a measure is exceedingly difficult and typically fraught with a host of arbitrary assumptions about subjective value, rates of use, viable alternatives, etc. In many aspects of law and economics, the tools of cost-benefit analysis are quite important. Evaluating the economic cost of personal injury or the impact of polluting factories, for example, is an essential part of a settlement.

However, there is a broader purpose of cost-benefit analysis, particularly as it applies to the economic analysis of law. That broader purpose is simply to understand and enumerate what the costs and benefits *are*, without dwelling on the numbers. If the impact of the law is to be evaluated, there is an informal economic accounting that will be very prominent in some cases and less prominent in others. A prime example may be found in the second chapter. In *Allard v. Andrus*, a Colorado district court was asked to rule on the constitutionality of a regulation prohibiting the sale of eagle feathers! The regulation was administered by the U.S. Department of Interior as part of a comprehensive federal legislation designed to save bald eagles from extinction. The very idea of searching for a monetary measure of the net benefits of this regulation is absurd, but principles of cost-benefit analysis provide important directions for productive thought.

For perspective, it is useful to think in terms of total benefits and costs. Saving the national bird from extinction must provide enormous public benefits, even if it involves very small benefits to each citizen. The losses from the commercial sale of the feathers lay mainly to those who owned and traded Native American artifacts. The ban entailed significant losses to a relatively small number of individuals. To say that one outweighs the other is an exercise in interpersonal comparison of utility, which has no scientific basis and reduces to matters of opinion. Nonetheless, a strong subjective argument can be made in favor of regulation, though not necessarily this particular regulation. The next step is to examine the relevant economic margins. The specific regulation was one component of a larger strategy. Without treading into the actual case material, the important questions relate to how the ban on commercial sale *adds to* the effectiveness of the regulation and how it *subtracts from* the property rights of the owners of the artifacts. These factors strike at the economic margin, but there is also a legal margin. The legal margin deals with the menu of the court's procedural alternatives, which might include striking down the regulation as unconstitutional, upholding the regulation but forcing the government to compensate the property owners for their losses, or upholding the regulation without any compensation to the property owners.

The compensation of property owners for economic losses sustained as a result of government regulations is a major theme underlying the next four chapters of this book. In light of the economic theory of cost-benefit analysis, that should be surprising—because the direct impact of compensating people for losses entails no net social gain or loss. Compensation is merely a transfer of money from government (taxpayers) to property owners. It follows that, if there is to be any economic rationale for awarding or denying compensation, that foundation lies in the indirect effects upon future behavior of the precedents established by the decision.

The following situations are examples of the implicit application of cost-benefit analysis by courts:

1. A city government seeks to condemn the homes of an entire ethnic community to provide land for an automobile plant. Constitutional protections require the city to pay "just compensation," but governments bear the additional burden of showing a **compelling** public purpose. In other words, before any formal analysis is applied to determining appropriate compensation, courts can block the entire process. The word "compelling" translates into sufficient public benefits that cannot be obtained by alternative means without incurring significantly higher costs. See *Poletown v. City of Detroit* in Chapter 2.

2. A cement factory emits smoke and noise pollution, disturbing a small number of property owners in close proximity to the factory. The court has the option of issuing a permanent injunction, essentially closing the plant unless its owners can negotiate with the neighboring property owners. The substance of the Coase Theorem suggests that the assignment of rights does not matter if transactions costs are negligible. To make an economically correct decision, the court must implicitly do *two* cost-benefit analyses. The primary one concerns whether the economic value of the plant outweighs the costs imposed upon its neighbors. If not, the injunction makes good sense; by imposing the efficient solution directly, potentially costly transactions are avoided. However, if the court judges the value of the plant to outweigh the environmental costs, the injunction risks an inefficient outcome (possibly with very high stakes). The second one concerns whether potential transactions costs might prevent a mutually beneficial bargain from transpiring. If not, the court

may go ahead with the injunction; if so, the injunction ensures an inefficient outcome. See *Boomer et al., v. Atlantic Cement* in Chapter 4.

3. A national drugstore chain signs a 30-year lease with a shopping center, with the stipulation that no competing drugstores occupy space in the same shopping center (a noncompetition clause). With 10 years remaining on the lease, the shopping center is threatened with a financially devastating vacancy. Accordingly, the owners of the shopping center attempt to fill the vacancy by entering into a lease agreement with a competing drugstore chain! At the same time, the owners admit to breach of contract, but ask the court to impose monetary damages. The owners of the (nonbreaching) drugstore chain ask for an injunction. The court can either do an explicit "cost analysis" to determine monetary damages or rely on the contracting parties to work out their own bargain. See *Walgreens v. Sara Creek Properties* in Chapter 8.

These three examples are representative of the kinds of subtle evaluations of economic costs and benefits that judges have to confront. Judges are reluctant to address the explicit numbers for the simple reason that they are arguably no more qualified than a jury to make such evaluations and very likely less qualified than the litigants. As a matter of principle, legal precedents tend to point toward delegating the task of evaluating costs and benefits to those in the best position to do the evaluating.

CHAPTER 2

PROPERTY RIGHTS

Private property is not an end in itself. Even as applied to hearth and home, private property rules derive their sanctity from two propositions. First and foremost, liberty *is* an end in itself. Second, liberty as applied to property combines with self-interest and rationality to yield a formula for success. I may not approve of the way that you run your household, but I am not harmed by your ineptitude. Private control of property enables the individual, who best knows his or her own tastes, to use the property in ways that maximize the value of the property to the one person who matters.

Particularly as it relates to the law, private "ownership" translates into a bundle of rights. The right to exclude (**exclusivity**) trespassers and thieves is the most fundamental attribute of private property. Without it, the connection between possession and value is disrupted, if not wholly severed. John Locke, the great natural law philosopher, conceded that the earth was the common property of mankind, but reasoned that the derivation of benefit from the common heritage required appropriation for individual use. Social rules affecting how and when individuals came to acquire property evolved along with the development of technology.

The right to sell or rent (**transferability**) is almost as fundamental. From an individual's perspective, part of maximizing value includes exchanging property for something of greater personal value. Those who would oppose private property on general principle find this principle particularly onerous because it goes hand in hand with the accumulation and concentration of wealth and power. However, the alternative would be to force property owners to abandon their land when they cease to be able to benefit from its use. The effect of such a rule would be to encourage initial owners to hold onto their land too long. From the perspective of society, allowing the sale of property enables it to gravitate toward its highest-valued use.

As applied to land, the connection between private property and liberty is visceral and emotional. However, the connection between private property and efficiency is more of a pragmatic issue—in J. S. Mills' terms, a "matter of convenience." It goes without saying that those who produce must have rights to the fruits of their endeavors; otherwise, the system is drained of incentives to produce. In the U.S. Constitution, property is not elevated to the status of inalienable right, except by inference as a component of the "pursuit of happiness." Accordingly, the extent of constitutional protection of property is a matter to be determined by law and circumstance. For example, it would be absurd to insist on private ownership of waterways or airways. The efficacy of a transport system relies on open access. Constitutional affirmation of private property is most prominent in the Fifth Amendment. Along with the protections against double jeopardy and self-incrimination, this amendment provides that "no person shall be deprived of life, liberty, or property without due process of law" and that property may not be "taken for public use without just compensation." The "due process" clause is repeated in the Fourteenth Amendment, which applies the same restriction to the state governments.

Ultimately, there are three important reasons not to insist on the universal application of exclusive and transferable property rights. One is that exclusivity may be inherently unproductive, as in the case of waterways or highways. Another is that they may be costly to enforce, as in the case of ocean fisheries. The third reason is a very broad one, involving externality. Promoting and enforcing the rights of one group may impinge upon the rights of others. Examples of competing groups abound: landlords and tenants, hunters and animal rights groups, industrialists and environmentalists.

The property issues involved in this chapter are not particularly complex, but they are fundamental to the creation, assignment, and transfer of property and of competing rights to the attributes of property. The first case addresses the initial assignment of ownership, how ownership rights affect productivity, and how the law might apply different principles depending upon economic circumstances. The next two deal with transfer of ownership. No sooner do we establish that voluntary sale of property encourages the transfer of property from lower to higher value than we find two ways to set aside the principle! In one case, the initial owner's right to sell eagle feathers is denied; in the other, owners are forced to sell their homes at a "fair market" price.

The forced sale of homes at a fair market price determined by the courts does have some economic justification. As addressed in the Fifth Amendment, it applies to the taking of private property for public use. There is, of course, a simple way to ensure just compensation when private property is taken for private use—allow the market to set the compensation by supply and demand. By implication, there must be some asymmetry (when public use is involved) to prevent the market from determining appropriate prices. The main asymmetry is that public use tends to require large amounts of contiguous land, the most obvious example being for the construction of a highway. Another is that governmental efforts to acquire land may not (by law) be conducted in secret.

Taken together, these factors tend to place governmental agencies at a strategic disadvantage when it comes to negotiating sales prices with each of a large number of individual property owners. In particular, each owner has incentive to "hold out" (that is, to delay accepting an offer until all other property owners have done so) in order to obtain a superior bargaining position over the government. The cumulative effect of this process would be to inflate prices above competitive (equilibrium) rates. Accordingly, the law of eminent domain exists as a measure to counteract what has come to be known as the **holdout problem**.

The kinds of rights that become subject to dispute fascinate the imagination, as does the mind of the law in addressing them. A central proposition of modern legal economics is that the common law evolves in the direction of efficiency. Like the efficiency of markets, the theoretical proposition is debatable and subject to a myriad of caveats. It is nonetheless very enlightening to analyze case law with this proposition in mind.

Thar' She Blows!

Ghen v. Rich
8 F. 159 (1881)

Simple Facts

In April of 1880, a whaling crew employed by Ghen shot and killed a whale. The whale then sank to the bottom of Massachusetts Bay, off the coast of Cape Cod. When the whale resurfaced three days later, it was discovered by Ellis, who subsequently sold it to Rich. Ghen sought damages for conversion, claiming that title to the whale is acquired when a hunter apprehends a beast. Rich countered that custom does not govern the acquisition of title.

Details

Archeological digs have uncovered evidence of primitive whaling in Japan as early as the second century, B.C. The practice began in Europe a millennium later, mainly in the Azores and Scandinavia, and sperm whaling found its way to colonial America in 1712. Long before the indiscriminate slaughter of the planet's largest mammal became politically and morally incorrect, the industry grappled with the technology of efficient killing.

ILLUSTRATION 2.1 Whaling crew in a small craft struggles to land a whale while the parent vessel hovers in the background.

ILLUSTRATION 2.2 Ghen shot and killed the whale near Provincetown. The whale resurfaced three days later on the beach in Brewster, 17 miles away.

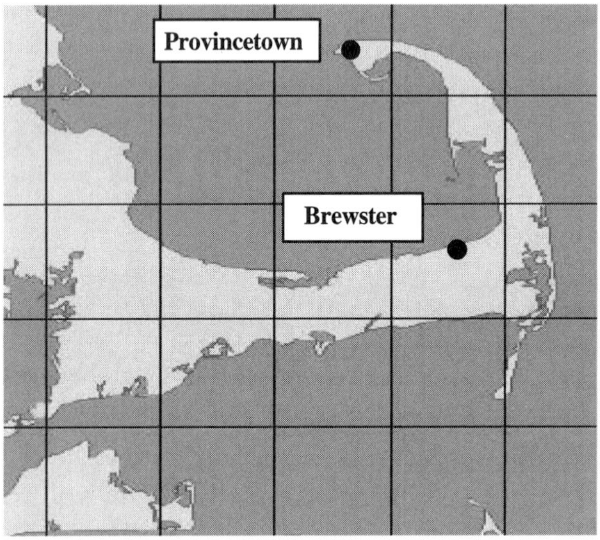

Harpoons date back to the thirteenth century, but someone's foot always got caught in the rope. More seriously, anyone who has read *Moby Dick* knows that harpoons do not kill whales, and the litany of complementary hardware might have made the Marquis de Sade a little queasy.

The problems inherent in capturing whales included penetrating tough blubber and getting close enough to effect a quick kill. Once a whale was harpooned, it would dive below the surface and sometimes carry the ship along with it. One of the more ingenious, and relatively less inhumane, devices was known as the bomb-lance. The bomb-lance was fired from a shoulder gun and, as the name implies, exploded upon impact. This method was more effective and less dangerous than harpoons. The primary disadvantage was that, if the kill was successful, the whale would immediately sink to the bottom of the sea. Although the whale would resurface in about three days, the device was not practical in the open sea.

The finback whale once frequented Massachusetts Bay in the early springtime. Whalers from Provincetown would pursue them from the shore, using bomb-lances. Recovery was a cooperative effort. When whales rose to the surface, some would be picked up by vessels and towed into Provincetown, others would float ashore at high tide, and a few would float into open seas, never to be recovered. Whaling was a capital-intensive venture that required considerable expertise, with exposure to risk and hardship. Each boat's crew had a peculiar mark on its lances that left an identifiable "brand" on the whale. When a whale was discovered on the beach, the finder would send word to Provincetown and receive a small fee from the owner.

On the morning of April 9, 1880, a crew employed by Ghen shot and killed a whale in Massachusetts Bay, near the tip of Cape Cod. Three days later, Ellis found the whale on the beach in Brewster, 17 miles from the spot where it had been shot. Bypassing custom, Ellis advertised the whale for sale at auction and sold it to Rich, who shipped off the blubber. While neither Ellis nor Rich knew the specific identity of the owner, both were familiar with the technology and therefore had the means of identification. Ghen learned of the finding, attempted unsuccessfully to claim the whale, and then sued Rich for unlawful conversion of his property.

Resolution of this dispute might appear to be easy. Numerous precedents supported the view that whales are the property of their captors, but "captor" usually implied something beyond mere killing. In one case, the words "anchored and left with marks of appropriation" were added. Another included "taken possession of by the boat" of the first taker. In *Bartlett* v. *Budd*,[1] the whale was anchored but set adrift. In returning the whale to the initial capturer, the court opined that:

> A whale, being *feroe naturoe* [untamed nature], does not become property until a firm possession has been established by the taker. But when such possession has become firm and complete, the right of property is clear, and has all the characteristics of property.[2]

If the court had woodenly adopted this rule, Ghen would not have acquired ownership merely by shooting the whale, despite clear evidence that he had killed the whale. To further complicate matters, other precedents acknowledged ownership even before the actual kill. Specifically, for whalers in the Arctic seas, custom assigned ownership on the basis of "first iron." The first harpoon to remain in the whale established ownership even if the crew lost hold of the harpoon. That custom was affirmed in the 1872 case of *Swift v. Gifford*,[3] in which two crews pursued the same whale. The whale was finally captured by the one that had not initially harpooned it. Apparently, a local court had sided with the "capturer," but Maritime law sided with the "harpooner," who eventually prevailed.

The unifying factor in all of the precedent cases was that local custom should determine the moment of appropriation. On the open seas, the first iron establishes ownership. In the present case, it was the bomb-lance. The moment Ghen's crew shot (and branded) the whale, Ghen owned it. The court awarded damages of $71.05 for lost profit plus interest.

Economic Analysis

1. Finding that "moment" of capture and/or possession is analogous to identifying a maximum point in economics. As applied to fugitive property, the pure economic problem is that of **technical efficiency**—organization of productive effort to maximize expected output for a given level of effort. Broadly defined, there are two primary tasks in hunting: search and pursuit. The immediate economic objective of search is discovery, and the immediate objective of pursuit is capture. Of utmost importance is the simple fact that *acquiring ownership* is something that is separate from both discovery and capture. Acquiring ownership is not a productive activity—it is merely distributive.

2. From the perspective of the individual hunter or whaler, the personal objective is to acquire ownership—specifically including the right of ownership that allows for sale and profit. For society as a whole, the objective is capture. Ownership is the economic reward for capture. If only one person were in control of the process of search, pursuit, and capture, there would be little reason to quibble over exactly how ownership is established. Whaling crews have captains and first mates who assign tasks to ensure a cooperative effort. Private and social objectives become essentially one and the same.

3. When two or more parties become involved in the process, the danger arises that private and social objectives will diverge from each other. Because ownership is at issue, the danger is that productive effort may be diverted from the social objective of capture to the private objective of appropriation. In the extreme, each hunter is indifferent between losing the prey and allowing the rival hunter to appropriate it. The economic dilemma is that assigning title upon discovery discourages the rival hunter from pursuing, but assigning title upon capture discourages both hunters from searching. We may speculate that ancient doctrine assigned title upon capture largely because the abundance of game very likely made discovery easy relative to the skill involved in capture with primitive weapons.

4. Once the whaling is insulated in the confines of a bay, harpoon technology is replaced by the bomb-lance. Discovery is less difficult than in the open sea, but mainly the bomb-lance vastly reduces the effort between discovery and kill. In other words, the correlation between discovery and kill was strong enough so as not to involve a distortion of incentives. Similarly, all problems of identification of the discoverer/killer were eliminated by the peculiar marks on the bomb-lances. In relation to discovery and kill, finding the dead whale after resurfacing involved minor costs. If it resurfaced in the confines of the bay, *someone* was likely to see it; if it floated ashore, *someone* was certain to find it. If it happened to resurface in open sea, searching for it might prove prohibitively costly. Awarding title to the finder would encourage excessive effort to the relatively unproductive search after the kill.

5. The broader effect of assigning title to the finder would be to sever the connection between hunting effort and reward. Title would become almost random. Ultimately, the socially inefficient harpoon technology would replace the socially efficient bomb-lance technology. To illustrate, suppose the commercial value (reflecting both private and social value) of a whale is $200; the expected costs of hunting are $95 if bomb-lance technology is employed or $125 if harpoon technology is employed; expected "finding" costs are $5 and $0, respectively. If rights are assigned to hunters, hunters use bomb-lances because the net payoff ($100) is higher than expected from using harpoons ($75). Moreover, these payoffs coincide with net social benefits. If rights are assigned to finders, social and private payoffs for hunting with harpoons are unchanged. However, hunters who use the bomb-lance technology would have to incur additional expenses to enforce their rights. In the extreme, the payoff to hunters would be –$95, and the only viable outcome would be for hunters to use harpoons.

6. The other two whaling cases provide an interesting contrast and vividly illustrate how property rights adapt to differences in technology and circumstance. Both

cases pertained to harpoon technology. One of them (*Bartlett v. Budd*) involved a dispute over a whale captured close to land, while the other (*Swift v. Gifford*) dealt with two crews chasing the same whale in open sea. The rule of first iron evidently applied in the open sea, but not close to land. First iron places a premium upon discovery, rewarding search and creating additional incentives for capture after discovery. By privatizing capture activity, the law reduces the incidence of destructive competition that might arise when two crews go after the same whale. The premium upon discovery encouraged competition in the search process, precisely where one would expect competition to do the most social good. All of the arguments in favor of first iron become less compelling as the whaling activities get closer to civilization. With a larger number of whaling vessels concentrated in a smaller area, search and discovery become easier relative to pursuit and capture.

7. The bomb-lance technology made capture (by someone) a virtual certain consequence of discovery. As a result, the *Ghen* court did not go into the subtle economics of harpoon versus bomb-lance technology, nor did it engage in any analysis of whaling in the open sea relative to the confines of harbors, bays, and inlets. It actually went one step further. In deferring to custom, the court was admitting that the subtle connections between technology, locality, and resource allocation cannot be ascertained "at the blackboard." Economists are very good at finding something that works in practice and determining that it works in theory. Local customs evolve, by trial and error, to something that works in practice. Deferring to local custom therefore trumps precedent on efficiency grounds.

8. This case is a microcosm of the economic theory of common law, particularly the common law of property. Like the rules pertaining to hunting and whaling, property rights are not just "assigned" by courts or by the state. To the extent that rights matter, they tend to evolve in ways that resolve subtle economic problems in the direction of efficiency.

Pilate Project

Poletown Neighborhood Council v. City of Detroit 410 Mich. 616 (1981)

Simple Facts

The city of Detroit invoked its power of eminent domain to facilitate the construction of a General Motors plant. Representatives of the homeowners maintained that the condemnation of land for use as a factory site goes beyond the scope of the power of eminent domain in that it takes private property for a private use. The city contended that the predominant effect of the action was to promote the public interest.

Details

The first of five companies that eventually combined to form General Motors was founded by Ransom E. Olds and produced the first Oldsmobile in 1897. Two years later, Olds built the first U.S. automobile factory on Jefferson Avenue in Detroit. The first version of General Motors was incorporated under the leadership of Will Durant in 1908. Olds, Buick, Pontiac, Cadillac, and Chevrolet shared the same corporate roof by 1916. Had bankers not refused to lend Durant a few million dollars in 1909, the list might have included Ford.

In 1949, executives of GM, Firestone, and Standard Oil were convicted (and fined $5,000) for their roles in a criminal conspiracy, the scope of which was to buy out over 100 electric surface-traction systems in 45 of the largest cities in the United States. The transit systems were subsequently dismantled and replaced with GM buses. The scandal did not deter President Eisenhower from nominating GM's president, Charles ("Engine Charlie") Wilson, to serve as his Secretary of Defense. When asked about possible conflict of interest during his confirmation hearings, Wilson replied, "what was good for the country was good for General Motors and vice versa." It was the press that subsequently garbled this remark into the adage, "what's good for GM is good for America." Like a majority of the citizenry, the Senate must have bought the message; Wilson served in Eisenhower's cabinet from 1953 until 1957.

As debatable as that adage might appear to be in retrospect, a much stronger case can be made for aligning the good fortunes of GM with those of the city of Detroit and the state of Michigan. In the spring of 1980, GM informed the city that it planned to close its Cadillac and Fisher Body plants within three years. The company offered to build an assembly complex if it could find a rectangular, 450- to 500-acre site with railroad and freeway access. Detroit found a site and set about to demolish a Polish-American neighborhood that had come to be known as Poletown.

Labor leaders, bankers, and businessmen aligned with the media and pollsters to climb aboard the civic bandwagon, succumbing to the sirens of the more than 6,000 jobs and tax revenues that would spring from the remains of an insignificant slum. Even the protection of the environment (social and cultural, that is) was brought into the equation. The slum denizens sued to enjoin the condemnation of their homes. By Christmas of that year, the circuit court had already dismissed the complaint. While the Michigan Wolverines were clobbering the Washington Huskies (23–6) in the Rose Bowl, the political football was quickly relayed upward through the court system. The Michigan Supreme Court complained about being rushed, but delivered an affirmation a few weeks before Easter.

The statutory basis for the city's action was the 1974 Economic Development Corporations Act, which cited alleviation of unemployment as one means of promoting the lofty goals of general health, safety, and welfare. In an opening salvo that is more reminiscent of Pontius Pilate than of Oliver Wendell Holmes, the court struck a blow for the legislative version of strict constructionism:

> The Legislature has determined that governmental action of the type contemplated here meets a public need and serves an essential public purpose. The Court's role after such a determination is made is limited. . . . [T]he determination should not be reversed except in instances where it is palpably and manifestly arbitrary and incorrect. . . . The United States Supreme Court has held that when a legislature speaks, the public interest has been declared in terms well-nigh conclusive.[4]

The majority opinion was delivered **per curiam** (by the court), meaning that none of the five concurring justices would admit to authorship.

In addition to the renowned guarantees against double jeopardy and self-incrimination, the Fifth Amendment to the U.S. Constitution prohibits the federal government from depriving any person of life, liberty, or property without due process of law and from taking private property for public use, without just compensation. The Fourteenth Amendment specifically extends these prohibitions to state governments. All state constitutions have similar provisions, including Michigan's. Like the federal constitution, Michigan's does not extend the phrase "public *use*" to include "public *purpose.*" Indeed, a 1952 Michigan Supreme Court decision explicitly stated that if "the intention to confer a private use or benefit forms *the purpose, or a part of the purpose* . . . , the power of eminent domain may not be exercised."[5]

The plaintiffs strongly emphasized the distinction between use and purpose, but the court deftly mixed a use/purpose cocktail with more than a dash of double-talk:

> We are persuaded the terms have been used interchangeably in Michigan statutes and decisions in an effort to describe the protean concept of public benefit. The term "public use" has not received a narrow or inelastic definition by this Court in prior cases. Indeed, this Court has stated that "[a] public use changes with changing conditions of society" and that "[the] right of the public to receive and enjoy the benefit of the use determines whether the use is public or private."[6]

Thus, in the great scheme of things, the benefit to General Motors and its employees was merely incidental to the accomplishment of the "essential public purposes of alleviating unemployment and revitalizing the economic base of the community." The court made it clear that the determination did not imply that every condemnation proposed by an economic development corporation should meet with similar acceptance. Quite the contrary, where benefits accrue to identifiable private interests, courts need to ensure that public benefits are not merely "speculative or marginal," but rather "clear and significant."

The dissenting opinions chastised the court for excessive deference to the legislature and, indirectly, to majoritarian whims. While conceding that unemployment in Detroit was of calamitous proportions and that the auto industry was the economic lifeblood of the city and the state, both jurists emphatically denounced the decision as a departure both from legal precedent and from constitutional principle.

A key bone of contention was the balance between *use* and *purpose*. Justice Ferguson pointed to Michigan's traditionally narrow stance and focused on condemnation for slum clearance as the only exception. In those cases, private property was transferred to alternative private use, but the private benefits were ancillary to the public purpose of maintaining standards of health and beautification. In contrast, the conversion of Poletown to an automobile factory involved public benefits that were ancillary to a private use and purpose. While this reversal of priority has some justification in taxation and spending policy, he saw it as a perversion of the power of eminent domain:

> Any business enterprise produces benefits to society at large. Now that we have authorized local legislative bodies to decide that a different commercial or industrial use of property will produce greater public benefits than its present use, no homeowner's, merchant's or manufacturer's property, however productive or valuable to its owner, is immune from condemnation for the benefit of other private interests that will put it to a "higher" use.[7]

Justice Ryan emphasized procedure. To justify condemnation of land for a private corporation, it is critical that the state retain some regulatory control. He singled out railroads, which were subject to a "panoply of regulations." Although General Motors no doubt had good intentions of providing upwards of 6,000 jobs, there was to be no public control after the transfer of the land; General Motors would be accountable not to the public, but to its stockholders. In effect, the city was simply acting as a conduit, while General Motors was invoking its powers of condemnation. The court had caved in to an "overwhelming sense of inevitability" that was attributable to the combination of a desperate city administration and an opportunistic corporate giant.

Economic Analysis

1. Okay, simmer down. On second thought, don't simmer down. Economics is at least partially emotional. Value derives ultimately from utility, and utility is largely about feelings. Even under the best of circumstances, forcing people out of their homes and businesses entails great emotional costs and personal upheaval. Much of the emotional cost goes uncompensated, as "just compensation" invariably gets translated into "fair market value," typically without remuneration for relocation expenses. Precisely because invoking eminent domain bypasses efficient market processes, the law traditionally required governments to demonstrate a "compelling public purpose" before being allowed to condemn private property. The *Poletown* decision diluted the meaning of the "public" portion of that phrase. However, the near unanimity of public opinion does suggest that the purpose was "compelling."

2. The impact of this case was not confined to the Wolverine state. For example, the Maricopa County Board of Supervisors (in Arizona) voted in 1995 to provide public funding and to condemn private property for the construction of what was later named Bank One Ballpark. The public purpose was to attract a major league baseball franchise, which (allegedly) would bring enormous economic benefits to the

metropolitan area of Phoenix. The public disagreed to the extent that a referendum on the stadium might well have been defeated. Although the success or failure of a referendum is not particularly important, public opinion is one indication of how compelling the purpose actually is.

3. The reader should become familiar with the Fifth and Fourteenth Amendments to the U.S. Constitution. They include guarantees of due process and just compensation with regard to the taking of private property for public use. As this case suggests, individual states have great latitude in the application of these principles. The rush to judgment borders on violation of due process and the taking is clearly for private use, but with indirect benefits to the public. All states have now stretched the reach of eminent domain.

4. The spirit of eminent domain, due process, and just compensation is to strike an economic balance between public necessity and individual property rights. In the *Poletown* case, there was at the very least a widespread perception of public necessity. On one hand (in contrast with the Arizona situation), an overwhelming majority of the population would have supported the decision. On the other, the Constitution exists to protect individuals from the government, and the umbrella extends to protection of minority rights from the tyranny of the majority.

5. On the side of public necessity, eminent domain avoids the "holdout problem." As applied to the present case, any public announcement of General Motors' (or the city's) intention to buy 500 acres of land in one area would have had a profound impact upon the market for individual properties. Each individual owner would have a strong incentive to "hold out" in an attempt to be the "last one" to sell and thereby extract a monopoly price. The holdout problem is not an absolute barrier to progress (e.g., a holding company might secretly buy up trolley systems in 45 major cities . . .), but it is an impediment that delays transactions and tends to bias their terms.

6. On the side of individual property rights, fair market value represents a minimum figure that completely ignores the basic economic concept of consumer's surplus. In other words, the fact that a person chooses to buy a particular home in a particular location and wants to stay there implies that the home is worth at least as much as all other alternatives and almost certainly worth more. In the case of an ethnic community, the individual consumer surplus is compounded by group synergy. In short, (a) the subjective individual values generally exceed fair market value and (b) the aggregate value tends to exceed the sum of the individual values.

7. Economists have a strong inclination to avoid "value judgments" and coyly point to employment as a *cost* (of foregone leisure), rather than a benefit to society. The value judgment implied by the *Poletown* decision is that the social benefits of the GM plant outweigh the social costs imposed upon the residents of the Polish community. Indeed, that presumption is almost blandly asserted as fact. The law recognizes that value judgments are an inevitable part of public policy, but harbors the economist's disinclination in the form of the due process clauses. The federal Constitution affords enormous latitude to individual states, but the main restraint is that (reasonably clear) procedures must be established and followed. Essentially, the states get to set their own rules, but the rules may not be administered capriciously.

No Redress for Headdress

Andrus v. Allard
444 U.S. 51 (1979)

Simple Facts

A series of statutes dating back to 1918 banned the sale of migratory birds and their parts. Native American artifacts containing feathers of birds killed prior to the act were subject to regulations administered by the Department of Interior. After two dealers were prosecuted for selling artifacts, they claimed that the ban amounted to an unconstitutional taking of their property.

Details

Benjamin Franklin staunchly opposed the designation of the bald eagle as the national bird. Despite its majestic appearance, Franklin considered the bird to be cowardly, lazy, and of "low moral character." Bald eagles, he contended, would perch on the limb of a tree and watch the labor of the fishing hawk. It was only when the diligent bird had caught a fish and was taking it to his mate and young ones that the bald eagle would rise up and take it from him. Franklin's opposition was doomed to failure. Living as it does on lofty mountaintops, the eagle is a symbol of freedom, long life, and great strength. The *haliaeetus leucocephalus* was officially adopted as the national emblem six years after its image was placed on the national seal of the United States on June 20, 1782.

At that time, there were as many as 75,000 nesting bald eagles in what came to be the lower 48 states. By the early 1960s, that number had fallen below 1,000. The bald eagle has suffered from habitat destruction and degradation, illegal shooting, and contamination of its food source. In 1967, bald eagles were officially declared an endangered species, an action that led to the banning of DDT and the use of lead shot for waterfowl hunting. An important element of protecting eagles from unlawful shooting was a ban on commercial sale of their feathers. Modern regulations in this vein ultimately derive their authority from the Migratory Bird Treaty Act of 1918 and the Bald Eagle Protection Act of 1940. The latter specifically states that:

> No person within the United States shall possess, sell, purchase, barter, offer to sell, transport, export, or import, at any time or in any manner, any bald eagle or any golden eagle, alive or dead, or any part, nest, or egg.[8]

The 1940 Act expressly permitted possession or transportation of bald or golden eagle parts taken prior to the effective date of coverage. Nonetheless, due to a myriad of amendments, the precise status of the law and its enforceability had reached a state of considerable complexity by 1975. Accordingly, the Fish and Wildlife Service issued a regulation effectively extending coverage indefinitely. Two years later, Allard and other dealers of Native American artifacts asked the District Court of Colorado to enjoin the Department of Interior from enforcing the regulation.

The basis for the initial complaint was twofold: (1) the statutes could not have been intended to apply to existing native art, and (2) even if they were, their enforcement amounted to a violation of the takings and due process clauses of the Fifth Amendment.

ILLUSTRATION 2.3 The North American bald eagle was considered by Benjamin Franklin to be cowardly, lazy, and of "low moral character."

© Photodisc/GETTY IMAGES

The Interior Secretary (Andrus) contended that it was impossible to distinguish feathers by age and that living birds are protected by eliminating markets for dead birds. By explicitly permitting only possession and transportation, the 1940 Act inferentially prohibited sale. Moreover, the laws were not *ex post facto* because the actual sale is something that is done after the enactment date. The district court granted the injunction in 1978, and the decision was appealed directly to the U.S. Supreme Court.

A key component of the dealers' argument was that, even if the age of feathers cannot be ascertained, it was still possible to date the artifacts themselves. Therefore, enforcement objectives could have been achieved by less onerous means than a ban on all sales (e.g., by requiring documentation of feathered artifacts). Addressing this argument head on, Justice Brennan replied that:

> This legislation is not limited to the sale of feathers as part of artifacts; it broadly addresses sale or purchase of feathers and other bird parts in any shape or form. The prohibitions of the statute were devised to resist any evasion, whether in the sale of feathers as part of datable artifacts or in the sale of separate undatable bird products. Moreover, even if there were alternative ways to insure statutory evasion, Congress was free to choose the method it found most efficacious and convenient.[9]

In familiar terms that would be echoed time and again in the future, the court maintained that the regulations did not compel the surrender of the artifacts and there was no physical invasion or other form of restraint upon them. The sales ban was a destruction of only one strand in the bundle of property rights possessed by an owner.

By 1995, the number of nesting pairs of bald eagles in the lower 48 states had risen back to 6,000, and the name of the national bird may soon be removed from the endangered species list. In November 1999, Timothy Kornwolf was arrested by an undercover U.S. Fish and Wildlife agent for attempting to sell an eagle feather headdress and a Sioux dance shield that had been acquired by his uncle, who had been in Buffalo Bill's Wild West Show in 1904.[10]

Economic Analysis

1. Although it may be just a single strand in the bundle of property rights, the right to sell is a fundamental one. Together with the presumption of efficient markets, it is the primary catalyst in the process of transferring ownership from lower- to higher-value use. This elementary economic principle applies generally to all commodities, as free exchange provides for mutual gain. In addition, a number of items may be elevated to "unique" status, perhaps the headdress owned by Mr. Kornwolf.

2. The costs of treating the artifacts as contraband thus are measured by the value of foregone opportunity. Whether the artifacts in question are ordinary or unique, the law has transformed their owners into quasi-owners and their value is diminished. If they are ordinary, large numbers of small losses in consumer and producer surplus add up to a significant sum. If they are unique, the loss to society may be dramatic. Magnificent headdresses owned and used by Native American icons probably find highest social value in museums where large numbers of people can see and enjoy them. Yet, even the Smithsonian Institute is prohibited from buying items containing protected bird parts.

3. Nonetheless, markets are not sacred. Unlike rights to life, liberty, and the pursuit of happiness, the right to sell is not inalienable; markets are means to ends. Preventing the butchery of bald eagles clearly lies within the police power of the legislature, and regulating the sale of feathers is one way of achieving that objective. As a matter of principle (on its face), the regulation was constitutional. As a matter of economics, government regulations can be very blunt instruments. Economists love to criticize regulations, but few would object to regulation on general principle.

4. By way of analogy, suppose you wanted to reduce the incidence of drunk driving, but had no police force. A (Pigouvian) tax on alcoholic beverages might help, as would a limitation on the percentage alcoholic content of liquor. Imposing severe penalties on offenders gets closer to the root of the problem, but only as a deterrent. A ban on production and sale is simple and direct, even though it punishes the majority of people who drink responsibly. Prohibition was not unconstitutional until repealed by constitutional amendment.

5. It is of some interest to consider the division of economic powers between legislative, executive, and judicial branches. The legislature gets to choose the means of regulation, while the executive branch gets to administer the regulation—essentially how far to extend the regulation. As applied directly to this case, Congress was "free to choose the method it found most efficacious and convenient" and the

Interior Department chose not to exempt the Native American artifacts. The judiciary gets to look at choice of variables (confiscation would have been unconstitutional), but does not get to second guess the executive branch's decisions, unless the diminution of rights is grossly out of proportion with the regulatory objective. This works both ways. The sales ban would fail the constitutionality test if it were the *only* measure taken to protect eagles (rather than part of a comprehensive plan that embraced policies relating to DDT, buckshot, habitat restoration, etc.).

6. In the context of the 1970s, the complete ban may have been the optimal regulatory choice. Given the threat of extinction of the bald eagle, the marginal benefits of regulation were enormous. In the absence of technology to determine the age of the feathers, allowing commercial sale of the artifacts would have provided a firm economic base for a black market for the feathers. Feathers are ideal for black market activity because they are easily transported and concealed. In contrast, Native American artifacts are specialty items that need to be displayed to a large number of potential buyers for inspection. As a result of these considerations, a ban on the sale of feathers would have been very difficult to enforce without the readily enforceable ban on the sale of artifacts. Ironically, forcing the government to pay compensation would border on a subsidy of the very market the regulation was designed to suppress!

7. In light of current conditions, the government should probably consider modifying the prohibition by exempting artifacts that contain only "old" feathers and parts. The bald eagle still merits protection, but the threat of extinction is much less critical. More to the point, DNA technology might permit effective enforcement of a selective ban. Despite the unanimity of the Supreme Court's decision, the outcome hinged on that point. If DNA technology had reached maturity by 1979, it is quite probable that the district court opinion would have been upheld.

Kohler's Last Strand

Pennsylvania Coal v. Mahon 274 Pa. 489, 260 U.S. 393 (1922)

Simple Facts

A Pennsylvania law prohibited the mining of coal where the mining might cause the subsidence of any improved property. The Mahons had acquired surface rights from the Pennsylvania Coal Company, but had signed a waiver of liability in exchange for a substantially reduced price. After enactment of the statute, the Mahons brought suit to enjoin the coal company from mining the coal under their land and thereby prevent the subsidence of their home. The coal company contended that the regulation amounted to a taking of private property without due process of law.

Details

The material that was gradually transformed into anthracite coal was deposited during the Carboniferous Geologic Period (400–250 million B.C.). At that time, most of what is now Pennsylvania was a hot, humid greenhouse of steamy swamps, towering trees, and spreading ferns. Property rights were not clearly defined.

The anthracite coalfield encompasses nearly 500 square miles across the eastern third of Pennsylvania. Economic and social development advanced along with the mining activity; by 1920, the many cities, boroughs, and villages sported a combined population of about one million people. When this locale was sparsely peopled, sporadic cave-ins were sources of personal and local tragedy, but not major public events. However, during the decade preceding this case, public welfare and safety were being threatened. Streets and buildings were collapsing, with substantial risk of injury and loss of life. At least that is what was suggested in the preamble of the 1921 Kohler Act:

> The anthracite coal industry in this Commonwealth has been and is being carried on in populous communities in such a manner as to remove the entire support of the surface of the soil to such an extent as to result in wrecked and dangerous streets and highways, collapsed public buildings, churches, schools, factories, streets, and private dwellings, broken gas, water and sewer systems, the loss of human life, and in general so as to threaten and seriously endanger the lives and safety of large numbers of the people of the Commonwealth. . . . [11]

Pennsylvania law had always held that the surface owner was entitled to support. However, owners frequently waived support rights when purchasing the surface rights from coal companies. In fact, a 1917 case[12] acknowledged a "support estate" that was distinct from the "subsurface" (mineral) and "surface" estates. A coal company had sold the surface property to a homesteader, maintaining the right to mine the coal without liability for damages. Eighteen years later, it conveyed the mineral rights to a steel company, but failed to transfer the waiver of liability. As a result, the support estate reverted back to the homesteader.

The Kohler Act prohibited coal mining where it might cause the subsidence of any improved property. It began by embracing a wide range of structures customarily

ILLUSTRATION 2.4 The anthracite coalfield encompasses nearly 500 square miles across the eastern third of Pennsylvania.

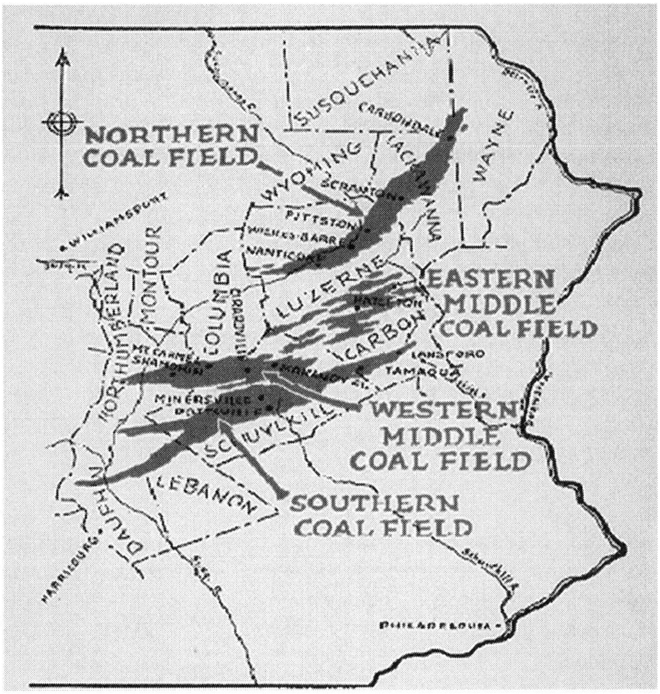

Courtesy, Mine, Safety & Health Administration

used by the public (e.g., churches, schools, hospitals, theatres, hotels, and railroad stations), but it eventually broadened its focus to include any structure used as a human habitation. The law exempted mining operations in sparsely populated towns and did not apply to cases in which coal companies owned both the surface and subsurface estates.

While the legislative ink was still drying, H. J. Mahon bought the house from his father-in-law (an executive of Pennsylvania Coal), and the terms of the sale explicitly addressed the support estate. Pennsylvania Coal then notified Mahon of its intention to mine beneath the domicile, whereupon the Mahons filed suit, seeking an injunction under provisions of the Kohler Act. Pointing to the existence of the support estate as separate property, the coal company maintained that the law was not merely an exercise in legitimate police power, but rather a taking of property without due process of law. In simple terms, the state transferred Pennsylvania Coal's property to Mahon.

The familial relationship suggests that this case was a deliberate test of the constitutionality of the Kohler Act; indeed, the case zigzagged its way to the U.S. Supreme Court. The court of common pleas denied the injunction, but was reversed by the Pennsylvania Supreme Court. The state court reaffirmed that Pennsylvania Coal owned the support estate and that its contract and property rights were constitutionally protected, but gave stronger emphasis to the "emergency" conditions "properly warranting the exercise of police power."

A vigorous dissent by Justice Kephart laid a firm foundation for appeal:

> While there are many cases of property damage due to subsidences, and people located thereabouts have been permitted to suffer because of what was then, and is now declared to be, a mistaken idea as to the power of an individual to sell property without surface support, yet that was the Commonwealth's blunder, and the Commonwealth should pay for its mistakes from general funds or use for this purpose the money now to be received from taxes on this very coal. No great hardship would follow that action. . . . [13]

Kephart cited a string of precedents upholding mining interests:

> We have . . . encouraged our citizens . . . to invest millions in these enterprises, until we have here developed the great anthracite industry, peculiar to Pennsylvania . . . The legislature stood by during all this time . . . , noted the subsidences, and did nothing. When this great anthracite industry reached its most flourishing state of prosperity . . . , contracts solemnly made on the faith of the word of the highest court of this State are swept aside, rights summarily destroyed, and property transferred to individuals without compensation.[14]

The appeal to the U.S. Supreme Court was a classic confrontation between private property rights and the police power of the state. Writing for the court was Oliver Wendell Holmes, Jr., a highly renowned jurist with strong liberal credentials. Justice Holmes began by acknowledging the great tradeoff:

> Government hardly could go on if to some extent values incident to property could not be diminished without paying for every such change in the general law. As long recognized, some values are enjoyed under an implied limitation and must yield to the police power. But obviously the implied limitation must have its limits, or the contract and due process clauses are gone. . . . [15]

His conclusion added little to the opening salvo:

> The general rule at least is, that while property may be regulated to a certain extent, if regulation goes too far it will be recognized as a taking.[16]

Holmes offered no guidance as to how this broad rule was to be generally applied. He was nonetheless very specific as to its application to this particular case:

> This is the case of a *single private house*. No doubt there is a public interest even in this . . . [but] a source of damage to such a house is not a public nuisance even if similar damage is inflicted on others in different places. . . . The damage is *not common or public*. . . . It is not justified as a protection of personal safety. This could be provided for by notice. Indeed the very foundation of this bill is that the defendant gave *timely notice* of its intent to mine under the house.[17]

Oliver Wendell Holmes, Jr.: *The natural tendency of human nature is to extend the qualification more and more until at last private property disappears. But that cannot be accomplished in this way under the Constitution of the United States. . . . The general rule at least is that while property may be regulated to a certain extent, if regulation goes too far it will be recognized as a taking.*

Louis J. Brandeis: *Every restriction upon the use of property imposed in the exercise of the police power deprives the owner of some right theretofore enjoyed. . . . But restriction imposed to protect the public health, safety or morals from dangers threatened is not a taking. The restriction here [merely prohibits] a noxious use. The property . . . remains in the possession of its owner.*

Without the personal safety issue, the sales contract prevailed. The Mahons had voluntarily exchanged the waiver of liability in return for a reduced price. Holmes then extended the same principle to the state:

> What makes the right to mine coal valuable is that it can be exercised with profit. To make it commercially impracticable to mine certain coal has very nearly the same effect for constitutional purposes as appropriating or destroying it. This we think that we are warranted in assuming that the statute does. . . . The rights of the public . . . are those that it has paid for. . . . The protection of private property in the Fifth Amendment presupposes that it is wanted for public use, but provides that it shall not be taken for such use without compensation.[18]

Given the equivalence between owning the coal and owning the right to mine it, the regulation did not merely diminish the value of the coal. The regulation went too far by entirely extinguishing its commercial value. In order to provide appropriate contrast, Holmes made reference to another regulation that required "pillars" of coal to be left along either side of the line between adjoining properties. In providing for the safety of employees, the law secured what Holmes called an "average reciprocity of advantage," even though the pillars amounted to approximately one-third of the coal deposits.

Economic Analysis

1. In the annals of economic history, it is hard to find a more pristine example of Coase bargains than those that existed between mining companies and homesteaders. The

state initially assigned rights to homesteaders—the owners of surface property—by holding mining companies liable for subsidence damage. At that point, private contracting took over. More often than not, the mining companies acquired the entire property that included the surface, subsurface, and support rights. Because the mining companies usually retained the support rights, initial ownership by the mining companies probably reduced transactions costs, as did the existence of the three separate estates. The price reduction for surface rights without support internalizes the externality in a sense: in theory, it represents the *expected* marginal costs of subsidence and marginal value of the coal. However, the real keys to internalizing the external costs are the clear definition of rights, the relatively low costs of negotiating and transacting, and the transferability of rights by individual contract.

2. Justice Holmes' contention that the case was about a single house emphasizes the one-on-one externality. Despite "similar damage inflicted upon others in different places" (large number of mines and large number of homeowners), the damage was not common or public because each pair of agents could negotiate its own unique bargain. As long as the externality is one-on-one, the transactions costs associated with a bargain may be presumed to be negligible. The reference to "timely notice" reinforces this principle. The notice gives the homeowner an opportunity to renegotiate.

3. If the Kohler Act had been upheld as constitutional, support rights would have been immediately transferred from subsurface to surface owners. This would have amounted to a huge transfer of wealth, but (probably) would not have resulted in a massive reallocation of resources. The logic is simple: if the coal is worth more than the house, the company will reacquire the support estate—the efficient outcome prevails independently of property rights. There are two reasons for the insertion of "probably" into the preceding statement. First, the "income effects" of transferring wealth essentially to homeowners might, at least in some instances, render the home more valuable (in terms of homeowners' willingness to pay) than the coal. A different efficient outcome prevails.

4. The second reason is more long-run in nature. The sudden shift in property rights might undermine public confidence. If the state can reassign rights at will, the rights can hardly be considered as "clearly defined." This point relates directly to Justice Kephart's dissent. The state of Pennsylvania successfully encouraged massive investment in coal reserves precisely because its citizens believed they could rely upon the law to uphold the mining incentives that it had created.

5. Beyond the mechanics of costless bargains, this case documents the evolution of property rights, from the steamy swamps through the coterminous development of mining technology, economic society, and the underlying legal relationships. Several important points emerge. First, the coalfield cut across a large number of small jurisdictional authorities. To the extent that there was a problem, it was up to the state government to address it. Second, property rights are not simply "assigned by the government" in some abstract "initial position." The opening paragraph aptly describes the initial position. Third, the law can be manipulated to tilt property rights in one direction or another.

6. The larger issue pertains to the tradeoff between private property rights and the police power of the state. Justice Holmes' question of how far a regulation may go before it constitutes a taking remained unanswered. However, the opinion strongly suggests that the issue rests upon matters of principle rather than upon dollar-and-cents comparisons of costs and benefits. For example, no social emergency excuses the state from its duty to pay just compensation. Quite the contrary, compelling public purpose is the rationale underlying eminent domain. Holding the state financially accountable is an important safeguard against potential abuse. Similarly, in justifying the regulation requiring pillars between adjacent mines, Holmes did not say that the reciprocal advantage was sufficient to compensate the mining companies for the coal that had to be left in the ground.

CHAPTER 3

ZONING AND REGULATION

Two cases from the preceding chapter provide important focal points for analyzing regulations pertaining to the use of land. In *Poletown*, the local government invoked its powers of eminent domain to transfer property from private use to an alternative use that satisfied a legitimate public purpose. Whether a GM plant constitutes a legitimate public purpose is now beside the point, which is that federal and state constitutions require that the government compensate property owners for their economic losses. In *Pennsylvania Coal*, a state law that effectively empowered regulators to close mines to protect surface property rights was held to be unconstitutional. Even though the regulation did not involve the actual condemnation of property, it went "too far" in context of the economic circumstances.

The purpose of this chapter is to consider how far land use regulations can go without bumping into constitutional restrictions. Three key issues apply: (1) whether the regulation has a legitimate public purpose, (2) whether the regulation effectively addresses that purpose, and (3) whether the public benefits expected to flow from the regulation are great enough to justify the costs imposed upon property owners. Subject to a number of procedural complexities, the law's three major options are to uphold the regulation as constitutional, to require compensation, or to strike down the law as unconstitutional.

The theoretical economic purpose of land-use regulation is to internalize externalities that cannot be effectively resolved by private arrangements. Therein lies the "legitimate public purpose." However, since governments are not necessarily fully enlightened, judicial review is important to ensure that the regulation fits the problem. Even then, there are no guarantees that the government remedy is a significant improvement upon the state of affairs that would unfold without intervention. Forcing governments to pay compensation induces officials to consider the costs of their actions. The general problem here is known as **fiscal illusion**. Without having to pay compensation, governments are encouraged to act under the "illusion" that the regulation imposes no costs upon property owners. In order to illustrate the dilemmas confronted by regulators and the judiciary, it is useful to consider two similar types of externality.

The Common Property Externality

Common property is the theoretical opposite of private property. Instead of having one owner with exclusive use rights, common property implies either multiple owners or no ownership at all. The more realistic versions entail property rights that conflict with one another because they are costly to enforce and/or difficult to define with clarity. Two classic paradigms are associated with this problem. One is the fishery with open access, meaning that any number of independent fishermen may enter. The other is the oil pool, where a number of independent owners each drill and extract oil from the same source that extends across legal property boundaries. The general proposition is that independent action results in excessive exploitation of the resource. That may translate into too many fishermen or too many oil wells relative to that which would maximize the value of the fishery or the oil pool.

The economic model of common property proceeds from a production function relating quantity of output (q) to a measurable input (x). The average and marginal product curves for an oil field are graphed in Figure 3.1 and illustrated numerically in the accompanying table. In the interest of simplicity, average product (q/x) is measured in terms of barrels of oil per well converted to dollars per well. In a competitive environment, exogenous prices exist for both the oil (p) and the wells (w). Under private ownership of the oil field, one entrepreneur determines how many wells to drill and maximizes rent (essentially, profit) at point M, where the value of marginal product (price × MP) is equal to the cost of the well (w). Using that point as a frame of reference, the predicted outcome is vastly different if a large number of independent owners have drilling rights to the same oil field. In the extreme, the number of wells rises to x_c, where the value of average product (p × AP) is equal to the cost of the well. The logic of this position is analogous to the "zero profit equilibrium" in perfect competition, but the underlying process is quite different. If exploited up to point C in the diagram, the oil field becomes socially worthless! The cost of the oil wells fully offsets the value of the oil.

Rather than interpreting this result literally, it is more important to focus on the underlying process. In other words, how can the institutional arrangement make such a difference in how resources get utilized? To understand the process, examine the accompanying table. As x rises, average productivity declines (10, 9, and 8) according to the law of diminishing returns. With two wells, each one yields nine barrels. The reason why marginal product (eight) is less than average product is that each well essentially reduces the productivity of the other by one barrel. With three, the effect is compounded; each reduces the productivity of the other two by one barrel.

Under private property, the single owner will take this effect into consideration. In deciding whether to drill a second or third well, the reduction of the productivity of other wells impacts directly and fully upon the owner. Under common property, independent owners of the individual wells have no direct concern about the impact of their decisions upon other owners in the group. A classic externality situation emerges, wherein individual rationality begets collective irrationality.

A great deal has been written about the **common property externality**, about the great chasm that lies between the abstract polar cases, and about its relevance to property law. The beauty of the model is that it lends structure to practical discussions of land uses that impact upon one another. However, things get messy very quickly once the practical application begins. In theory, the objective is to move the group from point C to point M in Figure 3.1. Following Pigou, a local government could impose a tax per well, equal to the difference between VAP and VMP at x*. Following Coase, intervention is unwarranted because bargaining has already solved the problem. If transactions costs impeded the bargaining process, the government could appoint a mediator. A third alternative is that the government could regulate the oil field and impose an administrative solution.

In practice, corrective taxation is not administratively feasible. Every oil field is unique in a number of respects. Even if a controlling authority could determine a solution resembling optimal usage, it would be more practical to impose an administered solution rather than to attempt to direct resources by something as clumsy as a tax.

FIGURE 3.1 Additional wells reduce the productivity of the others by the difference between AP and MP. Common owners tend to ignore this effect.

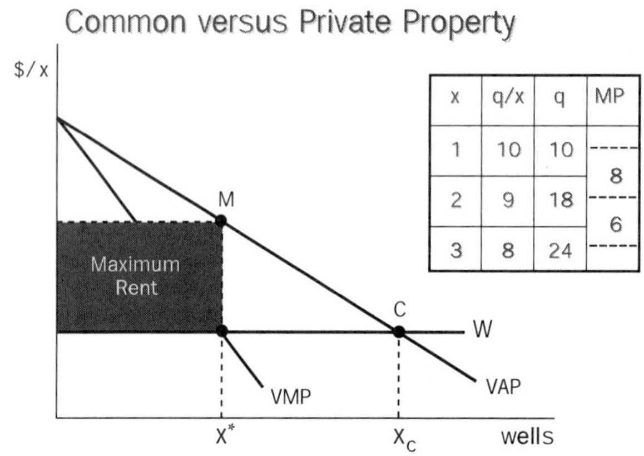

However, there is an even more basic reason than administrative infeasibility: the economic objective is not to encourage movement from a "point C" to a "point M." By the time a problem is recognized and understood by governmental authorities, the group is not at a point C because it has partially solved the problem by evolving to a workable arrangement. Workable arrangements may evolve through negotiation, local custom, tradition, or simple trial and error. The whaling customs described in the preceding chapter are a useful example.

A straightforward, though imperfect, solution to the common oil pool problem is zoning. In Texas and Oklahoma, state legislatures have specified minimum size restrictions for any land parcel housing an oil well. For example, the regulators could impose a restriction of one well per acre. Anyone owning less than an acre would have to negotiate with a neighbor to obtain a drilling permit. This kind of restriction essentially determines x for the oil field. One drawback is that different spacing might be appropriate for different fields, but variances from the rules can be granted. A second type of regulation pertains to a minimum distance between a well and any neighboring property. This is aimed at avoiding strategic positioning of wells in an attempt to exploit a neighbor's mineral rights.

Neither of these regulatory solutions should be regarded as "optimal" in the strict sense. However, in relation to the model, they are consistent with a movement in the direction of an optimal position. In this loose sense, the regulations may be regarded as "efficient." For example, the acreage restriction is consistent with a move from x_c to x^* in the diagram. The distance restriction is aimed at something that is not in the model. The very existence of a production function relating q to x presupposes **technical efficiency**, meaning maximum yield for any given number of wells. Given $x = 1$, for example, one would expect the well to be in the geographic center of the field. In general, approximate uniform distribution of wells would tend toward this ideal. Under private ownership, the entrepreneur is expected at least to attempt to do this; that is why theoretical production functions are presumed to embody technical efficiency. In sharp contrast, non-cooperative independent owners will be concerned with maximizing the yield of their individual shares. In short, whereas the acreage restriction is aimed at **economic efficiency** (optimal x), the distance restriction is aimed at *technical efficiency* (maximum q, for any given x).

Ideally, gainers compensate losers in such a way as to fashion a Pareto improvement. Indeed, if it were possible to identify gainers and quantify their gains, forcing governments to compensate those who are harmed by the regulation would seem wholly unobjectionable. Actually, the gainers would complain that the government has no right to make them pay for enforcing laws and the whole process smacks of bribery. Ruling out the notion of gainers compensating losers, we are left with a dilemma. On one hand, if the law does not force governments to compensate those harmed by regulations, we run the risk of fiscal illusion. On the other, if the law always requires compensation, we run the risk of fiscal insolvency because governments are not able to collect payment from those who benefit.

Congestion Tolls

A **crowding externality** is the first cousin of a common property externality. The mechanics of the two economic models are virtually identical. The unifying feature is that similar agents collectively impose costs upon one another. The most common example of the crowding externality is the congested road, where time cost (t) per vehicle is an increasing function of the number of vehicles (x) using the highway. As x increases, individual motorist consider only t, ignoring the incremental costs imposed on all other motorists. The textbook solution is to impose a congestion toll equal to the divergence between marginal private and marginal social cost, as shown in Figure 3.2. The point is to correct for overuse (from equilibrium at x_e to an efficiency point at x^*). This result holds up independently of how the proceeds of the tax are used, but the major options are to fund construction (or expansion) of the road. If the road size is exogenous, the straightforward disposition is neutral redistribution back to users.

Examples of crowding externalities abound in takings cases, but not in isolation. A group of homeowners located on an island impose costs upon themselves by building their homes too large, thereby obstructing views, impeding access to a common beach, or causing environmental damage to the sand dunes. The island merely adds emphasis to imposition of costs upon themselves; obstruction of view is a common problem for any neighborhood. Similarly, a *group* of mining companies extract coal from beneath the ground and the effect of (*aggregate*) mining activity weakens the structure of individual mines.

It can be very misleading to dwell on this particular aspect of any case; other facts and dimensions can hardly be classified as extraneous detail. However, it is far more misleading to ignore it entirely, for there are clean economic remedies. The most direct approach is to impose administrative restraints. If property owners are building excess housing, limits may be placed on the size of homes and/or the number of developable lots. Alternatively, a tax may be imposed upon building. One approach focuses on quantity, the other upon price. To the extent that quantity of housing is the sole source of the

FIGURE 3.2 On congested roads, motorists impose additional time costs upon one another. In theory, a congestion toll (EB) internalizes the externality.

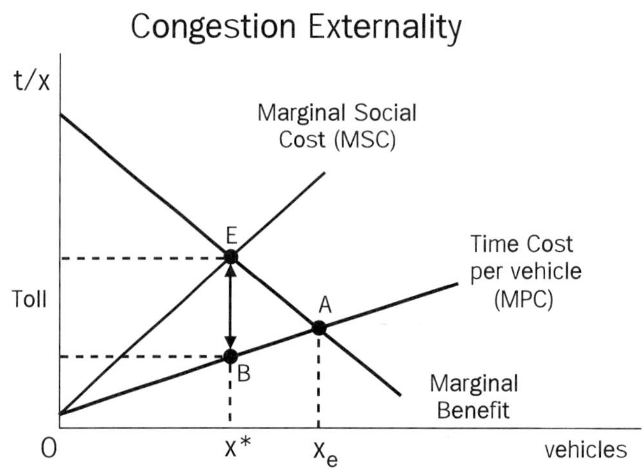

externality and that property owners have similar tastes, the two approaches are equivalent. The same sort of theoretical remedy applies to coal miners imposing subsidence damage upon one another by mining too much coal. The simple economic remedy is either to tax the coal or limit its extraction by regulatory decree. Again, to the extent that the quantity of coal is the sole source of the externality and that miners face similar technologies, the two approaches are equivalent.

Regulatory Dilemmas

This chapter is not about regulating oil wells or controlling traffic congestion, but there are several important perspectives to be drawn from the exercises. First, economic models paint abstract pictures of regulatory problems. Although economists sometimes appear to shelter themselves in the cocoons of unrealistic assumptions, the abstractions serve as a roadmap or checklist of regulatory objectives. Second, because they are abstractions designed for general applicability, models cannot determine or dictate the form of the regulations. Indeed, like the restrictions on acreage and distance, regulations will tend to be multidimensional. As a result, the specific form of the regulation will have some appearance of arbitrariness and almost always be open to criticism. Finally, an effective regulatory solution will tend to resemble the result of a corrective tax—even though actual corrective taxes are seldom used—and embody some accommodation for what may be broadly described as private bargaining. The end result is a net social gain, with some "losers," but with some conscious effort to avoid the imposition of excessive burdens upon a small minority.

When those harmed by regulation seek legal relief, the law affords considerable latitude to the government. As long as the regulatory plan is reasonably consistent with legitimate social objectives without effectively obliterating a property interest (as in *Pennsylvania Coal,* for example), the regulation passes constitutional muster and compensation is not required. When regulatory plans start to become inconsistent with rational or stated objectives, constitutional issues arise. For the purpose of evaluating the issues and explaining or predicting how the law operates, it is useful to have a model. Ultimately, if the regulatory plan is offensive to the spirit of the economic solution, facial unconstitutionality is a strong likelihood. If the plan fits the model, the government tends to prevail. In the cases detailed below, the reader should think about how the facts fit the models, look for unique features that go beyond the framework of the models, and attempt to interpret the judicial decision in terms of the models. Regulatory control of externality was a clear objective of the early zoning cases, of which *Euclid v. Ambler* is typical. By the 1970s, the environmental movement tempted municipal and state governments to seize property under the name of zoning (*Agins v. Tiburon* and *Lucas v. South Carolina Coastal Council*). We shall also return to the Pennsylvania coal fields (*Keystone v. DeBenedictis*).

Harmless Regulation

Village of Euclid v. Ambler Realty 272 U.S. 365 (1926)

Simple Facts

The Euclid Village Council adopted a comprehensive zoning plan in 1922. Extensive land holdings, acquired by Ambler for the purpose of commercial development, were designated for residential use. The realty company challenged the ordinance, alleging deprivation of property and liberty without due process. Despite inducing a significant diminution of the value of Ambler's land, the zoning plan was held not to be an unconstitutional taking of private property.

Details

The origins of this case are much less grandiose than those of *Pennsylvania Coal*. The earliest zoning-type ordinance—one that actually distinguished between "residential" and other uses—was passed in Modesto, California, in 1885. Its basis was the prohibition of public laundries (for draining water onto city streets). A similar regulation in San Francisco led to the arrest of unlicensed laundryman, Yick Wo. The California Supreme Court upheld Wo's conviction.

The Modesto ordinance evolved from land use restrictions aimed at specific activities, broadly conceived as nuisances or health hazards. The confinement of laundries was preceded by the regulation of slaughterhouses, cemeteries, and public privies. The closure of livery stables and brickyards (see *Hadacheck v. Sebastian* in Chapter 4) gave way to height and depth restrictions, lot sizes, and general empowerment with regard to nonconformity. By 1925, about a quarter of the states had passed laws enabling their towns and cities to exercise the police power to zone.

The village of Euclid, Ohio, was a suburb of Cleveland, with a population of 5,000 to 10,000 citizens. It occupied an area of about 14 square miles, the greater part of which was farmland or unimproved acreage. In 1922, the village council established a comprehensive zoning plan. The plan established general districts according to use, height, and area, with several categories within each district. It included six different use districts, numbered U-1 through U-6. Uses permitted in all districts with a lower number were also permitted in a higher-numbered district.

The Ambler Realty Company owned 68 acres of land, as shown in Illustration 3.1. About half the property was zoned U-6, essentially unrestricted. A small strip was zoned U-3, allowing for apartments, hotels, churches, schools, hospitals, and city buildings. The remaining portion was zoned U-2, which permitted only one- and two-family residences. Comparing current market land values, Ambler estimated a 75% diminution of value.

Other states were sending out mixed messages at the time. In the face of laws promulgating zoning, the Ohio court cited a Virginia case,[1] in which the establishment of uniform building lines in a single city block was held unconstitutional and void. Even cases with remote effects upon property (e.g., a minimum wage law for women in Kentucky and certain provisions of the Kansas Compulsory Anti-Strike Law) were being struck down as contrary to the Fifth and Fourteenth Amendments' protections of private property.

ILLUSTRATION 3.1 More than half of Ambler Realty's property was unrestricted (U-6), but the portion zoned as U-2 was diminished in value by about 75%.

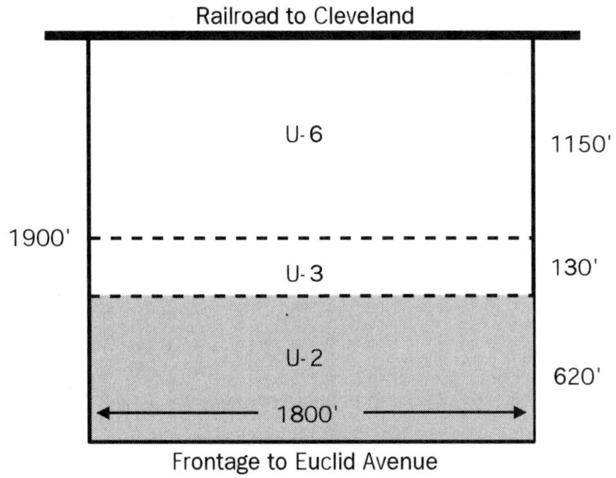

In finding for Ambler, the Ohio Supreme Court noted that the case "was destined to go higher." The extent of damage was in dispute, but acknowledged to be "substantial." The *Pennsylvania Coal* decision, barely four years old, clearly influenced the higher court, which cited Justice Holmes' ominous warning:

> [T]he natural tendency of human nature is to extend the [police power] more and more until at last private property disappears. But that cannot be accomplished in this way under the Constitution of the United States.[2]

The U.S. Supreme Court was not only unimpressed with the extent of damage, but also cited *Pennsylvania Coal* as only one of a number of prior cases addressing police power. While addressing the nuisance angle, the court carefully avoided nuisance control as the basis for this decision. The bottom line was to affirm the rights of municipalities to draw arbitrary lines between residential and industrial use, despite demonstrable financial losses incurred by investors. The court strongly implied that large numbers of actual and potential developments precluded case-by-case considerations. Regulations that seem arbitrary and unreasonable when scrutinized in minute detail must be viewed in a broader context:

> . . . the harmless may sometimes be brought within the regulation or prohibition in order to abate or destroy the harmful. The segregation of industries, commercial pursuits and dwellings to particular districts in a city, when exercised reasonably, may bear a rational relation to the health, morals, safety and general welfare of the community.[3]

It further emphasized that harm imposed upon residential property owners had (in contrast with simple nuisance activities) a multiplicity of possible sources:

> The establishment of such districts or zones may, among other things, prevent congestion of population, secure quiet residence districts, expedite local transportation, and facilitate the suppression of disorder. . . [4]

and, perhaps most importantly, that the harm was the collective effect of a range of activities that might otherwise be harmless in and of themselves:

> The exclusion of places of business from residential districts is not a declaration that such places are nuisances or that they are to be suppressed as such, but it is a part of the general plan by which the city's territory is allotted to different uses in order to prevent, or at least to reduce, the congestion, disorder and dangers which often inhere in unregulated municipal development.[5]

Other parts of the opinion stray from the central point, particularly an analogy to nonconforming uses with the "pig in a parlor."[6] Although zoning lines do keep specific nuisances out of residential areas, their primary purpose is to control quantities.

Economic Analysis

1. In this case, the courts are attempting not only to resolve a negative externality, but also to categorize it. "Nuisance"—which applied to the slaughterhouses and public laundries of yesteryear—suggests a noxious by-product tied to an otherwise legitimate business. "Congestion" is close, because the negative impact is the collective effect of the activities of individual members of a sizeable group. The appropriate word is "encroachment," suggesting that one group imposes costs upon another (e.g., commercial upon residential property owners) instead of upon themselves (e.g., oil producers upon oil producers).

2. Those who fancy double-entendres will appreciate the reference to "the danger of frittering away the constitutional guaranties by successive encroachments" in the U.S. Supreme Court opinion. The Court rattled off some 26 disparate state court opinions on similar issues. If there is a common purpose of modern zoning regulations, it is to separate industrial and residential land use. Along with many others, the Euclid plan implies that industrial land users impose costs upon residential users. The salient feature is that the lower-numbered groups, starting with residential, are permitted to locate in higher-numbered zones, rather than the other way around.

3. A textbook solution to the encroachment externality would call for a tax (t) on industrial use, combined with a simultaneous auction for land, with the stipulation that "I" users and "R" users will be segregated. The proceeds of the tax would be distributed uniformly, according to initial land ownership. For example, suppose 100 people initially own one acre each, to be sold at auction, with industrial property taxed at $1,000 per acre. Suppose further that 75 acres are acquired for resi-

dential use at a uniform price of p = \$4,000. The remaining 25 acres are acquired for industrial use at p + t = \$5,000. The tax proceeds (\$25,000) could then be distributed uniformly (\$250 each) to the 100 property owners.

4. The point is not to advocate Pigouvian taxation, but to establish two clean theoretical results. The first is that the auction, combined with an efficient tax, will result in higher average property values than the same auction without a tax. The second is that the same outcome would be generated by zoning the 100-acre tract with 75 acres for residential and 25 for industrial before allowing the auction to proceed.

5. The main difference between the tax plan and the zoning plan is that, under zoning, the auction would generate two different prices: p for residential and a higher p' (equal to p + t) for industrial. This outcome suggests that some of the initial owners might make more money than others. This is largely a distributive issue, of minor concern to the economist, with any number of theoretical ways to ensure equity to initial property owners. The realities of real land markets, actual zoning plans, and the pursuit of speculative profit tend to obscure the pure economics, but that is all the more reason to keep the allocative and distributive issues separate.

6. Ambler Realty was not simply an "initial owner" of land in a contrived auction. It was an active participant in a dynamic market. Without the suggestion of anything derogatory, Ambler was a "speculator." Speculators seek profit by keeping abreast of market conditions. As greater Cleveland began its encroachment upon Euclid, Ambler bought up properties, expecting to profit in the later "auction." Ambler failed to anticipate the new rules of the auction. Too bad; part of "keeping abreast of market conditions" is correct anticipation of regulation.

7. Although the courts chose not to address the extent of Ambler's losses, it is important to consider them. At the time, prime commercial property commanded a market price of about \$10,000 per acre, with an additional \$150 per foot premium for frontage on Euclid Avenue. Accordingly, the 68 acres with 1,800 feet of frontage had an estimated market value of \$950,000. The site map indicates that a little more than 22 acres were zoned as U-2, valued at \$2,500 per acre with a premium of only \$50 per foot for the frontage on Euclid Avenue. These figures suggest a paper loss of \$345,000—a diminution of some 36% of the whole parcel or about 71% in relation to the 22 acres zoned as U-2. It is not possible to determine how much Ambler originally paid for the property, or the extent of the positive impact upon residential values or other commercial values in neighboring communities.

8. Zoning has the potential for becoming a nasty political game, wherein bribes from speculators replace the Pigouvian taxes. There is also ample room for economically costly mistakes by well-intended public authorities. However, these potential negatives lay well outside the matters facing the court. In principle, zoning ordinances do not violate constitutional protections of private property. Indeed, they have the potential for enhancing the value of private property. Herein lies the larger economic tradeoff, the balance between protecting rights without trampling on them. That having been said, let the trampling begin.

California Schemin'

Agins v. City of Tiburon 447 U.S. 255 (1980)

Simple Facts

A city zoning plan imposed low density and open space requirements upon hillside property in Tiburon. The owner claimed that the plan was facially unconstitutional because it completely destroyed the value of the land. The city justified the ordinances as advancing the legitimate governmental goal of discouraging premature and unnecessary conversion of open-space land to urban uses.

Details

In 1968, Donald Agins acquired five acres of unimproved land on the Tiburon ridge in northern California. Those of us who have left our hearts in San Francisco have a special appreciation for Tiburon's environmental amenities. Nestled on a hillside peninsula beneath the great redwood forest of Mount Tamalpais, with breathtaking views of the Golden Gate Bridge and the City, Tiburon boasted the highest per capita incomes and property values in the Bay Area. Historical development had moved north along the peninsula away from San Francisco along both the flatlands and the ridge, with moderate density. Based on the pattern of development, one might extrapolate an expectation of 10–20 homes per acre.

In the early 1970s, the city council approved the sale of $1.25 million of municipal bonds. At the same time, it began eminent domain negotiations with Agins and other property owners to acquire the ridge for open space. The city soon discovered that it could not afford the property, so it rezoned the ridge for lower density, with strict requirements for open space. Ostensibly, the plan allowed for the construction of 1 to 5 homes per acre, but the city's clear intentions to block development were revealed by its prior actions.[7]

Instead of submitting a specific proposal for city approval, Agins went directly to court, requesting that the zoning ordinances be declared unconstitutional. He also initiated inverse condemnation proceedings, seeking $2 million in damages. Both claims were based on the contention that the city had taken the property without just compensation in violation of the Fifth and Fourteenth Amendments. The complaint alleged that the land value of Tiburon exceeded that of any other suburban property in California and that, by preventing residential development, the rezoning of the land had completely destroyed its value.

The California Supreme Court denied the inverse condemnation claim as a matter of procedure. For landowners challenging the constitutionality of a zoning ordinance, the appropriate remedy is not compensation, but declaratory relief. With regard to the Fifth Amendment claim, the Court also sided with the city—largely because Agins' claims so exaggerated the impact of the ordinance. The ordinance provided for construction of up to five homes per acre and therefore did not "completely" destroy its value. In granting *certiorari*, the U.S. Supreme Court addressed the *facial* constitutionality of the law—whether, as a matter of principle, the ordinance violated Agins' rights. It did not consider

ILLUSTRATION 3.2 The Tiburon lifestyle and its breathtaking views of San Francisco combined to produce the highest property values in California.

© Sandra Cannon www.sfbayimages.com

whether it was constitutional as applied to Agins' particular circumstances. Since Agins had not submitted a proposal, that issue was not "ripe" for a judicial ruling.

With regard to facial constitutionality, the Court established a two-prong test to be applied to zoning. A zoning ordinance is unconstitutional if it "does not substantially advance legitimate state interests" or "denies an owner economically viable use of his land." The zoning plan in *Euclid v. Ambler* survived both prongs, the focal point being the significant diminution of the value of the property. The Court still did not say how much diminution of value is tolerable. Inasmuch as other circumstances will always be relevant, it probably never will be specific on this issue. However, the Court did draw a line in the sand.

The Tiburon plan did substantially advance legitimate state interests:

> The State of California has determined that the development of local open-space plans will discourage the "premature and unnecessary conversion of open-space land to urban uses. . . ." The specific zoning regulations at issue are exercises of the city's police power to protect the residents of Tiburon from the ill effects of urbanization. . . . Such governmental purposes long have been recognized as legitimate.[8]

The Court emphasized that the plan would benefit Agins (!) as well as the public by "assuring careful and orderly development" and by providing for open-space areas.[9] Although these benefits would not fully offset the direct burdens, the law cannot require that *all* citizens benefit from a regulation. It also stressed that, while the plan limited the extent of development, it did not prevent the best use of the land nor did it "extinguish a fundamental attribute of ownership."

Economic Analysis

1. The zoning plan involved in this case is not classic encroachment of commercial use upon residential. Nonetheless, it does address encroachment of one kind of residential use upon another. The new development of the ridgeland (R) properties clearly affected the value of flatland (F) residences, not merely by increasing the quantity of housing, but also by altering the landscape. While some development of R would potentially enhance the value of F (a positive externality), unlimited development would almost certainly have a negative impact.

2. The scenario also involves a simple common property externality within the group of (competitive) developers of the ridgeland. Specifically, Agins' interests are limited to the value of his own five acres. In developing those five acres up to the point of maximum value, the tendency is to ignore the effects of less open space upon the value of similar tracts. This argument provides some theoretical basis for the Court's outrageous contention that the plan benefited Agins. The precise way of saying this is that the plan partially benefited the class of ridgeland developers, of which Agins was a member.

3. In principle, a zoning plan *could* increase total value of the combined properties. By internalizing the encroachment externality, the value of F is increased by more than the reduction in the value of R. The plan also provides partially compensating increases in the value of R by internalizing the common property externality. This vignette of economic theory justifies facial constitutionality, but says nothing about the Tiburon plan itself.

4. The alternative theory of the Tiburon plan is known as fiscal illusion. Under fiscal illusion, a government converts high-value private use to low-value public use. The net loss in economic welfare is rational for the government because the government does not have to pay for the land. The background facts, documented by William Fischel,[10] fit the fiscal illusion story quite well. The city began the eminent domain process, then discovered that the ridge property was too expensive, and then substituted zoning for condemnation. Fischel also mentions that the city rejected Agins' attorney's offer in oral argument to drop the case if the city would agree to one home per acre.

5. The state interests involved in this case include those of not only the city of Tiburon, but also the state of California. The foundation for California's interests reduces to environmental preservation as a general public good (beyond a means of enhancing private property values in individual communities). Within the community, environmentalists (E) comprise a third interest group. To the extent that general environmental preservation serves a legitimate public purpose, development should stop short of maximizing the value of private property.

6. This case raises two huge flags for private property interests. The first is the absence of lower limit (short of zero) on tolerable diminution of value. Coupled with the fact that environmentalist groups tend to be hostile toward development, the Court seems to be sending out an invitation for governments to treat environmental protection as a free good. To the extent that city planning boards have balanced representation among the important interest groups, this danger is mitigated.

7. The second flag is procedural. Superficially, the Tiburon plan appears to support the best use of the land, diminishing but not eliminating its value. However, the plan did not provide clear guidelines to property owners and essentially required them to keep submitting development proposals until they got one accepted. The danger here is that governments that are hostile to development either kill reasonable projects or make it very costly for property owners to obtain approval. This case apparently never became ripe for adjudication. The property remained undeveloped a decade later. Like a virus, fiscal illusion spread eastward in the direction of South Carolina.

Of Mice and Missiles

Lucas v. South Carolina Coastal Council 505 U.S. 1003 (1992); 112 S. Ct. 2886 (1992)

Simple Facts

In an effort to protect its beaches from erosion, a South Carolina law established critical areas where new construction was prohibited. Lucas, who owned two lots in a critical area, sought compensation on grounds that the law had denied him all viable use of the property. The state contended that the law was designed to protect the public from serious harm and, as an exercise of police power, did not require compensation.

Details

An online ad features a six-bedroom luxury vacation home with a private pool "sitting on a lagoon on the Harbor Golf Course located in the Marina of The World Class Renowned Resort Wild Dunes." The home rents at $5,000 per month during season. Second-row (from the beach) homes advertise "fourth-row prices" of $895 to $1795 per week depending on time of rental.

In the late 1970s, David Lucas and others began extensive residential development of the Isle of Palms, a barrier island situated eastward of the city of Charleston. Lucas bought two lots in 1986 in the Beachwood East Subdivision of the Wild Dunes. Testimony at trial indicated that he intended to put one home on the market for sale and retain one for his family. Lucas' lots were on the beach, where single-family homes now command rental rates of $5,000 per week.

South Carolina's interest in managing development in the "coastal zone" predated Lucas' purchase. The original (1977) version of the Coastal Zone Management Act required owners of land in "critical areas" (beaches and adjacent sand dunes) to obtain a permit before committing the land to development. In 1988, after Lucas had acquired the lots, the Beachfront Management Act redefined critical area in a way that included Lucas' two lots. Accordingly, the South Carolina Coastal Council refused to grant a building permit. It is important to emphasize that virtually all of the other lots in the subdivision were already developed.

Unlike Agins in the preceding case, Lucas did not challenge the constitutionality of the new law. He simply argued that the law, as administered by the Coastal Council, effectively deprived him of all viable use of his property. The Court of Common Pleas sided with Lucas and awarded compensation of $1,232,387.50. The Supreme Court of South Carolina reversed on grounds that the regulation was designed "to prevent serious public harm." That court noted the importance of the beach/dune system as a storm barrier, tourist attraction, and habitat for plant and animal species. It rattled off 10 reasons why a long-range comprehensive beach management plan was needed for the entire coast and cited a long line of "noxious use" cases. Since Lucas did not attack the legislature's contention that new construction would cause serious public harm, the court inferred a "nuisance-like" exception. It therefore concluded that Lucas was not entitled to compensation.

The dissenting jurist pointed to *Agins v. Tiburon*: "land use regulation can effect a taking if it does not substantially advance legitimate state interests . . . or denies an

ILLUSTRATION 3.3 In a 1994 photo taken by William Fischel, David Lucas' vacant lots stand out like two extracted teeth.

Courtesy, Professor William A. Fischel, Department of Economics, Dartmouth

owner economically viable use of his land." He added the opinion that the Beachfront Management Act did not have nuisance prevention as its primary purpose. Ultimately, the U.S. Supreme Court had to decide whether or not the potential environmental damage to the sand dunes constituted noxious use. In an effort to head off that confrontation after losing the initial battle (in the Court of Common Pleas), the state amended the Beachfront Management Act in a way that allowed Lucas and others to appeal denials of building permits. The state then argued that because of the newly created option to appeal, Lucas' claim was not ripe for a decision. The Court brushed aside this argument; unlike *Agins v. Tiburon* (see above), *Lucas v. South Carolina Coastal Council* was ripe for a decision, and it was time to draw lines in the sand.

Writing for the Court, Justice Scalia immediately focused on the subjective aspects of the case:

> One could say that imposing a servitude on Lucas' land is necessary in order to prevent his use of it from "harming" South Carolina's ecological resources; or, instead, in order to achieve the "benefits" of an ecological preserve. . . . [It] depends primarily upon one's evaluation of the worth of competing uses of real estate. . . .[11]

Antonin Scalia: *to win its case South Carolina must do more than proffer the legislature's declaration that the uses Lucas desires are inconsistent with the public interest. . . . Instead, as it would be required to do if it sought to restrain Lucas in a common law action for public nuisance, South Carolina must identify background principles of nuisance and property law that prohibit the uses he now intends in the circumstances in which the property is presently found.*

Dennis Brack/Bloomberg News/Landov

Harry Blackmun: *In the absence of "a final and authoritative determination of the type and intensity of development legally permitted on the property. . . ." there is no final judgment. . . . Petitioner can picnic, swim, camp in a tent, or live on the property in a movable trailer. State courts frequently have recognized that land has economic value where the only residual economic uses are recreation or camping.*

U.S. Supreme Court Historical Society

Scalia concluded from this observation that subjective definitions of noxious cannot serve as a touchstone for awarding or denying compensation. The steppingstone in his logic is that noxious is an absolute, rather than a relative term. In particular, he insisted (emphasis added) that whether an activity is noxious or not does not depend upon the nature or value of the activities that are harmed by it:

> Whether Lucas' construction of single-family residences on his parcels should be described as bringing "harm" to South Carolina's adjacent ecological resources thus depends principally upon whether the describer believes that the State's use interest in nurturing those resources is so important that *any* competing adjacent use must yield. [12]

Accordingly, Scalia looked for historical continuity of purpose (emphasis added):

> We emphasize that to win its case South Carolina must do more than proffer the legislature's declaration that the uses Lucas desires are inconsistent with the public interest. . . . Instead, as it would be required to do if it sought to restrain Lucas in a common law action for public nuisance, South Carolina must identify *background principles of nuisance and property law* that prohibit the uses he now intends *in the circumstances in which the property is presently found.*[13]

Scalia's insistence on "background principles of nuisance law" placed strong limitations upon arbitrary and self-serving designations. Without the "noxious use" argument, the state's case disintegrated: the state courts had already held that the regulation deprived Lucas of all viable economic use of the property; that holding was not under appeal; deprivation of all viable economic use is one of the "discrete categories of regulatory deprivations" that require compensation without case-specific inquiry.

The decision thus affirmed one principle and created a new one:

1. Subject to the "nuisance exception," a regulation that deprives the owner of all viable use of his property is a compensable taking;
2. A government may not brand an activity as a nuisance unless there is common law support in the form of "background principles of nuisance law."

Before this case, the principle regarding the deprivation of viable use was an abstract barrier. It was stated, but not applied, in *Agins v. Tiburon*. It had been applied to facial challenges (e.g., a Palo Alto ordinance designating private property as "open space" in *Eldridge v. City of Palo Alto*[14]) but not to inverse condemnation actions, where property owners sought compensation.

The decision provoked two dissenting opinions (Justices Blackmun and Stevens), a concurring opinion (Justice Kennedy), and a comment (Justice Souter). Both dissents began with the question of ripeness; Kennedy maintained that the case was ripe for a decision, and Souter claimed that it was not. The arguments against granting *certiorari* focused on the amendment to the Beachfront Management Act, allowing for appeals. A point in favor of *certiorari* was the fact that Lucas' development plans had already been postponed for several years. Consequently, the ripeness of his *temporary takings* claim was not affected by the amendment.

Part of the argument against hearing the case was the sentiment, expressed by Justice Blackmun, that the majority was "launching a missile to kill a mouse." That is, the majority could have found that the regulation "went too far" without creating such "bright-line" rules:

> Relying on an unreviewed (and implausible) state trial court finding that this restriction left Lucas' property valueless, this Court granted review to determine whether compensation must be paid in cases where the State prohibits all economic use of real estate. According to the Court, such an occasion never has arisen in any of our prior cases, and the Court imagines that it will arise "relatively rarely" or only in "extraordinary circumstances." Almost certainly it did not happen in this case.[15]

Blackmun went on to suggest that the land retained some value because "petitioner can picnic, swim, camp in a tent, or live on the property in a moveable trailer." He also made reference to the right to exclude and the right to sell all or part of the lots to neighbors. The point was that the category regarding deprivation of *all* viable use was artificial and unnecessary. Blackmun also objected to the high court's interference with a state's right to protect its citizens from harm. Justice Stevens echoed this sentiment, emphasizing that forcing states to rely on pre-existing common law nuisance principles effectively "freezes" the common law:

> Arresting the development of the common law is not only a departure from our prior decisions; it is also profoundly unwise. The human condition is one of constant learning and evolution—both moral and practical. Legislatures implement that new learning; in doing so they must often revise the definition of property and the rights of property owners. Thus, when the Nation came to understand that slavery was morally wrong and mandated the emancipation of all slaves, it, in effect, redefined "property." On a lesser scale, our ongoing self-education produces similar changes in the rights of property owners. . . .[16]

Stevens added that the Court was bestowing upon developers an artificial environment of certainty, sending out a distorted economic message:

> The Court today effectively establishes a form of insurance against certain changes in land-use regulations. Like other forms of insurance, the Court's rule creates a "moral hazard" and inefficiencies: In the face of uncertainty about changes in the law, developers will overinvest, safe in the knowledge that if the law changes adversely, they will be entitled to compensation.[17]

On remand, a subsequent trial in South Carolina resulted in a settlement. The state bought the lots from Lucas and then sold them to a housing developer to recover part of the costs of the settlement. According to Fischel, the price averaged out to $392,000 per lot. The owner of a home located next to one of the lots had offered $315,000 and promised to keep the lot undeveloped.[18]

Economic Analysis

1. Two externalities underlie this case. One pertains to the single island, where homeowners collectively impose costs upon one another ("upon themselves"). The other pertains to the South Carolina coastline in its entirety, where development threatens ecological harm. In the interest of simplicity, it is useful to treat the former as a congestion externality and the latter as an encroachment externality.
2. To the extent that development of the sand dunes causes erosion, individual property owners collectively impose costs upon themselves. The Isle of Palm was privately owned. The dunes may have prevented some storm damage to the property on the island, but any effect upon the rest of the state was less than negligible. Accordingly, the simple economic solution would have been to form a homeowners' or developers' association. An effective plan might have called for fewer homes at greater distances from the beach, with proceeds from higher aggregate values distributed equitably among the property owners. The key element of the solution is that the externality is internal to the island and requires little, if any, state intervention.
3. Whether the development plan should be implemented through a homeowners' association or a developers' association, by government mandate, or a cooperative effort between private and public authority, the key ingredients of a development plan go well beyond the number of lots developed. In other words, the economic problem cannot be reduced to a "quantity" of lots unless lot size, spacing, location and structural matters are addressed concurrently. Given the efficient resolution of those issues, Figure 3.2 becomes a reasonably accurate representation of the problem. The efficient number of developed lots rates to be less than it would be without effective planning. One would expect individual lots to be larger, with development set back further from the beach and perhaps more open space. Those who owned or retained private property would pay higher prices, though not in the form of an explicit "congestion toll."
4. With regard to the case itself, the economics are simple. The state attempted to take Lucas' property without paying for it. The effect of the taking was to destroy the land's value for residential purposes (an opportunity cost of $1.2 million or more).

In the aftermath of the decision, the state sold the lots to a developer for about $75,000 more than was offered by a neighbor who promised to leave the land undeveloped. This is a textbook example of fiscal illusion. The state was willing to deprive a property owner of a $1.2 million value to achieve an objective that was worth less than $150,000 to the state. Numbers aside, it was too late to save the Isle of Palms from development, and the marginal value of Lucas' lots for the purpose of environmental preservation and protection was negligible, perhaps even zero. If the neighbor had offered a dollar less than the developer, the state might still have sold to the developer.

5. Beyond the narrow confines of the Isle of Palms, the noble intentions of the Beachfront Management Act pertain to an encroachment externality: the *collective* effect of development has an adverse impact upon the large *group* of South Carolina's coastal islands. The disorderly conversion of sand dunes to high-rise edifices lies comfortably within the realm of legitimate state interest." The Court's language in *Euclid v. Ambler* (above) is particularly appropriate: "the harmless may sometimes be brought within the regulation or prohibition in order to abate or destroy the harmful." In seeking an efficient balance between private and public interests, it is counterproductive to label development as a noxious activity.

6. Justice Scalia's emphasis upon competing uses points directly to a quantity (D) of a scarce resource (dunes) that can be allocated for residential development (x) or preserved for environmental purposes (y). Any increase in x necessarily reduces y, so that the effect of additional development is to deny a benefit to the public—and vice versa. Two extreme positions bound the ideological spectrum. On the right, we may ignore the concept of an encroachment externality and insist that, if D is private property, the government has to pay for y (the portion mandated to remain undeveloped). On the left, we may call encroachment noxious and regulate private property out of existence ($y = D$) without compensation.

7. The competing use paradigm polarizes the analysis and, as the dissenters implied, the polarizing is largely unnecessary and misleading. Since regulations are generally not quantitative in nature, competitive bidding between private and public interests will not resolve the important questions. The liberal view is to scrutinize regulations on a case-by-case basis and to reduce the compensation issue to a simple yes or no. However, if a regulation essentially eliminates all viable use of a property, the issue essentially becomes quantitative; requiring compensation controls the problem of fiscal illusion. Fiscal illusion resurfaces with the noxious use paradigm, so that some objectivity requirements are necessary.

Pillars of Society

Keystone Association v. DeBenedictis 581 F. Supp. 511 (1984), 480 U.S. 470 (1987)

Simple Facts

An association of bituminous coal mining companies challenged the constitutionality of a Pennsylvania statute that was carefully crafted to regulate subsidence without crossing the line between a regulation and a taking. The statute survived the facial challenge—the *association* of miners was not given blanket protection of their rights to mine coal to the detriment of Pennsylvania society—but the door was left open for redress on a case-by-case basis.

Details

The reader should review the prior analysis of *Pennsylvania Coal v. Mahon* for appropriate background material. Five coal companies and an association challenged Pennsylvania's Bituminous Mine Subsidence and Land Conservation Act. They specifically asked for an injunction to prevent enforcement of three regulations of the Pennsylvania Department of Environmental Resources (DER) adopted under the act.

The Subsidence Act was carefully crafted to overcome the Court's prior objections to the Kohler Act. It prohibited mining that causes subsidence damage to public buildings and other protected structures like perennial streams, aquifers, and cemeteries. Companies were required to pay a reasonable sum to repair the damage. The act also contained a provision whereby owners of nonprotected properties might pay a reasonable price to purchase the coal that provides subsurface support to the structure.

The focal point of the complaint was upon a requirement that coal operators leave 50% of their coal in place for support under protected structures. Plaintiffs contended that the enforcement of this regulation amounted to an unconstitutional taking of private property. They also sought protection under the "contracts clause" (Article I, Section 10) of the Constitution, which prohibits state laws that impair private contractual obligations. In support of this claim, the association pointed out that regulation translated into 27 million tons of unmined coal—the entirety of the support estate, which they owned under Pennsylvania law.

The Pennsylvania court upheld the Subsidence Act, maintaining that its provisions overcame all three of Justice Holmes' 1922 objections to the Kohler Act. Specifically, the law was justified as a public safety measure; it seeks to prevent common or public damage; and no surface estate owner is excluded from the act. The court contended that the "support estate" was a "nebulous concept." Like the right to sell eagle feathers (*Andrus v. Allard*, see Chapter 2), the right to mine the 27 million tons of coal was only one strand, albeit the most valuable one, in the full bundle of rights.

The U.S. Supreme Court affirmed the decision by a 54 majority. The transcript provides a classic confrontation between liberal and conservative jurisprudence, with ample puffing from both sides. Whereas the liberal tendency is to lump all of the imperfections into one vat, the conservative tendency is to scrutinize each element in isolation.

Writing for the majority, Justice Stevens dwelled on the "nuisance exception" and the commonality of damage. He began with reference to the public purpose of the Act:

> to aid in the protection of the safety of the public, to enhance the value of such lands for taxation, to aid in the preservation of surface water drainage and public water supplies and generally to improve the use and enjoyment of such lands and to maintain primary jurisdiction over surface coal mining in Pennsylvania. . . .[19]

The reference drew attention to the *common property* aspects of the problem, but also provided fodder for a blistering dissent by Chief Justice Rehnquist, who cited similar wording in the Kohler Act:

> In apparent recognition of the obstacles presented by *Pennsylvania Coal* to the decision it reaches, the Court attempts to undermine the authority of Justice Holmes' opinion as to the validity of the Kohler Act by labeling it "uncharacteristically advisory. . . ." I would not so readily dismiss the precedential value of this opinion. . . . [T]he Court made clear that the mere existence of a public purpose was insufficient to release the government from the compensation requirement: "The protection of private property in the Fifth Amendment presupposes that it is wanted for public use, but provides that it shall not be taken for such use without compensation." [20]

Rehnquist emphasized the appropriation of 27 million tons of privately owned coal and decried "the ease with which the Court moves from the recognition of public interests to the assertion that the activity here regulated is 'akin to a public nuisance.' "

The lynchpin of the majority argument was to complete the dismantling of the support estate:

> The 27 million tons of coal do not constitute a separate segment of property for takings law purposes. Many zoning ordinances place limits on the property owner's right to make profitable use of some segments of his property. A requirement that a building occupy no more than a specified percentage of the lot on which it is located could be characterized as a taking of the vacant area as readily as the requirement that coal pillars be left in place. . . .[21]

The absolute figure, though impressive, exaggerates the burden imposed upon the coal companies. Since the actual landscape was not uniform, the 50% requirement was applied only in key locations. As a result, the regulation affected only about 2% of all coal deposits. Stevens addressed this issue head on:

> [E]ven if we were to accept petitioners' invitation to view the support estate as a distinct segment of property for "takings" purposes, they have not satisfied their heavy burden of sustaining a facial challenge to the Act. Petitioners have acquired or retained the support estate for a great deal of land, only part of which is protected under the Subsidence Act, which, of course, deals with subsidence in the immediate vicinity of certain structures, bodies of water, and cemeteries. The record is devoid of any evidence on what percentage of the purchased support estates, either in the aggregate or with respect to any individual estate, has been affected by the Act.[22]

John Paul Stevens: *Petitioners have acquired or retained the support estate for a great deal of land, only part of which is protected under the Subsidence Act. . . . The record is devoid of any evidence on what percentage of the purchased support estates, either in the aggregate or with respect to any individual estate, has been affected by the Act.*

Dennis Brack/Bloomberg News/Landov

William H. Rehnquist: *The Court attempts to undermine the authority of Justice Holmes' opinion. . . by labeling it "advisory. . . ." I would not so readily dismiss the precedential value of this opinion. . . . (T)he Court made it clear that the mere existence of a public purpose was insufficient to release the government from the compensation requirement.*

Jason Reed/Reuters/Landov

Lest the substance of the decision be lost in the flavor of the debate, we may summarize the holdings of the Court:

1. The enforcement of the Subsidence Act was a legitimate exercise of police power.
2. The support estate was not a separate piece of property for takings purposes.
3. The 50% requirement did not eliminate the profitability of coal mining.
4. The private contracts did not relate to common damage inflicted upon the public.

Taken together, the individual pieces paint the picture of a generic regulation that diminishes the value of private property, but does not destroy any of its fundamental attributes and, therefore, need not rely upon the concept of nuisance.

Economic Analysis

1. The model underlying *Pennsylvania Coal* was the one-on-one externality. The Court's references to a single private house, the existence of prior contracts, and the ability of the mining company to provide timely notice all pointed in that direction. As a result, the economic conditions underlying the Coase Theorem are met about as well as one could expect in a real world. If one views this case simply as a large number of one-on-one externalities, the 1922 precedent would apply. If the Kohler Act went so far as to constitute a taking, so did the Subsidence Act. For the same

reason, the Court tiptoed around the word "nuisance"; mining was "akin" to a public nuisance, but did not qualify for the "nuisance exception" to the takings clause.

2. The *Keystone* majority, in concurrence with the state court, viewed the externality as one of common property. In context of the circumstances, there are two interpretations of "common property." One interpretation relates to the collective effect of individual mining activities. To simplify, imagine two neighboring properties, each with one mine (M) and one house (H). Each pair of owners reaches a perfect bargain between themselves, but fails to account for Mine A's effect upon House B or Mine B's effect upon House A. Extending this to a large number of pairs adds up to the classic tragedy of the commons, or a congestion externality: members of the *group* of M's and H's *collectively* impose costs *upon themselves*. This type of externality is internalized by imposing a tax or quota upon each member of the group. The 50% quota is far simpler to administer.

3. The second interpretation of common property is that a portion of the subsidence damage accrues to publicly owned property, the prime examples being streets and waterways. Even if contracts between pairs of owners were perfect, they would cover only potential damage to private property. The free rider problem would preclude coverage of the public goods. This interpretation suggests a set of social costs imposed by the group of M's and H's upon others (P's) outside the group.

4. As Chief Justice Rehnquist noted, both laws were aimed at the public good and common property aspects of the problem. However, the theory of congestion and public goods suggests that *Keystone* is *not* a simple reversal of *Pennsylvania Coal*. First, notice what happens as the economy grows (more M's, H's, and P's). The one-on-one externalities do not become increasingly difficult to resolve, but the other externalities do. Accordingly, the same regulation that went too far in 1922 could be a "valid exercise of police power" in 1987. Second, the two statutes were administered differently. The Kohler Act authorized closure of individual mines as necessary, clearly directed to solving the one-on-one externality. Similarly, the Kohler Act exempted properties where surface and mineral estates were both owned by a coal mining company. The inference is that sole ownership by the coal company would not matter unless the problem was a one-on-one externality.

5. In contrast, the Subsidence Act reads like a "handbook of social engineering." Quotas internalize congestion, and liability rules internalize the damage to public property. Compensation at fair market value is applied to private property owners, addressing the portion of the externality that was covered by the private contracts. Even the liability imposed for damage to private property has a sound rationale. The Court clearly suggested that assigning liability to the mining companies for subsidence damage was an important enforcement tool:

> Petitioners argue that [requiring] coal companies to repair subsidence damage or pay damages to those who suffer subsidence damage, is unnecessary because the Commonwealth administers an insurance program that adequately reimburses

> surface owners for the cost of repairing their property. But this argument rests on the mistaken premise that the statute was motivated by a desire to protect private parties. In fact, however, the public purpose that motivated the enactment of the legislation is served by preventing the damage from occurring in the first place.[23]

Indeed, the system in its entirety is an elaborate set of incentives that is both consistent with efficiency principles and marked with compensatory payments to mitigate potential losses endured by the coal companies.

6. The dismantling of the "support estate" was a key element of the case. The state court dismissed it as a nebulous concept, but it is truly symbolic of the economic foundations of law. Without the expectation that some coal remains unmined, Pennsylvania society would cease to exist. The reference to "pillars" is more than just a casual metaphor. In fact, a 1914 case had upheld the state's right to cause boundary pillars "of sufficient width to safeguard the employees of either mine in case the other should be abandoned and allowed to fill with water." The coal that was ordered to be left unmined in the barrier pillar (singular) amounted to 734,147 tons. Exactly what portion of the 27 millions tons of support estate was actually owned by the mining companies therefore becomes highly speculative.[24]
7. In the final analysis, no model can determine what is reasonable. Given the state's prior regulatory interest in subsidence and the state's inferential right to the pillars, it follows that the mining companies did not have inalienable rights to mine all of the coal. Therefore, their rational economic calculations should have included the expectation of future regulation. In light of these considerations, the coal that was mandated to be left unmined was at least partly the property of the state. Because it was partly the property of the state, the Kohler Act was *facially* constitutional; because it was partly the property of the mining companies, the mining companies retained the option to seek compensation on an individual basis.

CHAPTER 4

NUISANCE EXTERNALITIES

The landmark cases about noxious activities cover the production and distribution of things that assault all senses. The list ranges from the production of beer[1] to the destruction of sand dunes on a privately owned island in *Lucas v. South Carolina* (see Chapter 3). Alcoholic beverages actually made Pigou's short list of externalities to tax, albeit with a strong caveat that such a tax would be a very crude way of getting to the root of the problem.[2] So is banning beer production, the regulatory equivalent to taxing it out of existence. The sand dunes did not make the list. This could say a lot about the power of Pigouvian economics, inasmuch as the law upheld the closure of Mugler's brewery but awarded compensation for regulating Lucas' dunes.

Both of these case examples represent outliers. Nineteenth-century morality led to stretching the definition of noxious because the consequences of unregulated spirits had a high subjective social cost. Late twentieth-century environmental mores tempted the state of South Carolina to do the same. Nonetheless, the differences between these two cases transcend a century of shifting social preferences. A clear statistical connection exists between a variety of social costs and the consumption of alcohol. The state's right to regulate it is clear; the main issue is how to regulate it, including the mix of restraints and penalties imposed on abusers. In a perfect world, the externality would be internalized by regulating the *abuse* of alcohol, with no reason to regulate all users equally by restraints on output. Even the abusers would not be restrained from harming themselves. In contrast, the harm to the sand dunes was either a matter of property owners imposing costs *upon themselves* or a matter so abstract as to lie outside a comfortable *economic* definition of nuisance.

Nuisance in Theory: An Economic Definition

In between these extremes, we find a host of examples in which the production of ordinary commodities generates annoying by-products. Smoke, dust, noise, vibrations, and stench clearly fit this description because they entail a direct assault on one of the senses. This by-product constitutes an additional variable (s) in the production equation, along with ordinary output (q) and inputs (x). Whereas outputs and inputs are marketable, the by-product tends not to be, although something like a price can be established through taxation, regulation, or bargaining.

The production possibilities essentially define a **potential nuisance**. A potential nuisance becomes an economic nuisance if others are harmed by exposure to the by-product. It is convenient to label those exposed to a nuisance activity as victims and the law frequently does just that. Once that term is accepted, there must be corresponding culprits. As a simple matter of fact, culprits directly control the production of s, and victims are exposed to s but cannot directly control its production. However, it is important to avoid the automatic attachment of connotations of guilt or innocence.

Nuisance stories come in all sizes and shapes. Although the dimensions of the problem lie on a vast continuum, it is useful theoretically to think in terms of the two discrete cases: public and private nuisance. The **private** (one-on-one) **nuisance** is a relatively simple legal-economic problem. If transactions costs are negligible (as they rate to be), there is no externality because the problem is resolved by bargaining. The simple role of the law is to clarify property rights, as in *Pennsylvania Coal* (see Chapter 2), for example. The **public nuisance** lies at the opposite pole: a large number of people (typically homeowners) are harmed by the activities of a single culprit. Air pollution comes to mind, but that tends to be the collective effect of a large number of agents. Either way, transactions costs tend to be high and some form of government intervention tends to be in order. However, another important aspect of pollution does not apply to nuisance: the tendency, at least in abstract models, for the substance to distribute itself uniformly into the atmosphere. Whereas a polluter (one of many) cannot control the radius of the harmful substance, the public nuisance can.

Nuisance Activities in Reality

The most common stories embody both private and public aspects. Typically, a single business (or a small number of businesses) produces a by-product that harms or annoys a relatively large number of homeowners or businesses within a certain radius. The large number of potential victims suggests public nuisance, but the confinement to a certain radius suggests private nuisance. In short, proximity to the source of the activity matters—the closer a victim is to the source, the greater the exposure to it and the greater the potential for harm. All nuisance situations therefore have three key dimensions: static, spatial, and temporal. It is useful to consider the three dimensions both separately and interactively.

In the static dimension, the main focus is on incentives to induce culprits to control s, with respect to both quantity and radius. Reducing output is the obvious way to accomplish this, but there almost always exist technological alternatives to reduce the ratio of s to q. Up to a point, such technological measures may even be profitable. From a social perspective, however, it is important to induce the firm to employ these measures beyond the point of maximum profit. One way or another, the firm must be made to pay the social costs of their actions. A secondary consideration relates to victim behavior. Victims must be encouraged to mitigate damages. For this reason, it is important not to compensate them for damages *per se*, even though some compensation for *exposure* to s *may* be appropriate.

The spatial dimension embodies similar principles to the static dimension, but is more long-run in nature. Culprits must be encouraged to isolate themselves and to seek low-cost victims. The primary enforcement tool is forced closure or relocation. Herein lies the economic foundation for the so-called nuisance exception: if the state has the right to tax externalities, it has the right to tax them out of existence if the external costs are large enough. Forced relocation without compensation for loss of property is the administrative equivalent to taxation out of existence. With regard to victims, the same caveat about compensation applies. The main objective is to encourage low-cost victims and to discourage high-cost victims from locating in economic proximity to the nuisance.

The temporal dimension is arguably the most complex of the three. It is impossible to cover this topic in the abstract, except in the form of broad principles to be applied to individual cases. Perhaps the most important principle is that the rights and duties that apply to culprits and victims are not, and generally should not be, dependent on which party was "there" first. In particular, a key component of culprit technology is the potential for harm that exists whether or not there is a victim close enough to be harmed. Culprits must therefore be held responsible for anticipating or forecasting the general direction of economic progress, including its random components. Indeed, culprits are usually there first precisely because *rational* culprits attempt to isolate themselves. The second important principle applies to the potential for strategic behavior. Because the law tends to force culprits to make the first move, they are entitled to some protection against premature encroachment by victims, particularly if the victims have good alternatives.

Twilight Zone

Hadacheck v. Sebastian 239 U.S. 394 (1915)

Simple Facts

A city ordinance prohibited the manufacture of bricks in residential districts, on grounds that the noise and smoke generated by the factory was a noxious activity. The factory, which initially lay outside city limits, had been in operation for eight years prior to the passage of the ordinance. Even though the action effectively destroyed all viable use of an $800,000 property, it was upheld as a legitimate exercise of the government's police power.

Details

Spanish occupation of California began in 1769. Gaspar de Portola led an expedition to develop a trail between San Diego and San Francisco. That trail, which came to be known as *El Camino Real,* would set the infrastructure for the 21 missions founded by Padre Junipero Serra. Father Serra was a member of Portola's expedition, along with Father Juan Crespi. The group entered Los Angeles via the modern-day Elysian Park and camped by a river which Father Crespi named *El Rio de Nuestra Senora la Reyna de Los Angeles de Poriciuncula*—the river of Our Lady, Queen of the Angels of Porciuncula.

Nothing about LA lies in the realm of ordinary. Before the expedition broke camp, it had experienced three earthquakes, but Father Crespi still envisioned greatness for that inspirational river basin. Although the Gold Rush of 1849 diverted the pioneers north to Sacramento and San Francisco, the water would ultimately be diverted to the south. It was to be only a matter of time before the basin exploded outward as severely as its name contracted inward. The completion of the Southern Pacific and Santa Fe railroad lines into Los Angeles in 1883 ushered in the tourism, citrus, oil, and motion picture industries. As land speculators conspired to harness the waterways of the West, population doubled during the 1890s and tripled in the decade that was to follow.

In 1902, J. C. Hadacheck acquired an eight-acre tract of land for the purpose of operating a brickyard. The tract contained a bed of rich clay deposits that were ideally suited for the manufacture of fine quality bricks. Hadacheck made a considerable investment in capital equipment (kilns and machinery) and operated the brick factory for nearly eight years. He claimed a value of at least $100,000 per acre, or about $800,000 for the entire tract. Because of deep excavations on the property, much of the land was unusable for residential or any other economic purpose. Inasmuch as transportation of the clay was economically infeasible, the value of Hadacheck's facility was inseparable from its clay deposits. At the time of Hadacheck's acquisition, the tract lay entirely outside the Los Angeles city limits.

In 1909, the city of Los Angeles adopted one of the first zoning ordinances in the United States. The ordinance called for seven industrial districts. The other areas were zoned for residential use, with provisions for residential exceptions. The latter was a sort of twilight zone where certain unobjectionable industries were permitted. The ordinance in question was retroactive. It not only forbade the creation of any brickyards in the future in this residential district, but also required all existing brickyards to cease operating.

The ordinance did not immediately affect Hadacheck because his tract still lay outside the city limits. In 1910, however, the city annexed the surrounding land and zoned it all as residential. At the time, the LA city limits encompassed over 100 square miles. The parcel that was annexed included only three square miles and was sparsely settled, containing large tracts of unoccupied land. Nonetheless, since the brickyard lay inside a residential district, the ordinance effectively mandated its immediate closure. Hadacheck defied the ordinance and was twice arrested and fined. Sebastian was the LA chief of police.

Because Hadacheck had defied the ordinance, the California Supreme Court reviewed a *habeas corpus* petition on the criminal complaint. The essential elements of Hadacheck's case were as follows: (1) the property was "far more valuable for brick making than for any other purpose," (2) viable use of the property was essentially eliminated, (3) the property was outside the city limits when he acquired it, and (4) no one expected the city either to pass the restrictive zoning law or to annex the surrounding property. In addition, Hadacheck alleged that other brick factories were operating in more populous areas within the city limits. Indeed, several hundred residents had signed a petition claiming that other brickyards were nuisances and the city had not attempted to regulate them.[3]

The city did not deny any of these allegations. In particular, it was clear that Hadacheck would be compelled to abandon his business if the ordinance remained in effect. The major point of contention was whether the manufacture of bricks was a noxious activity. Referring to the California Civil Code relating to nuisances, Hadacheck denied that his business could be "dangerous or detrimental to health or the morals or safety or peace or welfare or convenience of the people of the district or city." As one might expect, he denied that the factory was noisy or that it emitted noxious odors and claimed that "an extremely small amount of smoke is emitted from any kiln and what is emitted is so dissipated that it is not a nuisance. . . ."[4] During its seven years of operation, no complaints were filed, and the city did not attempt to regulate it.

The California court affirmed the right of the legislature to exercise police power despite severe diminution of the value of prior investments. The matter before the U.S. Supreme Court was mainly concerned with the denial of due process. In particular, was the police power exercised arbitrarily and discriminatorily? The Court drew a fine line on this issue. The actual administration of an otherwise legitimate police action is largely beyond the scope of the judiciary. The fact that other brickyards continued to operate in residential areas did not justify the conclusion that the ordinance in question was anything other than a regulation intended to control a nuisance activity.

The fact that Hadacheck had been in business for a substantial period was not relevant. The restriction met the city's burden of bearing a "a reasonable relation to some legitimate purpose within the purview of the police power." In contrast, Hadacheck's burden was overwhelming; he had to demonstrate that his business did not affect the health or comfort of *anyone*.

Economic Analysis

1. The dust, smoke, and noise from the brickyard add up to a classic nuisance externality. The number of potential victims is large enough to warrant the label of

"public nuisance," the main effect being that the prospective costs of transacting with actual and potential residential neighbors were prohibitive. Moreover, the technology of manufacturing bricks is relatively simple; there is very little potential for reducing the side effects without reducing the output. For practical purposes, the harmful side effects may be considered proportional to the output. This case brings out all three dimensions (static, spatial, and temporal) of the nuisance problem.

2. The static problem thus fits comfortably into a Pigouvian framework. We may envision a one-dimensional graph, with brick output and proportional "nuisance" output on the horizontal axis and marginal costs and benefits on the vertical. Given the sparse population, there are few victims and the externality is negligible. Once the city annexes the surrounding land, the population does not immediately change, but the city lays plans for a housing development. The prospect of having a large number of victims spells divergence between private and social costs. In theory, the city could tax the bricks or the dust, but the tax would be so high as to drive Hadacheck out of business. Closure is a straightforward administrative alternative to taxation. Within this narrow context, the issue of compensation is not relevant, but the government's right to tax or regulate a nuisance strongly suggests that the property owner should not be compensated for economic losses.

3. The issue of compensation becomes economically relevant in relation to matters of timing and location. From a social perspective, the loss may be specified in terms of unsalvageable plant and equipment, along with the clay deposits that cannot feasibly be transported. Assuming that the land is more valuable for housing than for brick making, the economic question turns to whether the brickyard should have been built at all. Even with hindsight (*ex post*), that answer would be yes if the (time-discounted) value of the bricks manufactured over the eight-year payback period (from 1902 through 1910) exceeded the cost of the initial investment in plant and equipment. However, the important economic perspective lies at the point of the investment decision in 1902 (*ex ante*).

4. Since the only feasible means of regulating brickyards is the blunt instrument of closure or relocation, the appropriate *ex ante* social calculus is to consider the stream of value (annual brick output) discounted according to the *probability of being permitted to operate*. To simplify, imagine an initial outlay of \$150 for capital that lasts for exactly two years, with projected net return of \$100 per year. Operation during the first year is a certainty, but neighboring development may (with probability p) force closure during the second year. The expected social return (ignoring time value) from the investment is: $W = 100 + 100(1 - p) - 150$. If $p > 0.5$, the plant should not be constructed. As simplistic as this example might be, it provides an important insight about the compensation issue. This figure is also a correct measure of expected profit only if the government is *not required* to pay compensation. Payment of compensation encourages the investor to act as though $p = 0$ (even though it is not) and thereby issues an invitation for socially excessive investment.

5. This argument against compensating Hadacheck places the risk of being harmed by regulation on an equal plane with the general class of entrepreneurial risk. Just as

farmers run the risk of crop destruction by bad weather, businesses that produce outputs with potentially harmful by-products run the risk of closure. This analogy is harsh, particularly as applied to a decision made in 1902 when zoning laws were in their infancy. More to the point, the analogy is imperfect because bad weather is not the result of human decision. Accordingly, the law must provide some safeguards (under the broad heading of due process) against exposing businesses to the risk of regulation by bad government.

6. As a general matter, neither city planners nor entrepreneurs are capable of perfect foresight and timing. On one hand, entrepreneurs must base their decisions on expectations regarding the timing and direction of growth. On the other, city planners should provide reasonable signals about their intentions. In practice, the city's administrative plan appears to have been far from perfect. Whereas the land surrounding Hadacheck's factory was sparsely populated, other brickyards were allowed to continue operating in mature developments whose residents had complained about dust and noise. This evidence, together with the plant's proximity to the rich clay deposits, suggests that the city closed the factory with the lowest social cost!

7. The expansionary motives of the Los Angeles city government had become reasonably clear and generally understood by 1900. In the midst of violent change and rampant land speculation, the annexation of small cities and unincorporated tracts was a complex undertaking. As a result, the rapid expansion was chaotic and random in the sense that the city, in competition with speculative interests, seized opportunity when it arose. This ties in directly with the p in the social investment formula. The timing of the annexation of the land surrounding the brickyard was the result of general market conditions. In retrospect, the city may have closed the wrong brickyard, but the process was not tainted. The higher courts have no expertise that qualifies them to determine whether or not better parcels of land were available or whether other brickyards should be closed. Acquiring those other parcels was part of the city's long-range development plans, and closure of the other brickyards was largely a matter of time.

Confluence of Doctrines

Spur Industries v. Del Webb Development Co. 108 Ariz. 178 (1972)

Simple Facts

The expansion of a retirement community collided with the expansion of a nearby feedlot. The feedlot's daily processing of tons of steer manure created a potential health hazard to residents and prospective residents of the community. The developer obtained an injunction forcing closure of the feedlot. The Arizona court upheld the injunction on grounds that the feedlot was a public nuisance, but remanded the case back to the trial court for determination of appropriate compensation for relocation expenses.

Details

Sun City, Arizona, is a master-planned retirement community and the brainchild of the Del Webb Corporation. Founded in 1960, Sun City is world renowned for its active, resort lifestyle and has set the standard for a modern phenomenon. Sun City is the largest retirement community in the United States, sporting a population of about 45,000 citizens and bustling with 11 golf courses and several recreation centers. Although self-contained with a wide variety of retail centers and restaurants, the town is unincorporated and depends on Maricopa County for law enforcement, street repairs, and zoning protection. At least one member of the household must be 55 years of age, and only recently was anyone under that age permitted to live there. Needless to say, school bond appropriations are not a high priority item.

In 1956, the Northside Hay Mill and Trading Company established feedlots in an area between the confluence of the Agua Fria and New Rivers. The two rivers were usually dry so the area was (as noted in the court opinion) well suited for cattle feeding. By 1959, the operation was feeding about 7,000 head of cattle per day on the 35-acre tract. Spur acquired the property in 1960. Shortly before Spur's acquisition (May 1959), Del Webb began planning the community that came to be known as Sun City. Webb acquired 20,000 acres of farmland at a very favorable price ($15 million, or $750 per acre) relative to land prices in the nearby Phoenix metropolitan area, some 15 miles to the southeast. By early 1960, Webb was constructing a golf course and advertising homes. The first 500 units were about 2.5 miles north of Spur. According to the court opinion, "Del Webb did not consider odors from the Spur feed pens a problem and . . . continued to develop in a southerly direction, until sales resistance became so great that the parcels were difficult if not impossible to sell."[5]

To complicate matters further, just as Webb was expanding to the south, Spur began expanding the feedlot to the north! As in all textbook examples of externality, prevailing winds were from south to north. By 1967, the two operations were within 500 feet of each other, and Spur was feeding 20,000 to 30,000 head of cattle and processing an estimated one million pounds of manure per day. Accordingly, Del Webb filed for an injunction, complaining that Spur was a public nuisance because of the flies and the odor that drifted over the southern portion of Sun City.

Writing for the court, Justice Cameron admitted that the result of the appeal might appear "novel." The court briefly addressed the nuisance issue, but the fact that Spur's operations amounted to a public nuisance was largely a given. The court emphasized that Webb would not have been granted injunctive relief if Webb were the only party injured:

> Plaintiffs chose to live in an area uncontrolled by zoning laws or restrictive covenants and remote from urban development. In such an area plaintiffs cannot complain that legitimate agricultural pursuits are being carried on in the vicinity, nor can plaintiffs, having chosen to build in an agricultural area, complain that the agricultural pursuits carried on in the area depreciate the value of their homes. The area being *primarily agricultural*, any opinion reflecting the value of such property must take this factor into account. The standards affecting the value of residence property in an urban setting . . . cannot be the standards by which agricultural properties are judged.[6]

However, the court had little choice but to grant the injunction, inasmuch as Webb was essentially suing on behalf of all of the residents of Sun City. The substantive question was whether to compensate Spur for relocation expenses. Like the two rivers that bounded the properties, the case embraced a confluence of doctrines:

> Were Webb the only party injured, we would feel justified in holding that the doctrine of "coming to the nuisance" would have been a bar to the relief asked by Webb, and, on the other hand, had Spur located the feedlot near the outskirts of a city and had the city grown toward the feedlot, Spur would have to suffer the cost of abating the nuisance as to those people locating within the growth pattern of the expanding city.[7]

In short, the fact that the apparent victim "came to the nuisance" does not provide blanket protection for the apparent culprit. In practice, nuisances seldom come to their victims. Accordingly, the court sought a balance among the following factors: (1) Spur could not have anticipated that a new city would spring up alongside the feeding operation; (2) Webb encouraged people to purchase homes in Sun City; (3) Webb took advantage of the lower land prices and availability of large tracts of land; and (4) the land was previously set aside for agricultural use. The balance that it found was to sustain the injunction, but to compensate Spur for relocation costs.

Economic Analysis

1. The distinction between public and private nuisance is economically important because it relates to the possibility of resolving the externality by bargaining. From the standpoint of Webb and Spur, we may envision the one-on-one externality; from the standpoint of the community, Spur (like Hadacheck in the preceding case) is imposing costs upon a large number of independent agents. Neither Webb nor Spur attempted to initiate negotiations. Perhaps both thought the law was on their side (property rights unclear). It is hard to imagine that neither party (particularly Webb) foresaw the problem. Indeed, Spur surely would not have expanded its operations if rights had been clearly specified and understood. Given that the relocation was eminently foreseeable, the expansion of the feedlot was an avoidable economic mistake.
2. The language of the court opinion reflects a clear appreciation for what Coase called the "reciprocal" nature of externalities. The odor from the feedlot imposes costs on the residents, but Webb imposed costs upon Spur by encouraging people to locate in Sun City. Given the location of Sun City next to the feedlot, the efficient solution

was to relocate the feedlot. In that narrow context, which party pays for the relocation is a largely irrelevant "income effect." In the broader context of locational choice, however, the compensation issue is critical. Compensating Spur encourages similar businesses to anticipate development and to consider social costs as well as private costs. In particular, the choice of location involved *a sacrifice of present and future profit to avoid or reduce potential external costs.*

3. Feedlots and brickyards must locate somewhere. As indicated in the court opinion, Spur's predecessors chose a location that was "well-suited" for a feedlot. The economic translation of well-suited could be "socially optimal." They may not have planned their location down to minute details, but they acted as if they were maximizing long-run profit net of external costs. The dry riverbeds were poorly suited for planting crops and perhaps ideal for the movement of cattle. Most importantly, they were isolated. There was no reason to tax or regulate Spur because the potential nuisance had no actual victims. At the time, Phoenix was expanding mainly eastward (in the direction of Mesa, Tempe, and Scottsdale).
4. It is useful to compare Spur's choice of location to that of Hadacheck in the preceding case. Hadacheck's choice of location was dictated by the immovability of the clay deposits. Ironically, a prime reason advanced in favor of compensation is the key factor against compensation. Hadacheck may have thought development would not come as soon as it did, but he took no extraordinary efforts to avoid civilization. In short, it would be wrong to say that Hadacheck made an *irrational* choice of location—at the *margin,* he made no choice at all—but he failed to go the extra mile that might have justified compensation.
5. Although the courts tend not to be explicit about their economic rationale, it seems clear that the issue of locational choice was the driving factor in explaining the divergence of the two decisions—why Hadacheck was not compensated for his losses, but Spur was indemnified for its relocation expenses. Except for the dimension of locational choice, the facts of the two cases are parallel: (1) Hadacheck could not have anticipated the annexation; (2) the city of Los Angeles encouraged development of the area; and (3) the city may have taken advantage of the lower land prices. The fact that Webb is a profit-oriented business and Los Angeles is a city government ought not to be relevant.

Cedar Rust

Miller et al v. Schoene
146 Va. 175 (1926), 76 U.S. 272 (1928)

Simple Facts

Cedar trees in Virginia were infected with a fungus known as cedar rust. In an effort to prevent communication of the fungus to neighboring apple orchards, a law mandated that infected cedars within a two-mile radius of apple orchards were to be cut down. The law branded the cedars as public nuisances and provided no compensation to owners of the cedar trees.

Details

The first botanical specimens of the *juniperus virginiana* came from Virginia, but the tree is widely dispersed throughout North America. The slender columns of the red cedar tree provide food and cover for more than 50 songbirds and game birds, including grouse, pheasant, morning dove, quail, and the cedar waxwing. The unique scent of the cedar was especially popular among colonial Americans, who manufactured cedar chests to protect their clothing and roof shingles to repel termites. The tree defends itself against harmful parasites by producing biochemical ingredients that repel harmful parasitic bacteria and fungi.

Cedar rust is an infectious plant fungus. Its life cycle has two phases alternating from red cedar to apple trees. The fungus was not communicable between trees of the same species, only from cedar to apple and back to cedar. Expert testimony revealed that a single cedar tree produces millions of spores annually, in the springtime (see Illustration 4.1). Carried by wind to the apple trees, the spores impart the cedar rust on the fruit, producing more spores to be carried back to uninfected red cedar trees in a perpetual cycle. Unless the galls containing spores were removed in the early spring of each year, the only feasible way to protect the apple trees was to destroy all infected red cedar trees located within two miles of apple orchards.

Although the red cedar has some use as lumber, its primary value is aesthetic and ornamental. In particular, its commercial value is insignificant relative to that of the apple tree. The cedars in question grew wild, mostly on grazing lands and the main commercial use at the time was for fence posts. Some evidence even suggested that the land is more valuable without them. Apple orchards were a major agricultural commodity in Virginia, were exported in large quantities, and provided employment for a large segment of the population.

The circumstances effectively forced the state to choose between two classes of private property. Logically, it chose the one with the higher value. The Virginia legislature passed the Cedar Rust Act in 1914. The act empowered the state entomologist (Schoene) to conduct official inspections and to condemn infected cedars. The statute branded the infected cedars as public nuisances, declared it unlawful to own them, and required owners to cut them down, without compensation. Inasmuch as all red cedar trees could host plants of cedar rust, it was not necessary to wait for absolute infection before the cedars could be destroyed.

ILLUSTRATION 4.1 Brown kidney-shaped galls (upper left) swell to bright gelatinous spore horns (lower right), which are carried to apple trees in the springtime, infecting leaves and fruit (upper right).

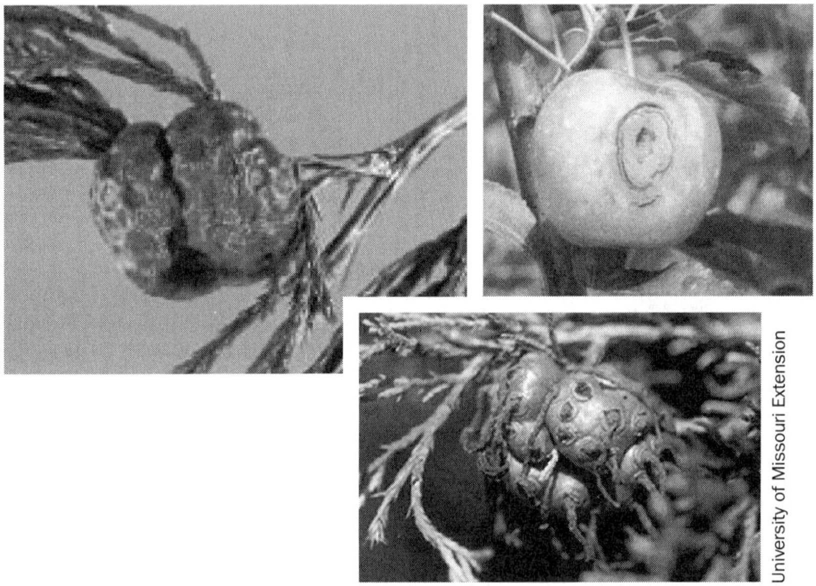

University of Missouri Extension

University of Missouri Extension

University of Missouri Extension

Miller and other plaintiffs sought compensatory damages of about $7,000 for diminution of property value from the loss of ornamental trees. Their main contention was that the government was destroying private property, not for public use, but for the promotion of the *welfare* of *individuals.* They argued that the statute was not concerned with the rights of anyone, other than the owners of the orchards and the cedar trees. In particular, since there was no threat to health or safety, it was inappropriate to brand the cedars as public nuisances.

The Virginia Supreme Court had no problem with the nuisance issue. While conceding that the red cedars have a scenic value if properly trimmed and kept in order, it held (emphasis added) that: "an infected cedar tree is not merely dangerous to apple trees within two miles of such cedar tree. If the infected cedar tree infects an orchard, this orchard will infect previously uninfected cedar trees, and thus this *dangerous disease* is widely disseminated."[8]

The U.S. Supreme Court sidestepped the question of whether the infected cedars constituted a nuisance. It simply held that the state was exercising its legal police power. Specifically, since the choice was unavoidable and the social policy was not unreasonable, there was no denial of due process. However, the Court did make an oblique connection with nuisance, pointing out that the injury to property was no more serious, nor the public interest less, than in *Hadacheck* and similar cases. On the issue of public purpose:

> It will not do to say that the case is merely one of a conflict of two private interests and that the misfortune of apple growers may not be shifted to cedar owners by ordering the destruction of their property; for it is obvious that there may be, and that here there is, a preponderant public concern in the preservation of the one interest over the other.[9]

Plaintiffs were awarded no compensation, except $100 for the removal of the trees.

Economic Analysis

1. As in the preceding case, the high-value commercial enterprise endures. The destruction of the infected cedars to save the apple orchards is clearly an efficient action. Were the values reversed, the law would have found a suitable mechanism for maintaining the cedars, akin to the land servitude arrangement in *Boomer v. Atlantic Cement* (see the following case).

2. Prior cases witnessed victims coming to the nuisance and nuisances coming to victims. This one seems to involve a nuisance that came to the culprit. Indeed, some analysts have referred to the cedar rust as an "act of God," maintaining that the question of compensating the owners of the cedar trees is a close call. The answer lies in the "technology" of the externality—how it is produced, transmitted, and absorbed.

3. Before considering the technology, there are a few red herrings to cull from the discussion. The main one is the plaintiff's argument that the rust is not a public nuisance because the harm accrues only to other owners of *private* property. Another is the state court's reference to the rust as a "dangerous disease," apparently for the purpose of lending credence to the "public nuisance" label. "Strike three" is the reference to the aggregate number of people employed by the commercial apple industry. Other things being equal, the more people that are employed by the industry, the more costly the enterprise and the less inclined the public should be to favor apple trees to cedars. The common error of equating employment to social benefits is palatable only because of the correlation between employment and productive output.

4. Cedar rust is to cedar trees as dust is to bricks and stench is to manure. Neither cedars, nor bricks, nor fertilizers are noxious. However, the *by-product* is noxious and it *invades* surrounding properties. Whether the invasion extends far enough to warrant the label of *public* nuisance is relevant to the determination of an appropriate remedy, but not to the issue of compensation. The fact that infestation is a random event is similarly irrelevant; if only one brick out of every 10 generated dust, the owner of the factory would still be responsible for the dust.

5. There are two apparently minor points buried in the state court opinion. One is that the red cedars "are supposed to possess a scenic value" if "properly trimmed and kept in order."[10] This was the basis for the contention that the land might be worth more without them. The other is a simple qualifying clause. Destroying the infested cedars is the only feasible way of protecting the apple orchards *unless* the galls containing spores were removed in the early spring of each year. These "diamonds

in the rough" are the things that the economist looks for among the obscure Latin phrases and footnotes. There is now an alternative to destroying the cedars.

6. Except for the passing reference to the pruning, the court viewed the development of the cedar rust as "an act of God." That sentiment was echoed by Warren Samuels and Richard Epstein in their analyses of the case and not challenged by James Buchanan in his analysis of the property rights issues.[11] While the initial development of the fungus was unavoidable, the transmission of the fungus to apple trees was avoidable. Uninfected trees simply are more costly to maintain than infected ones. Unlike the dust from the brickyard or the stench from the feed lot, the "s" per cedar tree is an economic variable. Cedar owners' behavior ranges from passivity (neglect) to regular trimming (to maintain aesthetics) to careful attention (timely removal of galls). Neglected trees are public nuisances. They will be noticed and the 10 freeholders will notify the authorities. Regularly trimmed cedars are private nuisances, which might harm an occasional apple tree and attract attention. Given regular trimming, each individual owner weighs the marginal aesthetic value with the marginal cost, including the risk of losing trees to the entomologist's saw.

7. This alternative was not even mentioned in the court opinion. Its absence suggests that the ornamental value of the trees may not have been significant. If the ornamental value is important, the cedars require attention. A natural extension would be to check the trees for the galls and to remove them before the spores develop. If the owners keep the trees free of rust, the entomologist does not order them to be cut down. If they do not, we may infer that the ornamental value is not worth the effort to maintain the trees.

Damage Control

Boomer et al. v. Atlantic Cement 26 N.Y. 2d 219 (1970)

Simple Facts

Eight plaintiffs, each operating small businesses, filed suit to force the closure of a cement plant. The noise and pollution emitted from the plant was found to constitute a nuisance, despite the fact that the plant employed state-of-the-art pollution control technology. The trial court awarded compensatory damages in lieu of an injunction.

Details

In 1962, the Atlantic Cement Company began operation in Coeymans, New York, about 11 miles south of Albany. The initial investment value of the plant exceeded $40 million, including about $1.6 million for pollution abatement. The company employed more than 300 workers. The plant continued to operate until August 1967, at which time, eight plaintiffs filed a class action suit seeking an injunction to close the plant.

The plaintiffs owned the lands and were operating their businesses before the cement plant began its operation and claimed that the respondent was polluting their properties and causing a general nuisance of vibration from the plant's operation. These combined activities led to loss of business for the plaintiffs involved. The businesses included a dairy farm, an auto body shop, and a small distillery. The estimated value of businesses and homes was about $350,000 when the plant opened in 1962.

The trial judge noted that Atlantic had taken "every available and possible precaution to protect the plaintiffs from dust," but held that the factory did create a nuisance:

> The discharge of large quantities of dust upon each of the properties and excessive vibration from blasting deprived each party of the reasonable use of his property and thereby prevented his enjoyment of life and liberty. . . .[12]

Accordingly, the court had the *power* to grant the injunction. The judge refused to do so on grounds that the injunction would "produce great public hardship."[13] In lieu of the injunction, the plaintiffs were awarded permanent damages. The aggregate sum was about $200,000, including diminution of property values and damage to automobiles.

The appellate court noted a long history of enforcing injunctions despite large "disparity in economic consequences."

> The ground for the denial of injunction, notwithstanding the finding both that there is a nuisance and that plaintiffs have been damaged substantially, is the large disparity in economic consequences of the nuisance and of the injunction. This theory cannot, however, be sustained without overruling a doctrine which has been consistently reaffirmed in several leading cases in this court and which has never been disavowed here, namely that where a nuisance has been found and where there has been any substantial damage shown by the party complaining an injunction will be granted.[14]

Ultimately, the court upheld the concept of permanent damages while technically reversing the lower court. It emphasized that the judgment, "by allowance of permanent damages imposing a servitude on land, which is the basis of the actions, would preclude future recovery by plaintiffs or their grantees." The implied message to the lower court was that the basis for damage assessment was incorrect.

The final resolution involved lengthy testimony about subjective factors, with clear implication that surrendering servitude of the land entitled the defendants to more than just estimated reduction in fair market value. In determining permanent damages, the trial court noted: (1) temporary damages already found, (2) damage from September 1962 to December 1972, (3) fair market value with and without the nuisance, (4) consideration of plaintiffs' (subjective) theories, and (5) future damages. The owners of the dairy farm eventually accepted a lump sum of $175,000. Settlements for other plaintiffs were not disclosed.

Economic Analysis

1. Without explicitly admitting it, the New York courts brokered a bargain. In so doing, they made it clear that the proceedings related only to the private aspects of the nuisance—the costs imposed on the small group of plaintiffs seeking the injunction. The appellate court emphasized that the "relief granted is a limitation only within the four corners of these actions and does not foreclose public health or other public agencies from seeking proper relief in a proper court."

2. It is important not to confuse the bargain brokered by the court with a Coasian bargain. Whereas the court-imposed bargain had a strong taint of coercion, the latter is a purely voluntary agreement. The procedure adopted by the court reveals a strong reluctance on the part of the judiciary to do cost-benefit analysis. Indeed, even though a rule of imposing damages is *vastly superior to a permanent injunction*, the decision was not unanimous and the dissent (against allowing polluters to buy rights) was passionate. The short-run outcome of permitting the plant to continue operations clearly serves the interests of efficiency. Long-run implications are more complex. It is therefore important to consider this decision in context of both the past and the future.

3. Atlantic's choice of the Coeymans location appears to be an efficient one because of the small number of apparently low-cost victims. Given that location, the firm faced three administrative options: (a) to seek government cooperation; (b) to negotiate directly with the neighboring property owners, individually or collectively; and (c) to build the plant and accept the legal consequences after the fact. Option (a) probably would have failed; Coeymans was not Detroit and Atlantic Cement was not General Motors (see *Poletown v. Detroit* in Chapter 2). Option (b) is a Coasian bargain, which almost certainly would have been mutually beneficial.

4. The Coasian bargain failed to materialize because of high transactions costs and/or unclear property rights. In 1962, there was no Environmental Protection Agency (EPA) to set pollution standards. Environmentalism was far from a "movement," and standards varied considerably from one locale to another. Transactions costs might appear to be low because the number of affected parties was small, but an agreement with eight different parties would be hampered by the holdout problem. The holdout problem might be severe in this case because of the tendency for each of the seven small claimants to seek equal bargaining status with the dairy.

The alternative of attempting to strike eight separate bargains is not only time-consuming, but also risky and more costly because of the need to maintain secrecy to avoid the holdout problem. Finally, the group of affected parties was not clearly identified until 1967 when they filed suit and the court limited the claimants to *Boomer et al.*

5. In choosing to go ahead and build the plant without any legal guarantees, Atlantic pursued a risky strategy with at least the trappings of economic sophistication. In effect, the company put much of its $45 million investment at risk of permanent closure. The straightforward economic explanation of this action is that Atlantic (figuratively) *expected to pay an efficient Pigouvian tax!* In contrast to the brickyard in *Hadacheck v. Sebastian* (see case earlier in chapter), an efficient tax on the cement plant would not be so high as to warrant closure. Accordingly, the rational firm expected an efficient government to charge an appropriate fee for the costs imposed upon its environment. Subject to the procedural wrangling, that is essentially what the government did.

6. In anticipation of the prospect of regulation, Atlantic behaved as if it expected to pay an emissions tax. The company invested $1.6 million in state-of-the-art pollution abatement technology. Although there is no observable reduction in output, we may infer that its plant capacity was designed to an approximately efficient size, given the full social costs of operating it. Politically, that investment might also be interpreted as a gesture of good faith to deter the law from taking a more hostile position.

7. The expectations of the culprit are only half of the social equation. Long-run efficient use of land is largely independent of who gets there first. Whether the victim comes to the nuisance or, in this case, the nuisance comes to the victim, both should behave as though in response to a known set of efficient incentives. The presumption that all parties have (reasonably) correct expectations provides the economic link between past, present, and future. Very likely, the victims did not anticipate that a cement plant would one day disturb their pastoral environment. But transport costs preclude cement plants from locating far from populous areas. Atlantic Cement chose its victims—arguably those least harmed by the noise, vibrations, and dust. Without having to pay damages, Atlantic would choose victims indiscriminately. More importantly, occupants of the land are transitory.

8. Precisely because occupants of land are transitory, the use of a property rule (payment for servitude) instead of a liability rule (compensation for diminution of market value) bristles with efficiency implications. The compensatory payments are owed to "the land" in addition to its current occupants. Even though the servitude is permanent, future owners are not harmed by it because market prices will accurately reflect the lower value of the land. What the lower land prices do is compensate future victims on the basis of *exposure to potential harm.* Compensation based on actual harm would encourage an economic absurdity—the location of high-cost victims next to the plant!

9. Economic purists should be bothered by the fact that Atlantic's payments were lump sum. Unless the pollution is taxed directly, simple theory implies that the rational

cement company will respond with inefficiently high rates of pollution. While there is no doubt some truth to this caveat, Atlantic had already designed its factory on the expectation of having to pay an emissions tax. Without having implemented the abatement technology, Atlantic might well have had to close the factory. All things considered, Atlantic's long-run behavior is highly consistent with that of a competitive firm responding to correct market prices and efficient Pigouvian taxes. Moreover, the rights acquired by Atlantic are limited to a servitude over a few neighboring properties. Should Atlantic wish to expand the scope of its operations, it would have to ensure that the pollution did not extend beyond the boundaries of the acquired rights. If it did, the firm would then be subject to additional sanctions.

CHAPTER 5

PUBLIC GOODS

Textbook examples of public goods are lighthouses, television entertainment, and national defense. Without dwelling on the examples, they are defined in terms of the absence of two key characteristics: rivalry and excludability. **Rivalry** implies that one person's consumption precludes consumption by anyone else. **Excludability** implies that suppliers (providers, producers, owners) can withhold a private good from any potential consumer, typically those who do not pay for it. These two properties characterize *private* goods. They relate directly to the basic question of why a price mechanism is efficient or important. Prices serve three broad purposes: (1) a rationing mechanism; (2) an incentive structure, and (3) a source of information.

Rivalry, Nonrivalry, and Rationing

The **rationing** purpose relates directly to the notion of rivalry and merits strong emphasis: *prices ration scarce goods to their highest valued uses*. The economic assumptions embodied in this proposition are that prices are competitively determined and that value is synonymous with willingness to pay. Accordingly, price will rise to a level such that high- and low-value consumers identify themselves naturally and voluntarily by the simple acts of buying and refusing to buy or by accepting and declining offers. Without prices as a rationing device, some potential value is lost as low-value replaces high-value. Moreover, alternative means of rationing (e.g., waiting in lines) may be far more costly. All of this changes if the commodity is nonrival. Using a price mechanism as a means of rationing becomes totally pointless.

The classic economic example, first analyzed by Jules Dupuit in 1844, is a bridge. Within bounds set by physical dimensions, large numbers of vehicles can utilize the bridge at negligible cost; hence, it is nonrival. At relatively low cost, a barrier can be erected, enabling a controlling authority to monitor and regulate use; thus, the bridge is excludable. The simple purposes of the barrier are to impose a price and to collect revenues. Given the hypothetical demand conditions underlying Figure 5.1, a toll of $5 per person could generate revenues of $2,500 (say, per day), which might be sufficient to finance construction of the bridge. Moreover, the 500 people who use the bridge are the ones who place the most value upon using it.

The dilemma is that the toll also discourages use—500 of the 1,000 potential users choose to forego the benefits. At a user charge of zero, 1,000 people would use the bridge, for an economic surplus of 5,000 (area under the marginal benefit curve). Surplus is reduced by 1,250 if the 500 marginal users do not use the bridge. Although the people who comprise this group are clearly the low-value users, the small loss to individuals may add up to a significant social loss. The overriding point is that those additional benefits could have been generated *without cost*. The user charge sends out the message that crossing the bridge "costs" $5. If the message were correct, the price

FIGURE 5.1 Pricing generates revenue (up to $2,500), but discourages beneficial use that could be generated without additional cost.

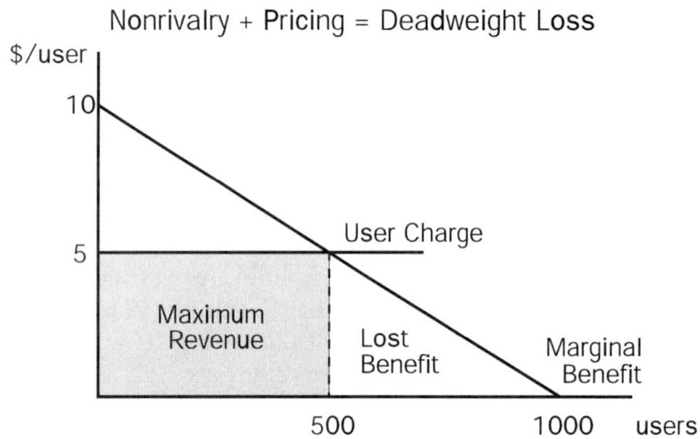

mechanism would have performed a useful social function by rationing use only to those whose value of use (known only by the individual) exceeds the cost of use. However, the message is a false one because no additional resources are expended by the simple act of crossing the bridge.

A common fallacy about this concept is that allowing free use of the bridge would be costly to the owner in the form of lost revenue, $2,500 in the example. The statement is correct as far as it goes, but the fallacy lies in omitting the other side of the balance sheet. The owner's loss is the users' gain—the $2,500 is just a transfer of money. If the bridge is owned and operated by a government, the transfer is between citizens and their government. The same reasoning applies to ownership by private business, but there is an added dimension. Without the power to tax, the profit motive to produce the bridge is severely compromised.

Exclusion and Financial Incentives

The bridge paradigm provides the starting point for all discussions pertaining to excluding people from using public goods. The simple principle is that exclusion is wasteful. A competing principle is that exclusion for the purpose of financing is expedient and (in light of the fact that arranging for financing is seldom without cost) might be less wasteful than other alternatives. As applied to exclusion, the word "expedient" is used in the administrative sense. People are excluded in the sense that they may exchange payment for access. That procedure is generally accepted, straightforward, and uncomplicated.

Exclusion may also be impossible or prohibitively expensive to implement. Tollbooths are easy for bridges, but cumbersome for highways with exit and entry points every mile or so. Perhaps nothing is impossible, but preventing ships from using the services of a lighthouse comes close. It was for this reason that, in 1883, Henry Sidgwick chose the lighthouse as the paradigm for what came to be called the **pure public good**—the nonrival, nonexcludable good that must be provided by a government (directly or indirectly) if it is to be provided at all. As applied to lighthouses and national defense, that caveat is about as true in reality as it is in theory.

Without the ability to exclude as a means of enforcing payment of user charges, profit-oriented businesses have to seek alternative means of financing. One alternative is government subsidy, which doesn't count because private provision through government subsidy is essentially equivalent to government provision. Another is enforcement of the right to collect payment after the fact. For example, the British crown commissioned private companies to build lighthouses, with limited rights to assess fees to operators of ships using harbor facilities. Similarly, software piracy may not be preventable, but detection has recently become feasible, so that copyrights are more enforceable than they once were.

Whether the right to exclude or collect payment is enforceable or not, the key point is that users have virtually no purely economic incentive to make voluntary contributions toward the financing of a good that provides them with benefits. In game-theoretic terms, voluntary payment is a **dominated strategy**—individuals are worse off for having contributed, whether others contribute or not. If others do contribute, the public good gets produced, and the noncontributor enjoys the benefits without having to pay for them. If others do not contribute, the public good is not produced, and the contributor loses the amount of the contribution without enjoyment of any offsetting benefits. The solution to the game is that no one contributes, and the good is not produced.

This theoretical result—that public goods will not be provided by voluntary contribution—is known as the **free rider problem**. As applied to practical circumstances, this result is not absolute; the softer version is that free riding tends to result in *under*-production of public goods. Either way, it is a barrier to provision by the private sector and an argument in favor of provision by government. However, it is wrong to conclude that the free rider problem is solved by government provision. Quite the contrary; the free rider problem re-emerges in a different form.

Free Riding and the (non) Revelation of Preferences

To illustrate how the free rider problem applies to governmental provision, we may apply the same data contained in Figure 5.1 and assume that exclusion is not feasible. For example, the project is not a bridge, but a bike path that costs \$3,000, including land and construction. Assuming that everyone would be permitted to use the path without direct payment, the consumer surplus would be \$5,000—so that a simple comparison of benefits and costs suggests that the path should be constructed. Accordingly, the city holds a referendum in which everyone (1,500 citizens) votes on whether to impose a \$2 tax per person to construct the path. This "tax price" is not the same as a user charge. If the measure passes and funds are allocated to the construction of the path, all citizens are forced to pay the tax whether they use it or not.

The effect of the tax price upon voting behavior is illustrated in Figure 5.2. As the marginal benefit curve indicates, 1,000 of the citizens would use the path at a user charge of zero, but the remaining 500 would get no benefit at all. The outcome is predictable. A majority (800 out of 1,500) votes in favor of the tax. However, a closer examination of impact of this outcome identifies gainers and losers. The clear gainers

FIGURE 5.2 At a "tax price" of $2 per person, the referendum passes, 800 to 700. At the higher price of $3 per person, the referendum fails.

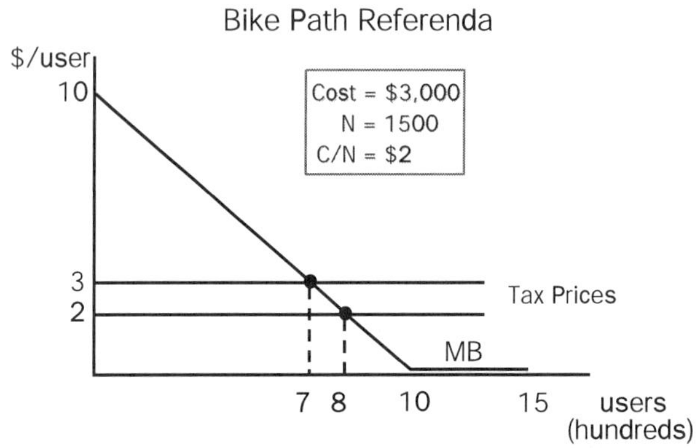

are those in the majority whose benefits exceed the tax price. The losers are the 700 citizens who comprise the minority. Most of them (500) get no benefits, but pay the tax anyway. The other 200 use the path, but benefit by less than the $2 tax. This group is not deterred from using the path because use is not conditioned on payment.

In this example, efficiency is served at some cost in terms of equity. The majority has imposed its will upon the minority and the constitutional tolerance of this process is not unlimited. In addition to considerations of equity, efficiency is not guaranteed. As a counter example, suppose the path costs $4,500. The 500 nonusers still vote against the referendum, but the tax price has risen to $3, inducing another 100 of the would-be users to change their votes. The measure fails; the new majority of 800 votes against the project, even though the benefits outweigh the costs.

Assuming that this outcome is undesirable, the problem can be overcome by creative financing. One way is to impose a larger tax burden on the high-demand users; this is a pragmatic possibility, but (strictly speaking) the free rider problem prevents it from happening. The other way is to impose a larger tax burden on those who are already voting against it. The imposition of disproportionately large burdens on specific individuals or groups will be the subject matter of two of the cases to be discussed later in the chapter. The issue is partly a matter of simple justice, but also a matter of efficiency. The same tactic could be used, in principle, when social costs exceed social benefits. Ultimately, the free rider problem applies to both groups. Governments are not mind readers and cannot distinguish between high-value users, low-value users, and nonusers with any substantial degree of confidence.

Referenda provide some guarantees against overzealous governments, but most of the important issues surrounding the provision of public goods are too complicated to be decided at the ballot box. Dimensions of size, quality, durability, and location are at least as important as the simple yes or no. In the abstract, all of these quantitative dimensions may be lumped together into one measure of quantity, so that we may

FIGURE 5.3 The theoretical optimal quantity (q*) of a public good is determined at point E, but finding optimal solutions in practice is not a realistic possibility.

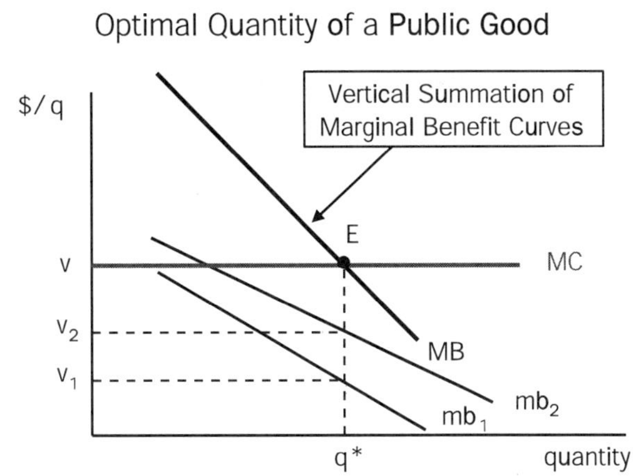

consider the question of "how much" of the public good should be produced. In Figure 5.3, marginal benefits are represented as decreasing functions of quantity, for each of two individuals—of course, that number is invariably much larger than two. The optimal quantity is thus determined by adding up marginal benefits and equating the sum to the marginal cost. That rule translates into a vertical summation of the individual marginal benefit curves. It is a theoretical prescription for efficiency that is virtually impossible to implement with any degree of precision. Along the vertical axis, individual valuations generate an aggregate "v," equal to marginal cost, but the individual valuations are only implicit prices. They cannot be actual prices because everyone is consuming the same quantity whether they pay the price or not.

The fact that optimal solutions are impossible to implement in practice does not imply that governments should not use the theoretical solution as a guideline. In practice, the rigid conditions that define pure public goods are rarely satisfied. Nonrivalry often applies only up to a threshold level, giving way to crowding or deterioration of quality. Similarly, exclusion is almost always *possible*, particularly if extraordinary measures are undertaken. Once exclusion becomes feasible, provision by the private sector is expanded beyond the realm of voluntary contributions. The economic focus shifts away from the ability to exclude, to the right to exclude. The dilemma is that exclusion and pricing may deter efficient use, but limiting the right to exclude encourages free riding and reduces the incentive to produce.

Cases dealing with public goods ultimately relate to social incentive structures. The law seeks to find appropriate compromise with regard to the dimensions of use, provision, and information. This chapter will be concerned not with lighthouses or national defense, but with the provision of waterways, bike paths, flood relief, skyscrapers, and historical landmarks.

Ahupua'a

Kaiser Aetna v. United States
444 U.S. 164 (1979)

Simple Facts

Construction of a channel was privately funded by a housing developer, with prior approval by the Army Corps of Engineers. The channel provided a navigational link between a privately owned pond and the Pacific Ocean. After construction of the channel was completed, the Corps asserted public access under the doctrine of navigational servitude.

Details

Hawaiian fishponds were part of a complex aquaculture system developed in the late Pleistocene Period, near the end of the ice age. They included both man-made and

ILLUSTRATION 5.1 Hawaiian fishponds were part of a complex aquaculture system developed in the late Pleistocene Period, near the end of the ice age.

Courtesy, J.M. Farber

natural enclosures of water in which fish were raised and harvested. Early Hawaiians built the ponds out of stones piled up to make walls. A large number of people would form a line from a rock quarry to the pond and pass the rocks from one to another. The boundaries of the ponds were usually marked by an altar (*ahu*) with the image of a pig (*pua'a*) and the surrounding land thereby came to be called *ahupua'a*.

Traditional law was a reflection of the scarcity of fresh water. The laws, known as the *kanawai*, imposed strict regulations upon the use of water and severe punishments for damaging irrigation systems or harming the water source. Fishing was permitted only at certain times of the year.

Kuapa Pond is contiguous to Maunalua Bay on the island of Oahu. Until 1961, its waters were used exclusively for fishing. However, it is somewhat misleading to call it a fish pond, inasmuch as it covers 523 acres and extends inland from Maunalua Bay a distance of approximately two miles. Kuapa Pond's private ownership dates from the Great Mahele of 1848, wherein King Kamehameha III granted large land units to his chiefs. It was part of an *ahupua'a* that eventually became part of the Bishop Estate, which leased a 6,000-acre tract to Kaiser Aetna. As part of the Hawaii Kai subdivision, Kaiser Aetna constructed a marina and dredged a channel to provide access to and from Maunalua Bay. Kaiser Aetna controlled access to and use of the marina.

Before embarking on the project, Kaiser Aetna notified the Army Corps of Engineers of its development plans. The Corps advised Kaiser Aetna that the company was not required to obtain permits for the development of the marina. With regard to the channel in particular, the Corps granted its full approval, except for noting that the channel might cause erosion of the beach.

In 1972, a dispute arose concerning whether Kaiser Aetna needed authorization from the Corps for future construction in the marina and, more importantly, over the developer's right to deny public access to the pond. The Corps made authorization contingent upon Kaiser Aetna's granting an easement for public access. Ultimately, the Corps invoked the doctrine of navigational servitude, claiming that the pond was "navigable water of the United States."

The district court conceded that the pond was navigable for the purpose of placing it under Congress' regulatory power, but refused to grant public access. However, the court of appeals held that the conversion of the pond into a marina and the connection with the bay did indeed create navigational servitude, thus giving the public a right of access to what was once private property. Kaiser Aetna appealed.

The U.S. Supreme Court sided with the district court, affirming the government's right to assert public access, but required the government to pay just compensation under eminent domain. Writing for the Court, Justice Rehnquist (emphasis added) drew a clear distinction between Congress' authority to assure the public a free right of access to the Hawaii Kai Marina and whether the exercise of that right constitutes a taking of private property:

> The owner of what was once a *private pond*, separated from concededly navigable water by a barrier beach and used for aquatic agriculture, has *invested substantial amounts of money* in making improvements. The Government contends that as a result of one of these improvements, the pond's connection to the navigable water in a manner approved by the Corps of Engineers, the owner has somehow lost one of the most *essential sticks in the bundle of rights* that are commonly characterized as property—*the right to exclude* others.[1]

Rehnquist also called attention (emphasis added) to the timing of the government's actions:

> We have not the slightest doubt that the Government could have refused to allow such dredging on the ground that it would have impaired navigation in the bay, or could have *conditioned its approval* of the dredging on petitioners' *agreement to comply with various measures* that it deemed appropriate for the promotion of navigation. But what petitioners now have is a body of water that was private property under Hawaiian law, linked to navigable water by a channel dredged by them with *the consent of the Government.*[2]

The opinion cut across traditional liberal-conservative lines, most notably with Justice Stevens concurring. A dissenting opinion by Justice Blackmun advocated strict interpretation of the concept of navigable waters, citing the substantial federal interest in maintaining "common highways, . . . forever free."[3]

Economic Analysis

1. The remarkable community effort in constructing the ponds reveals that the native Hawaiians were not significantly encumbered by the free rider problem. Aside from that, the most fascinating aspect of this case is that of role reversal: a private business provides a public good, while the government exhibits the classic free rider behavior! Accordingly, it provides a unique scenario for addressing the three allocative problems (use, provision, and financing) associated with public goods. We may start with use of the good and the case for free riding.
2. The strongest case for the government is to invoke navigational servitude on grounds that the channel is a nonrival good—allowing public access does not diminish homeowners' ability or capacity to enjoy the channel. That case is somewhat weakened by the potential for crowding and congestion, as well as by fundamental issues of privacy and security. In principle, however, navigational servitude relates directly to the nonrivalry as applied generally to waterways. Blackmun's dissenting opinion focused almost exclusively on this dimension.
3. With regard to provision, the important difference between government and private enterprise is the right to tax. Without the power to tax, the developer has two sources of revenue. One is to impose user charges (docking fees at the marina); the other is to extract indirect payment through higher prices for the developed lots in the subdivision. Public access does not eliminate these sources of revenue, but can reduce them in innumerable ways (e.g., crowded facilities and compromised security). These are difficult to evaluate. Moreover, the revenues collected by Kaiser Aetna are, at best, imperfect measures of homeowners' willingness to pay for the channel.
4. The fact that this channel is already constructed does not eliminate the provision question. If Kaiser Aetna had known in advance about the public access rights, it may have done some things differently. In relation to Figure 5.3, the "mb_1" and "mb_2" curves pertain to potential benefits to homeowners (represented by Kaiser Aetna) and the general public (represented by the Corps of Engineers). A major

component of demand remained *unrevealed*. The Corps either willfully withheld its intentions or failed to anticipate the extent of public interest in the project. Either way, the effect was to "conceal their true preferences." Rehnquist's reference to what the Corps "could have done" is more than an oblique reference to government shenanigans.

5. Primarily as an affirmation of an intrinsic connection between private property and the right to exclude, Kaiser was awarded just compensation. As a matter of efficiency, the outcome finds a nice balance among the three allocative dimensions. Failure to force the government to pay compensation would be a clear invitation for free riding, thereby discouraging future private provision of public goods. The fact that the public use probably imposed some form of congestion costs (e.g., loss of privacy or threat to security) upon the homeowners strengthens the case against the government.

Coelum et Inferos

United States v. Causby 328 U.S. 256 (1946)

Simple Facts

During World War II, the government contracted for use of a municipal airport for various military purposes. Army and Navy planes began regular operation of frequent, low altitude use by heavy bombers. Plaintiffs claimed that the government had taken their property by rendering it unfit for the operation of their chicken farm and (almost) for habitation.

Details

Thomas Lee and Tinie Causby opened a commercial chicken farm in Greensboro, North Carolina, in 1934. At the time, a small airfield existed a little more than one-third of a mile from the farm. The airfield and chicken farm peacefully coexisted until 1942, at which time the United States contracted to use the airfield for military flights. The government intended to use the airfields throughout the National Emergency, now known as World War II. In addition to increased traffic, low-altitude flights became common—bombers approached at heights of 83 feet, just 18 feet above the trees.

The frequency and severity of noise and the glare from the flights frightened Causby's family, as well as the chickens. On a typical night, six to 10 chickens would fly frantically into walls and die. Also, the productivity of the surviving chickens dropped dramatically, forcing Causby to shut down the chicken farm. Initially, the court of claims determined that the severity of the damage caused by the flights amounted to a taking of an easement. Accordingly, it awarded compensatory damages of $2,000.

On appeal, the U.S. Supreme Court seized the opportunity to clarify a general principle about landowners' rights to superadjacent airspace. Although "ancient doctrine" asserted that common law ownership of land extends indefinitely upward, the Court held that such doctrine "has no place in the modern world."[4] Without the clear understanding that airspace is a "public highway," every commercial flight would subject the operator to "countless trespass suits."

This holding lent substantial support for the government's contention that, when flights are made within the navigable airspace without any physical invasion of the property of the landowners, there can be no taking of property. Specifically, Causby did not own exclusive rights to the superadjacent airspace, nor had he subjected it to possession by the erection of structures or other occupancy. The government added a technicality: even if the United States took airspace owned by Causby, the damages were merely consequential and, therefore, not compensable under the Fifth Amendment.

The Court refused to accept this argument. The government had conceded on oral argument that there would have been a compensable taking if the property had been rendered uninhabitable. Extending the hypothetical, the Court maintained that there was "no material difference between the supposed case and the present one, except that here enjoyment and use of the land are not completely destroyed . . . [and] that does not seem to us to be controlling."[5] Although the airspace is a public highway, the landowner must have exclusive control of the "immediate reaches" of the enveloping atmosphere:

> While the owner does not in any physical manner occupy that stratum of airspace or make use of it in the conventional sense, he does use it in somewhat the same sense that space left between buildings for the purpose of light and air is used. The superadjacent airspace at this low altitude is so close to the land that continuous invasions of it affect the use of the surface of the land itself. We think that the landowner . . . has a claim to it and that invasions of it are in the same category as invasions of the surface.[6]

Accordingly, the majority upheld the substance of the lower court's findings. Causby was entitled to compensation. On remand, the court of claims reduced the damage award to $1,435 because the land servitude was not permanent. The $1,435 included $1,060 for rent of the easement and $375 for the chickens.

Justice Black's dissenting remarks are noteworthy:

> The concept of taking property as used in the Constitution has heretofore never been given so sweeping a meaning. The Court's opinion presents no case where a man who makes noise or shines light onto his neighbor's property has been ejected from that property for wrongfully taking possession of it. Nor would anyone take seriously a claim that noisy automobiles passing on a highway are taking wrongful possession of the homes located thereon, or that a city elevated train which greatly interferes with the sleep of those who live next to it wrongfully takes their property.[7]

Economic Analysis

1. For centuries, the common law doctrine was *ad coelum et ad inferos*—literally, "to the sky and to the depths." Ownership of surface land carried with it the complete control over everything above and below the property. The coal mining cases (*Pennsylvania Coal v. Mahon* and *Keystone v. DeBenedictis*) discussed in Chapters 2 and 3 addressed the *inferos*; this one is tinkering with the *coelum*.
2. Ancient doctrines emerged along with land scarcity and the development of agrarian society. However, the scarcity to which the doctrine applied was *horizontal*, rather than *vertical*. As a starting point, we may imagine three completely separate land estates in the horizontal direction. Along the ground level, land is parceled out according to area. Exclusive rights are strongly enforced because use of the surface land is rival. The same principle applies to the subsurface mineral rights, again because one person's extraction and use of the minerals precludes the extraction and use by others. In stark contrast, use of airspace is a public good in virtually the same sense as bridges, highways, and waterways.
3. The "public highway" analogy is useful in two respects. First, to the extent that flight paths remain uncongested (as they were in the 1940s), airspace is nonrival in a practical sense. Second, flight paths are indivisible. Use for air transportation requires, essentially, that each aircraft have access to the entire airspace (though, of

course, not simultaneously). The 1926 appropriation of the airspace under the Air Commerce Act was clearly in the public interest. It was also not a taking, *precisely because surface property rights were not materially affected.*

4. The foregoing horizontal relationships are illustrated in Figure 5.4. Pricing and markets govern the use of the surface and mineral estates because users compete for quantities of scarce space. Because space is rival in both of these dimensions, it is more than sensible that the same person have initial ownership *ad inferos* as well as the right to sell one or the other. For example, the full realization of economies of scale in mining would be encumbered by tying ownership of the two estates together. The same principle does not extend *ad coelum* because parceling out airspace is both unnecessary (because airways are nonrival) and counterproductive (because of the indivisibility of use).

5. Figure 5.4 also draws attention to the vertical dimensions, which are not covered by laws relating to the horizontal. To the extent that the pursuit of mining interests interfered with enjoyment of surface property rights (by creating subsidence), the law had to deal with the potential externalities. Although the Air Commerce Act did not have explicit provisions to cover a vertical "buffer zone," the existence of such a zone may be inferred from how the law related to mining.

6. Determining the exact vertical boundary of surface land is somewhat arbitrary and surely ought to vary according to circumstances. The precedent established in *Causby* is that the landowner owns "at least as much of the space above the ground as he can occupy or use in connection with the land, even though he does not occupy it in a physical sense by buildings and the like." The larger point is that a conceptual

FIGURE 5.4 In the horizontal direction, surface and mineral rights are rival and divisible, but use of airspace is rival and indivisible.

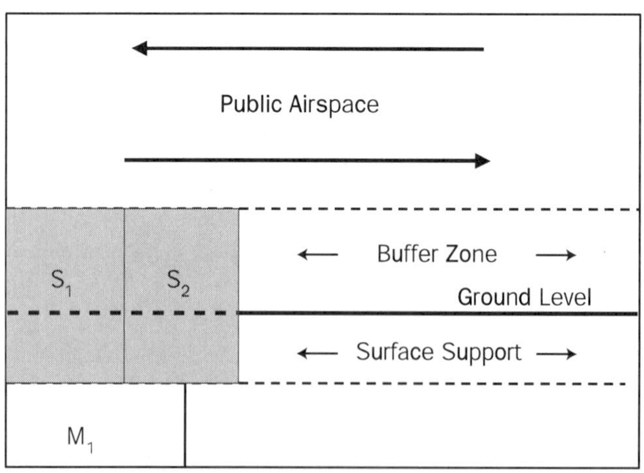

boundary does exist and that the permanent or semi-permanent invasion of it amounts to a servitude on the land. As in *Boomer v. Atlantic Cement* (see Chapter 4), the property owner was entitled to rent for the use of his land.

7. The government attempted to create an alternative paradigm, crafting an analogy to a zoning regulation, wherein the favoring of one use (aviation) over another (commercial/residential) merely caused a diminution of Causby's property. That analogy fails by logical contradiction. Specifically, the government appropriated the airspace for general and commercial aviation—bypassing both the market and the eminent domain courts—via the premise that use of the airways did not materially interfere with surface property rights. Indeed, that premise was not really at issue in this case: aviation in general was not interfering with surface rights in general. Once the zoning paradigm fails, the nuisance paradigm takes over and analysis proceeds as though the government and the Causbys were neighbors along the *horizontal* plane. Accordingly, the payment for temporary servitude was analogous to fair market value in an eminent domain proceeding.

8. Justice Black's dissent misses the same point. The hypothetical noisy neighbors to whom Black refers are the sole owners of the adjacent property. Although they could not be evicted from their property for making noise, they could be enjoined from making excessive noise and jailed or fined for contempt if they failed to comply. Similarly, the government acquired the land for the highway either by purchasing it or by invoking its powers of eminent domain. If the government had invoked eminent domain and paid just compensation for converting private airspace to public airspace, "adjusting the boundary" might qualify as a noncompensable regulation.

The Nollan-Dolan Nexus Blues

Dolan v. City of Tigard
512 U.S. 687 (1994)

Simple Facts

Florence Dolan of Tigard, Oregon, applied for a permit to expand her store and pave the parking lot. The city planning commission conditioned approval of the project upon Mrs. Dolan's dedicating a portion of her land for a public greenway to mitigate flood damage and for a pedestrian/bicycle pathway intended to relieve traffic congestion. Dolan contended that the land dedication requirements were disproportional to the (adverse) economic impact of the proposed development.

Details

Florence Dolan operated a plumbing and electrical supply store in the central business district of Tigard, a community of about 30,000 residents on the southwest edge of Portland, Oregon. Mrs. Dolan applied to the city for a permit to redevelop the site, located along Fanno Creek in the southwestern corner and along the western boundary. In her application, Mrs. Dolan sought permission to pave a 39-space parking lot, to double the size of her existing building to 17,600 square feet, and to build an additional structure on the northeast side for complementary businesses.

The City Planning Commission conditioned the approval of her permit on the requirement that Mrs. Dolan dedicate the portion of her property within the 100-year floodplain of Fanno Creek as greenway and an additional 15-foot strip of land adjacent to the greenway for use as a public bike path. In total, the requirement amounted to 7,000 square feet, approximately 10% of Mrs. Dolan's parcel of land. The 10% dedication was not a complete loss to Dolan because it satisfied a 15% open space requirement imposed upon all property owners in the Central Business District by the Community Development Code (CDC).

Following a denial of her application for a variance from the CDC requirements, Dolan appealed to the Land Use Board of Appeals (LUBA), claiming an uncompensated taking of her property because the dedication requirements were unrelated to the proposed development. Citing the city's findings that the expansion of the building and the paving of the parking lot would increase the amount of impervious surfaces and resulting runoff into Fanno Creek, LUBA concluded that a "reasonable relationship" existed between the city's development plans and the requirement to dedicate the land along the creek for a greenway. With respect to the pedestrian and bike pathway, LUBA again cited city findings that a significantly larger retail sales building and parking lot would attract larger numbers of vehicles and that the bike path would alleviate the additional congestion.

The dedication requirement was upheld through the Oregon courts, the key precedent being *Nollan v. California Coastal Commission*, in which the Commission had conditioned a building permit upon a pedestrian easement. Nollan prevailed in that case due to the absence of any "essential nexus" between the commission's objectives (the commission argued that the building would limit view of the ocean and thereby limit access to the public who had full rights to use the beach) and the easement (alleged to compensate for obstructing the view).[8]

The U.S. Supreme Court had established the essential nexus test in 1987 and applied that standard to Dolan's circumstances, but held that essential nexus was merely a necessary hurdle for the city. In addition to the nexus, the government must also demonstrate a "rough proportionality" between the exactions and the anticipated impact of the proposed development. Writing for the Court, Chief Justice Rehnquist maintained that:

> [T]he conditions imposed were not simply a limitation on the use petitioner might make of her own parcel, but a requirement that she deed portions of the property to the city.... Under the well settled doctrine of "unconstitutional conditions," the government may not require a person to give up a constitutional right—here the right to receive just compensation when property is taken for a public use—in exchange for a discretionary benefit conferred by the government where the property sought has little or no relationship to the benefit.[9]

Rehnquist particularly emphasized that the purpose of the takings clause was to prevent governments from "forcing some people alone to bear public burdens, which in all fairness and justice, should be borne by the public as a whole."[10]

The Commission's findings did not satisfy the rough proportionality requirement because (a) the city never showed how a *public* greenway was required in the interest of flood control, when a *private* greenway could fulfill the same purpose and (b) the city failed to demonstrate that the additional number of vehicle and bicycle trips generated by the development would be reasonably affected by the pedestrian and bicycle pathway condition.

In dissent, Justice Stevens contended that the new test focused too narrowly on a landowner's right to exclude, that it imposed a "novel burden of proof on a city implementing an admittedly valid, comprehensive land use plan."[11] Stevens also complained that the majority opinion failed to consider Dolan's gains from the exchange:

> Dolan's acceptance of the permit, with its attached conditions, would provide her with benefits that may well go beyond any advantage she gets from expanding her business.... [T]he improvement that the city's drainage plan contemplates would widen the channel and reinforce the slopes to increase the carrying capacity during serious floods....[12]

There was also some ambiguity as to the burden of proof being imposed upon the government. Rehnquist (emphasis added) specifically held that "no precise mathematical calculation is required, but the city must make *some sort of individualized determination* that the required dedication is related both in nature and *extent* to the impact of the proposed development." Seizing on the chief justice's use of the word "extent," Stevens inferred a significantly stronger burden: "a city must not only 'quantify its findings—' and make 'individualized determination[s]' with respect to the nature *and* the extent of the relationship between the conditions and the impact—, but also demonstrate 'proportionality.'"[13]

Economic Analysis

1. This case involves three issues of public concern: traffic congestion, flood relief, and a bike path. The combination of one externality and two public goods provides an opportunity not only to explore the economic meaning of "rough proportionality,"

but also to apply it. As Chief Justice Rehnquist remarked, proportionality pertains to both the *nature* and the *extent* of the burden imposed upon the individual. Despite Stevens' inferences about quantifying individual determinations and demonstrating proportionality, the process need not be an exercise in advanced econometrics, but rather one of applying judgment and perspective.

2. The focal point of the economic model is the provision of a public good. There are three general components of demand for it: recreation and aesthetics, flood control, and congestion relief. It is important to note that the bike path might not be the best way to solve the flooding problem or the congestion problem individually, but the economies involved in the combined effort make the city's choice reasonable. Similarly, there are alternative (and better) ways to model the problem and frame the issues, but this framework is consistent with the city's choice.

3. Flood and congestion relief are literally nonexcludable and user charges for the bike path would be absurd. So the path must be financed via "general tax revenues." For a city government, that essentially means some combination of sales and property taxation, but extra sales taxes could be imposed on all downtown merchants in accordance with their impacts upon congestion and water runoff. A wide range of alternatives lay within the city's constitutional rights, but taking Mrs. Dolan's land without compensation is not within the city's options. This is why the law imposes a burden of proof upon the city.

4. Meeting that burden starts with the fact that the proposed expansion of Mrs. Dolan's store is contributing to the flood and congestion problems. Thus, to some extent, she does owe a larger burden than the average citizen, and it *might* be reasonable to collect that debt through the exaction of the easement. The "might" depends on nexus and proportionality.

5. With regard to flood control, paving the lot adds to runoff problems. Therefore, the city has the right to regulate the development of the parking lot. A law requiring that 15% of the lot remain undeveloped would be reasonable and well within the police powers of the government. Alternatively, the city could allow development with the stipulation that the runoff be offset by appropriate drainage. This might be more complicated and expensive than it appears. However, bike paths and parking lots are made of similar substances. Therefore, if the parking lot adds to the runoff problem, so will the bike path; if the path can be drained properly, so can the parking lot. Therefore, *there is no essential nexus between the city's plan and the flood control.*

6. With regard to the congestion, expanding the store does contribute to the traffic congestion, which would be partially alleviated by the bike path. Actual numbers were speculative, but a reasonable guess is that the public benefits from alleviation of traffic congestion rate to be a minute portion of the public benefits associated with the path. If the land for the path is a significantly larger portion of the total costs, the city plan fails rough proportionality (even though it passes essential nexus). This casual analysis may be wrong, but the law places the burden of proof on the city because there is a plausible alternative theory to explain the city's behavior (an attempted "end run" around the Fifth Amendment).

7. It may be (as Justice Stevens implied) that Dolan would be better off in spite of having to donate her land against her will. But as a citizen, she is entitled to a reasonable share of the net benefits of the project. That does not mean an equal share; perfect distribution of net benefits is both arbitrarily subjective and administratively impossible. Condemnation via eminent domain allows the city to acquire the land for a sum that is approximately equal to its opportunity cost, avoiding the holdout problem that would encourage individual owners to inflate the value of their property. Forcing compensation at fair market value keeps the government honest, avoiding the problem of fiscal illusion.

Lead Us Not into Penn Station

Penn Central v. New York City 438 U.S. 104 (1978)

Simple Facts

New York City's Landmarks Preservation Commission designated Grand Central Terminal an historic landmark, the exterior of which was to be maintained without alteration except with Commission approval. The Landmarks Law was challenged when the Commission refused to approve the construction of a multi-story office building over the Terminal.

Details

"On a drizzly Monday morning in October of 1963, the jackhammers arrived, piercing the pink granite of New York City's Pennsylvania Station and the monumental act of vandalism began."[14] Thus began Lorraine Diehl's poignant eulogy of a great railway station. In the aftermath, the city passed its 1965 Landmarks Preservation Law, credited with saving many

ILLUSTRATION 5.2 Visitors approaching Grand Central Terminal from downtown New York behold statues of Hercules, Minerva, and Mercury.

of New York's other important buildings and fostering an increasing awareness throughout the country of the importance of the preservation of classic architecture.

The first building to be saved by the law has been called a cathedral with trains. Visitors approaching 42nd Street and Park Avenue from downtown will be facing a magnificent facade, featuring a 50-foot pediment with statues of Hercules, Minerva, and Mercury surrounding a 13-foot clock. This triumph of *Beaux Arts* design was created by architect Whitney Warren in 1913. The interior of Grand Central is a breathtaking sight with over a dozen levels, graced with grand staircases, elegant balconies, and glass walkways.

Under its authority granted by the Landmarks Law, the city's Landmarks Preservation Commission designated Grand Central Terminal an historic landmark, the exterior of which was to be maintained without alteration except with Commission approval. The Landmarks Law was challenged when the Commission refused to approve the construction of a multi-story office building over the Terminal, finding that such a structure would be destructive of the Terminal's historic and aesthetic features:

> [We have] no fixed rule against making additions to designated buildings; it all depends on how they are done. . . . But to balance a 55-story office tower above a flamboyant *Beaux Arts* facade seems nothing more than an aesthetic joke. Quite simply, the tower would overwhelm the Terminal by it sheer mass.[15]

Penn Central observed that the airspace above the terminal was a valuable property interest (citing *Causby*) and claimed that the commission was depriving them of any gainful use of their "air rights." Despite the value of the remainder of their parcel, the city's action constituted a taking of their right to this superadjacent airspace, thus entitling them to just compensation measured by the fair market value of these air rights.

The case was complicated by a creative feature of the city's zoning laws, which permitted property owners to transfer development rights to contiguous parcels in the same city block. In short, the city acknowledged that Penn Central owned development rights to the airspace above the terminal, but contended that the transferable development rights (TDR's) to adjacent properties provided sufficient in-kind compensation as to invalidate the takings claim. At least eight other properties owned by Penn Central, including the Waldorf-Astoria Hotel and the Pan-American Building, qualified for TDR's (because of prior regulations, Penn Central did not own development rights to the airspace above the adjacent properties).

Although the trial court originally decided in favor of injunctive and declaratory relief for Penn Central, the New York Supreme Court, New York Court of Appeals, and the U.S. Supreme Court all ruled that no taking had occurred. Writing for the Court, Justice Brennan began with the observation that designation as a landmark permitted continued use as a railroad terminal:

> Its designation as a landmark not only permits but contemplates that appellants may continue to use the property precisely as it has been used for the past 65 years: as a railroad terminal containing office space and concessions. So the law does not interfere with what must be regarded as Penn Central's primary expectation concerning the use of the parcel. More importantly, on this record, we must regard the New York City law as permitting Penn Central not only to profit from the Terminal but also to obtain a "reasonable return" on its investment.[16]

William J. Brennan: *Their ability to use these rights has not been abrogated. New York courts here supportably found that . . . the rights afforded are valuable. While these rights may well not have constituted "just compensation" if a "taking" had occurred, the rights . . . mitigate whatever financial burdens the law has imposed on appellants. . . .*

U.S. Supreme Court Historical Society

William H. Rehnquist: *The . . . proposed office building was in full compliance with all New York zoning laws. . . . The rubric of "zoning" has not yet sufficed to avoid the . . . proposition that the Fifth Amendment bars the government from forcing some people alone to bear public burdens which . . . should be borne by the public as a whole.*

Jason Reed/Reuters/Landov

The lynchpin of the Court's argument was that Penn Central was not denied all use of even the preexisting air rights. As articulated by Brennan:

> Their ability to use these rights has not been abrogated; they are made transferable to at least eight parcels in the vicinity of the Terminal, one or two of which have been found suitable for the construction of new office buildings. . . . New York courts here supportably found that, at least in the case of the Terminal, the rights afforded are valuable. While these rights may well not have constituted "just compensation" if a "taking" had occurred, the rights nevertheless undoubtedly mitigate whatever financial burdens the law has imposed on appellants. . . .[17]

Justice Rehnquist's dissent was partially philosophical, but focused on the magnitude of Penn Central's lost opportunity. Penn Central had a lease agreement with UGP Properties, Inc., under which UGP would construct and operate the office building cantilevered above the terminal. Under the terms of the lease, Penn Central was to receive $1 million per year during construction with a minimum rental of $3 million per year for the next 50 years. In Rehnquist's view, this burden was excessive:

> The record is clear that the proposed office building was in full compliance with all New York zoning laws and height limitations. . . . The rubric of "zoning" has not yet sufficed to avoid the well-established proposition that the Fifth Amendment bars the government from forcing some people alone to bear public burdens which, in all fairness and justice, should be borne by the public as a whole.[18]

In short, the restriction went beyond zoning limitations, building a skyscraper is not a noxious activity, and Penn Central is bearing a disproportionate share of the costs of the provision of a public good (preservation of the terminal). Therefore, in Rehnquist's estimation, a compensable taking occurred.

Economic Analysis

1. In isolation, the public goods dimension screams for compensation. Penn Central owned the development rights, and the denial of the building permit destroyed all viable use of the airspace above the terminal. The value of the facade as a landmark is undeniable, but Penn Central is clearly bearing a disproportionate share of the cost. More importantly, the decision seems to be a clarion call for fiscal illusion, encouraging other governments to ignore the opportunity costs of landmark preservation.

2. In theory, compensation could be paid either in money or in kind. In practice, the city transferred development rights to an alternative site. The theoretical basis for compensation would therefore seem to be the simple difference in assessed valuations, but there are two hurdles. The first concerns the city's ownership of the development rights, in particular *the right to use TDR as compensation.* Establishing this right is, itself, a constitutional hurdle to be addressed in items 3 and 4 that follow. Then, if that hurdle can be cleared, the second concerns the precedent that would be set if the Court engaged in a simple appraisal of the two properties.

3. The city had "acquired" the development rights to the neighboring properties by zoning them away from Penn Central. This is economically justifiable as a means of internalizing a congestion or encroachment externality. If all sites were homogeneous entities, height and density restrictions would suffice. Just as in *Euclid v. Ambler* (see Chapter 2), the expected result would be an increase in aggregate property value, and the city should have neither the responsibility to compensate the "losers," nor the right to extract rents from the "winners."

4. However, the right to zone does not automatically transfer full property rights to the city. What makes the TDR program economically palpable is that it encourages the substitution of high-value development for relatively low-value development. For example, if the Waldorf Astoria were the more valuable development site, Penn Central would have voluntarily traded rights to develop the terminal for the rights to develop the Waldorf. Clearly, it would be inefficient to prohibit transferability as a matter of principle.

5. It would also be inefficient (not to mention absurd and outrageous) to allow the city to charge Penn Central for the difference in values. This would encourage the city to deny development permits to high-value sites, in hope of cashing in later on. Though less obvious, the awarding of compensation on the basis of the difference in assessed values would have essentially the same effect! City planners would come to learn how to ease their Fifth Amendment burdens by squirreling away development rights to high-value properties.

6. Ultimately, the outcome rested on a delicate "*ad hoc* balancing" of three major incentive issues. First, failure to compensate Penn Central discourages the creation of landmarks in the future; property owners will be less inclined toward fine architecture and more inclined to preempt landmark designation by redevelopment. Second, the avoidance of paying compensation encourages city planners to ignore

the opportunity cost of landmarks. Third, awarding full or net compensation encourages inefficiently aggressive zoning. *Penn Central* remains a watershed case because there are strong efficiency arguments on both sides.

7. Justice Brennan captured the essence of the issues when he said that, "[w]hile these rights may well not have constituted 'just compensation' if a 'taking' had occurred, the rights nevertheless undoubtedly mitigate whatever financial burdens the law has imposed on appellants. . . ." There were also at least three offsetting factors that point toward siding with the city. One is the set of intangible benefits (to Penn Central) associated with the landmark designation. These benefits might be relatively small, but the point is the government is not allowed to collect payment from those who benefit from regulation. Another is that those who claim to be harmed have incentives to provide inflated estimates of the harm. Without real "investment-backed expectations," the \$50 million "loss" borne by Penn Central may be little more than a bluff designed to extract compensation from the city.

8. The final offsetting factor is Penn Central's historical status as a regulated monopoly. In return for its monopoly position, the firm is guaranteed a fair or normal rate of return on its capital. Theory suggests that regulated monopolists capture some excess profits in the form of costly amenities. A magnificent facade, featuring a 50-foot pediment with statues of Hercules, Minerva, and Mercury surrounding a 13-foot clock, is a prime example of a costly amenity. In a real economic sense, the citizens of New York City had already paid for the terminal.

CHAPTER 6

INTELLECTUAL PROPERTY

It is sometimes said that patents and copyrights create property. This is not literally correct; the patent and copyright laws create and enforce ownership rights to the fruits of creative activity. Generally speaking, **patents** cover (the implementation of) creative ideas and copyrights cover creative expression. Patents are more difficult to obtain and are of limited duration (usually, 17 years in the United States); **copyrights** are relatively easy to obtain (for things like books, music, and software) and are not subject to expiration.

In one very important sense, creating and enforcing ownership rights do create property. In providing support for commercial exploitation, the law encourages creative activity. Without patent protection, new ideas would be discovered by accident, but there would be much less effort actually directed toward the discovery and development of new ideas and technology. Similarly, authors, musicians, and artists would create for their own enjoyment or draw their support from patrons or voluntary contributors.

The downside of protecting intellectual property is that ownership creates exclusivity. Ideas and information are essentially public goods that can be utilized without marginal cost. The traditional monopoly diagram (Figure 6.1) aptly illustrates the tradeoffs. Under (perfectly) competitive conditions, **market price** (P_c) would be driven down to **marginal cost**, which includes the costs of implementing the idea or reproducing the book, but not the costs of the creative effort. The good news is that production levels would expand to Q_c, and consumers would enjoy all of the potential gains from trade. The bad news is the absence of market incentives to create. The theoretical effect of patent or copyright protection is to support a **monopoly price** (P_m), enabling the creator to extract a profit (π). The consumer's share of the economic surplus is reduced to the triangle (S) above P_m; and, more importantly from the pure economic perspective, a portion (L) of the net benefits is "lost" by virtue of the reduced production.

Even within the comfort zone of the graphics, there is no simple policy conclusion. On one hand, reduced surplus is better than none at all, so creative effort warrants protection. On the other, the idea may have eventually been discovered by accident. Beyond the graphics, the additional dimensions of the problem are virtually limitless. Two examples are particularly worthy of mention. The first draws from destructive competition. The existence of patent laws creates a "winner-take-all" race for valuable rights, which encourages wasteful duplication of effort, unproductive secrecy, lawsuits, and a general climate of uncooperative gamesmanship.

The second is based on the dynamics of the problem. It is important to understand that the demand side of the market does not consist only of consumers or industrial users of the intellectual property. Technological progress is cumulative; new inventions are built upon the ideas embodied in old inventions. Similarly, literature, musical compositions, and theatrical scripts all borrow plots and characters or melodies and chord progressions from creative works of the past. For this reason, strengthening patent or copyright protection does not necessarily increase the flow of

FIGURE 6.1 Intellectual property rewards creative activity with monopoly rents (π) at the cost of welfare loss (L).

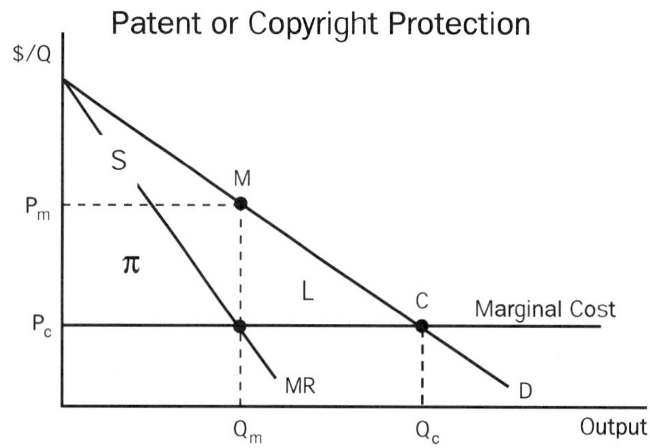

creative activity. At some point, higher profit expected to result from *future* monopoly power gets outweighed by the higher development costs accruing from the existence of *prior* patents and copyrights.

The generic question concerns how liberally protection should be extended. This chapter will simply examine some of the more interesting dimensions of the problem. The focal point of all the cases is whether or not someone wrongfully appropriated someone else's legally private property. The underlying policy questions are more dynamic: should the "property" be privately owned or left in the public domain? If so, for how long? Is there enough consistency in the law for rational people to form reasonably correct expectations about these matters before they actually arise?

Spice of Life

Cheney Brothers v. Doris Silk Corp. 35 F.2d 279 (1929)

Simple Facts

Cheney Brothers designed original dress patterns for production and retail sale. The designs had a short economic life and could not be patented or copyrighted. A competitor, Doris Silk, marketed exact copies of successful designs and undercut Cheney's prices. Cheney sought to protect its creative efforts under a theory of common law patents.

Details

Cheney Brothers was a designer and manufacturer of silk dresses. During a typical season, the company would create a large number of new patterns in an effort to broaden its market. Attempting to produce novelty or beauty was a risky enterprise—so risky that only 15–20 percent of its creations would be popular, and the popularity seldom endured beyond a single season of eight to nine months. While the aggregate success rate was predictable, the success or failure of any specific pattern was largely random. Cheney had to rely on profit from the successful patterns to offset the losses on the failures.

The nature of the product was such that it "fell through the cracks" between the patent and copyright laws. Patent applications require detailed descriptions of the invention design and support for the claim that the invention is novel and useful. It was therefore not practical to secure design patents on all of the patterns, and the unpredictability of success made it pointless to pursue patents selectively. Beyond the logistics, the extent of originality might not have qualified for patent protection anyway. Copyright protection, on the other hand, is intended to protect "creative expression." Originally restricted to literature, music, and art, its limits have expanded and continue to expand with technological advances, but dress patterns do not qualify.

It was also easy to copy a design pattern and mass-produce the dresses. Failing to qualify for either patents or copyrights, Cheney found itself without protection of any sort for its creative efforts. Taking advantage of this situation, Doris Silk copied one of the popular designs in the season beginning in October 1928 and undercut Cheney's price. Cheney brought suit, seeking "common law protection" of a temporary nature, during season.

Cheney's case relied heavily on the 1918 precedent of *International News Service v. Associated Press*[1] involving the reproduction of news articles. In that case, the U.S. Supreme Court struck a balance between giving Associated Press a right to monopolize the distribution of the news and preventing competitors from reaping the fruits of its efforts and expenditures. It held, essentially, that "fresh" news was protected under rules of "fair competition." Like the dress patterns, news stories did not satisfy the creative expression requirement for a copyright, and patents were obviously out of the question. Any differences between the two activities, Cheney contended, were solely matters of degree.

The Court concurred, but held that the "matters of degree" were significant. With reference to exception granted for newsgathering, it held that:

> [W]e agree that, if it meant to lay down a general doctrine, it would cover this case. . . . While [the law] ordinarily speaks in general terms, there are cases where the occasion is at once the justification for, and the limit of, what is decided. . . . [W]e think that no more was covered than situations substantially similar to those then at bar. The difficulties of understanding it otherwise are insuperable. We are to suppose that the court meant to create a sort of common-law patent or copyright for reasons of justice. Either would flagrantly conflict with the scheme which Congress has for more than a century devised to cover the subject matter.[2]

To the extent that public policy dictates protection of the sort of enterprise in which Cheney engaged, it would be up to Congress to amend the copyright law. The Court pointed to limitations on the power of the judiciary and emphasized that gaps and omissions (like the design of dress patterns) must be presumed to have been deliberate:

> Congress might see its way to create some sort of temporary right, or it might not. Its decision would certainly be preceded by some examination of the result upon the other interests affected. Whether these would prove paramount we have no means of saying; it is not for us to decide. Our vision is inevitably contracted, and the whole horizon may contain much which will compose a very different picture.[3]

Accordingly, Cheney's property rights were limited to the "chattels" which embody the invention.

Economic Analysis

1. The market arena in which Cheney, Doris, and many other similar firms compete may loosely be characterized as monopolistically competitive. The theory of **monopolistic competition**, the brainchild of Harvard economist Edward H. Chamberlin, was hatched in the early 1930s to fill an ever-expanding hiatus between the models of monopoly and perfect competition. Its salient feature is a large number of firms offering similar, but not identical, products. The keyword is **product differentiation**, which connotes actively striving to distinguish one's product.

2. In relation to Cheney Brothers' activities, product differentiation consists of producing "variety" and catering to differences in tastes across consumers and to changes in tastes over time. The asymmetry wherein Cheney creates and Doris copies was not part of the model, but not because that sort of competition was regarded as "unfair." Rather, the exact imitation of a competitor's product would be irrational because there would always be an unfilled niche in the market to provide better profit opportunity. This was a logical inference from the implicit assumption that the *costs* of developing slight product changes were negligible.

3. The economic variables that were of prime importance to Cheney were subtle ones that are typically assumed out of the formal models. Cheney incurred costs in an effort to get a feel for the pulse of the market and to discover the little things that mattered to enough individuals as to generate a "hit." Whether or not to provide

legal protection for this sort of creative effort is a microcosm of the policy issues that generally underlie intellectual property. Without protection, Cheney (and others) will tend to provide less variety, but consumers will pay lower prices for items that remain on the product menu. Parasites like Doris are good for consumers in the short run, but may harm consumers in the long run.

4. It is useful to consider why a "common law patent" was granted to the Associated Press but not to Cheney Brothers. As the Court noted, if there were a general doctrine of common law patent protection, it would cover this case. The key difference is that news stories can be copied instantaneously and without cost. If the INA's of the market were permitted to pirate news stories indiscriminately, newsgathering would have no profit potential. Like the classic free rider problem, for-profit provision of the public good would be eliminated. In contrast, Cheney's designs had to be embodied in dresses, which have a cost of production. Profit potential is reduced, but not eliminated. Indeed, since Doris copied only the profitable patterns, Cheney must have earned some return on its efforts.

Dancing around the Law

Midler v. Ford Motor Co. 849 F.2d 460 (1988)

Simple Facts

Renowned entertainer Bette Midler turned down a lucrative opportunity to sing in a commercial for Ford Motor Company. Ford's advertising agency then hired another singer to do a vocal impersonation of Midler's signature tune and used the impersonation in a commercial that was broadcast on national television for six months. Midler contended that Ford had, in effect, stolen her voice.

Details

One of her hundreds of unofficial Web sites heralds the "divine" Bette Midler as the ultimate diva, an astonishing legend with an unforgettable voice. Indeed, there is little left for Midler to accomplish as an actress and singer. She won her first Grammy in 1973 and received an Oscar nomination in 1979 for her portrayal of another legend, Gypsy Rose Lee, in *The Rose*. She has been called "outrageously original" and "the most dynamic and poignant singer-actress of her time."

Midler's first record album, "Bette Midler—The Divine Miss M," was released in 1972. The first song on the album is "Do You Want To Dance." Midler regularly performed the composition in live concert tours for over a decade. Many of these concert performances were recorded, and her rendition of the song was released for a second time in a 1977 album entitled "Bette Midler, Live At Last."

The copyright to "Do You Want To Dance" is owned by Bobby Freeman, who composed the tune and lyrics in 1958. Besides Midler's version, the song has been recorded by such luminary performers as John Lennon, The Mamas & The Papas, and The Beach Boys. Nonetheless, to Midler's legions of admirers and the millions who wanted to dance in the 1970s, it's *her* song, her "signature" performance.

In early 1984, the advertising firm of Young & Rubicam created an ad campaign for Lincoln-Mercury automobiles. The strategy underlying the ads was the recreation of romantic moods. Among the popular songs selected for the ads was, of course, "Do You Want To Dance." It obtained a license from Bobby Freeman Music to synchronize and record for commercial adaptation. The music producer then contacted Midler's agent, but the divine one made it clear that she did not do commercials. Period. The answer was no.

Young & Rubicam next contacted Ula Hedwig, a one-time member of Midler's backup group, the "Harlettes." Hedwig's close familiarity with Midler's style enabled her to recreate a virtually perfect impersonation of a Midler performance. The commercial, with Hedwig's rendition of Midler's signature song, was aired extensively over nationwide television during the first six months of 1986. The intention to recreate Midler's unique style was clear. Naturally, Midler was divinely and litigiously outraged.

Midler's complaint, covering a variety of actions from invasion of privacy and infringement of right of publicity to unfair competition, sought injunctive relief and compensatory damages. The complaint centered around California Civil Code § 3344, which held liable for damages any person who "knowingly uses another's name, voice,

ILLUSTRATION 6.1 The "divine" Bette Midler received an Oscar nomination in 1979 for her portrayal of Gypsy Rose Lee in *The Rose*.

Molly Riley/Reuters/Landov

signature, photograph, or likeness" for purposes of advertising goods or services, without prior consent.[4]

The district court's problem with the complaint was basic. Ford's behavior was likened to that of the "average thief," but the commercial did not use Midler's name, voice, signature, or photograph! Midler's claim focused on likeness, contending that her voice was so unique that the public would automatically associate the excellent imitation with her endorsement of the product. The court specifically disagreed that the statute provided protection against voice imitations. The ruling appeared to boil down to the placement of a comma. In citing the statute, the judge included the comma between "likeness" and "photograph," but then proceeded to ignore it:

> [W]ith the inclusion of "or likeness" the protection of section 3344 was extended to cover simulacra. That is, the statute precludes the use of methods that clearly evoke one's visage when the visage itself is not being used. On the other hand, when the California legislature placed the word "voice" in section 3344, it did not go on to indicate that the imitation of a voice was also covered, and, at least in normal usage, it would be surprising to find that the word "likeness" refers to voice in the context of the statute.[5]

Once the application of likeness was limited solely to visage rather than to general attributes, section 3344 was "out" and Midler's complaints were summarily dismissed.

The search for an effective legal principle to support Midler and to punish Ford continued at the appellate level. First Amendment primacy of freedom of speech and expression generally protects the media in the reproduction of likenesses or sounds. As in *Cheney Brothers* (see case earlier in chapter), federal copyright law preempts much of this area. Quoting notes from a Senate Judiciary Committee hearing, "Mere imitation of a recorded performance would not constitute a copyright infringement even where one performer deliberately sets out to simulate another's performance as exactly as possible."[6]

Indeed, the law had already sided with Young & Rubicam in a suit brought by Nancy Sinatra over an ad featuring an impersonation of her rendition of "These Boots Are Made For Walkin'." In that case, the defendants had paid for the copyright license, and Sinatra had merely alleged unfair competition.[7] A successful suit was brought by actor/comedian Bert Lahr (of "Cowardly Lion" fame) over the use of an imitation of his voice together with a cartoon of a duck.[8] Lahr prevailed on an unfair competition claim, but his market was minute in relation to Midler's—a series of one-minute commercials could not begin to saturate Midler's market.

The court also rejected code section 3344 as no help to Midler, referring again to the passage about the person's "name, voice, signature, photograph or likeness," this time with the comma edited out. However, the statute did refer to these things as "property rights" and turned to cases that treated the appropriation of common law property rights as a tort. Citing a 1974 case involving a cigarette ad, the Midler court found an invasion of her "proprietary interest" in her own identity. The ad made use of an edited picture of a racecar driver's *car* to establish a subtle linkage between the driver and the product. The driver, Luther Motschenbacher, was actually in the car, but the court held that his physical presence in the commercial was irrelevant.[9] The ad suggested his presence by emphasizing signs or symbols associated with him. In the same way the defendants here used an imitation to convey the impression that Midler was singing for them. Getting to the crux of the matter, the court asked and answered the key questions:

> Why did the defendants ask Midler to sing if her voice was not of value to them? Why did they studiously acquire the services of a sound-alike and instruct her to imitate Midler if Midler's voice was not of value to them? What they sought was an attribute of Midler's identity. Its value was what the market would have paid for Midler to have sung the commercial in person.[10]

The court went on to maintain that a voice is more distinctive and personal than a racecar and, indeed, one of the most prominent ways in which identity is manifested. Especially for a singer of Midler's stature, the impersonation of her voice was tantamount to pirating her identity:

> We need not and do not go so far as to hold that every imitation of a voice to advertise merchandise is actionable. We hold only that when a distinctive voice of a professional singer is widely known and is deliberately imitated in order to sell a product, the sellers have appropriated what is not theirs and have committed [the tort of misappropriation] in California.[11]

The case was remanded back to the district court for trial but evidently settled out of court.

Economic Analysis

1. This case involves a passionate struggle between economics and the law. It is about finding a valid legal reason to assign rights to Midler for *something*—because, whatever "it" was, Ford took it from her. Moreover, Ford took it after Midler's agent explicitly told Young and Rubicam that she was unwilling to sell it at any price! Economics is on Midler's side, but the letter of the law appeared to be (and might have been) with Ford.

2. Even the economics can get complicated if one indulges in speculation about "why's." Why the same person would buy insurance and engage in gambling is one of the more enduring examples in economics. Why a celebrity's endorsement lends value to a product is another. In the final analysis, "why" is beside the point; Ford offered Midler millions for doing the commercial. Why Midler turned it down is another mystery; she doesn't do commercials as a matter of principle. Again, her reasons are irrelevant. Midler refused Ford's offer. The simple economic inference is that the right was worth more to Midler than to Ford.

3. On strict efficiency grounds, the harder case is Motschenbacher. There is no way to determine whether the value added to the cigarette commercial was worth more to R. J. Reynolds than the subjective costs to Motschenbacher because there was no attempt to structure a contract. Of course, that is the point. *Ex ante*, negotiating a contract was the simple way to determine relative value and to ensure that the right was put to its more valuable use. Bypassing normal market channels is what links RJR and Ford to the "common thief."

4. There is sound economic reason not to grant copyright protection to a performer's *rendition* of a song. That would interfere with copyright of the song itself by creating unnecessary transactions costs. The economic value of the copyright would dissipate in a fashion analogous to common property resources. Similarly, the costs of enforcing rendition rights would very likely be prohibitive, due to the inherent subjectivity of what would constitute an infringement. Finally, "rendition rights" tend to be self-enforcing. Much of the commercial value associated with being a professional entertainer lie in uniqueness and originality. Consequently, the incentives for widespread imitation are likely to be minimal.

5. If Ford had identified Ula Helwig as the actual performer, the impersonation itself would probably have been legal, perhaps even if the identification had been in fine print. In focusing on the identity theft, the court emphasized the simple economic effects of deluding viewers into thinking that Midler was performing in the commercial and implicitly endorsing the product. In so doing, Ford appropriated Midler's property for its own use. The ethical issues transcend both the law and the economics. Ford's actions were inefficient because the property right was worth more to Midler than to Ford.

Cell to the Highest Bidder

Moore v. The Regents of the University of California 51 Cal. 3d 120 (1990)

Simple Facts

Patient John Moore was hospitalized at the UCLA Medical Center for leukemia treatment, including removal of his spleen. Unbeknownst to Moore, his blood cells were uniquely suitable for a research program that led to multi-million dollar patents for the university. Discovering that his body had been harvested, Moore claimed unlawful conversion of his property.

Details

A normal human spleen is about five inches long by three inches wide, one and a half inches thick, and weighs about six ounces in a healthy adult. When it becomes enlarged from malaria or other diseases, it can weigh a hefty four pounds or so. When John Moore came off the Alaska pipeline seeking treatment for leukemia in 1976, his spleen had expanded to just over 14 pounds! Dr. David Golde at the UCLA Medical Center told Moore that his life was in immediate danger and recommended that the spleen be removed.

Approximately 1% of the population, including *NBC Tonight Show* host Jay Leno, are spleenless, the main disadvantage being greater susceptibility to infection. Tucked under the left side of the diaphragm, the spleen filters blood from the heart to the liver. Spleens contain two types of blood cells, B and T lymphocytes. The B-cells serve a memory function; the T-cells monitor blood for invading cells and produce lymphokines (proteins) that regulate the immune system. Moore's T-cells were interesting to Dr. Golde because they overproduced certain lymphokines. Moore's lymphokines were not unique—they have the same genetic code in all humans—but their large numbers made genetic material easier to identify. Consequently, they were very useful for Golde's research, though not if taken directly from the body. Golde needed the spleen itself.

Before the operation, Golde informed Moore that he was engaged in academic and scientific research and made arrangements to obtain portions of the spleen following its removal and to take them to a separate research unit. Golde gave no indication that he had any commercial or financial interest in the research. Surgeons at the center removed the infected spleen on October 20, 1976, and Moore recovered. At Golde's direction, Moore returned to UCLA from his Seattle home several times over the following seven years. Golde made it clear that these visits were necessary and required for his health and well-being. On each occasion, Golde withdrew additional samples of blood and other fluids.

Dr. Golde failed to mention that the university had secured a number of valuable patents as a direct result of his research. Moore became suspicious in 1983, when his doctor pressed him to sign over all rights to cell lines taken from his spleen. He refused and later discovered that the "Mo line" had been sold to a biotechnology company for $1.7 million. This was not just a case of failure to disclose, but one of ongoing and conscious deceit. During the periodic visits, Moore directly inquired about potential commercial or financial value of his fluids, or whether the researchers had discovered anything valuable. The answer was always no, and the doctors apparently discouraged this line of inquiry. In a magazine interview, Moore said that the doctors had staked a claim to his genetic essence and humanity and viewed him as a mine for biological material. His body had been harvested.

Moore's lawsuit pursued 13 causes of action that included fraud and deceit, infliction of emotional distress, and unjust enrichment. In substance, they reduced to two general complaints. The first was directed primarily at Dr. Golde, for breach of fiduciary duty. A physician who treats a patient in whom he also has a research interest has potential conflicts of interest. Moore contended that he was entitled to know the extent of the research and financial incentives that might influence Golde's medical decisions. The second complaint named the board of regents, a genetics research institute, and a private pharmaceutical corporation, along with Golde and Dr. Shirley Quan, a researcher employed by UCLA. It alleged unlawful conversion of Moore's property. The doctors had staked a claim on his body, and Moore was staking a claim on their patent royalties.

The California Supreme Court ultimately sided with Moore on the matter of breach of fiduciary duty. Despite some legal technicalities, the ruling was relatively straightforward and consistent with a long line of precedents:

> [M]edical treatment decisions are made on the basis of proportionality—weighing the benefits *to the patient* against the risks *to the patient*. . . . A physician who adds his own research interests to this balance may be tempted to order a scientifically useful procedure or test that offers marginal, or no, benefits to the patient. The possibility that an interest extraneous to the patient's health has affected the physician's judgment is something that a reasonable patient would want to know. . . . [12]

Although Golde maintained that the scientific use of excised cells cannot possibly affect the patient's medical interests, the point is that the *intended* use after the surgery can compromise the medical decision. The fact that the information would not have changed this particular decision is beside the point. Moreover, it almost certainly would have figured into the decision regarding seven years of commuting between Seattle and LA.

The conversion claim, however, was as unique as the property that was allegedly converted. No court had ever applied conversion liability for the use of human cells in medical research. Indeed, the tort of conversion evolved from a common proceeding (trover) against a person who had found someone else's property (a horse) and kept it. Finding and keeping a lost horse is far removed from making use of diseased body parts which have no inherent use to the patient. Numerous regulations, in fact, deal with the proper procedure for sanitary disposal of excised parts, and these regulations severely limit patients' property rights.

The court rejected theories related to proprietary interest in one's persona (like Midler's in the preceding case). Moore advanced the theory that the genetic sequences embodied in his cells were his own tangible property. That argument failed, mainly because the genetic code for lymphokines does not vary from individual to individual. The court expressed grave concerns over the public policy implications of the case. Moore was, in effect, asking the court to impose an enormous duty upon research scientists, that of investigating the "consensual pedigree of each human cell sample used in research." The court drew a clear distinction between the cellular material and the patents derived from it:

> [T]he patented cell line is both factually and legally distinct from the cells taken from Moore's body. . . . Federal law permits the patenting of organisms that represent the product of "human ingenuity," but not naturally occurring organisms. . . . It is this *inventive effort* that patent law rewards, not the discovery of naturally occurring raw materials. Thus, Moore's allegations that he owns the cell line and the products derived from it are inconsistent with the patent, which constitutes an authoritative determination that the cell line is the product of invention.[13]

In short, (1) Moore's claims to ownership of the excised parts were tenuous and of minimal value and (2) the patented cell line and the products derived from it cannot be Moore's property.

Economic Analysis

1. The legal claim of breach of fiduciary duty is largely a contract matter. The physician has an obligation to inform the patient not only of the relevant medical conditions, but also of conflicts of interest that might bias medical judgment. The economic foundation is a compound, complex version of consumer sovereignty. Consumers buy treatment and diagnosis from health care providers. Inasmuch as rational consumers do not place blind faith in diagnoses (indeed, it is common to seek second opinions), a part of the diagnosis includes some sense of degree of certainty and reliability.

2. Without getting too specific about this matter, the appropriate economic remedy is compensatory (and, perhaps, punitive) damages, but not a share of the patents. Compensatory damages induce providers to consider the full costs of their actions. With regard to the removal of Moore's spleen, it is clear that a full disclosure of Golde's economic interests would not have affected the medical decision. Hence, there is no basis for compensatory damages. With regard to the post-operative treatments, it is very likely that the treatments were excessive and that they could have been conducted in Seattle. Accordingly, some compensation for Moore's time and travel expenses would be warranted.

3. The legal claim of conversion is, strictly speaking, a tort matter. If the excised body parts were Moore's legal property, the appropriate remedy would be restitution or compensation at fair market value. Neither remedy works very well in this case. Restitution is impossible, and there exists no market—certainly not an organized (no pun intended) competitive one—for the materials in question. Without prices of comparable exchanges, the correct economic approach would be to impute a value based either on Moore's marginal cost or the defendants' marginal benefit. The marginal cost is arguably negligible; people have no more use for their excised body parts than for old oil removed from the crankcase of their cars.

4. The marginal benefit to the researchers is more interesting. The correct framework is to guesstimate an *ex ante* value of marginal product. Several factors are involved. First, the outcome of the research is uncertain, and, even if the research product is

socially beneficial, there are no guarantees of patents or of the value that might be derived from them. Second, there are two generic inputs, materials and scientific expertise, in the production function for the research output. The material input is worthless without the expertise input, but there are substitutes for the material input. Moore's cells essentially reduced genetic search costs, so that expected cost reduction would be the basis for evaluation. The court's assessment of Moore's claim on the patents mirrors this line of reasoning.

5. In choosing between Moore's marginal cost (negligible) and the researchers' imputed marginal benefit (high, but well below patent values) as a basis for imputed value, the prime consideration is whether Moore had the right to free appraisal services. In other words, beyond the simple fact that the UCLA Medical Center was involved in research, Moore is not entitled to the information that the cells have special value to the center. The fact that Golde informed Moore that a portion of the spleen was being transferred to the research facility effectively opened negotiation. If Moore wanted to exact a price, it was his responsibility to determine potential worth. What makes this issue particularly complicated is that Golde owed Moore additional information as part of the patient/physician relationship, but not as part of the buyer/seller relationship.
6. Beyond transferring wealth out of the research community, the main economic effects of assigning this kind of property right to patients would be to create unnecessary transactions costs. The court's reference to the duty to investigate the consensual pedigree is a dramatic example, but one that could generally be solved by waivers signed upon admittance. A more serious problem is potential damage to the doctor/patient relationship. The case addresses conflict of physician interest, but the same could be said of patient conflicts. Patients should be encouraged to seek second medical opinions, but not to engage in purely rent-seeking expeditions.
7. Assigning the rights to the "research community" is a good example of a loosely-stated corollary of the Coase Theorem. If transactions costs are significant, welfare can be enhanced by assigning rights to the party that would ultimately purchase them. If applied cautiously, adhering to this policy increases the chances that the property will find its most valuable use and avoids the incurrence of unnecessary transactions costs.

Piracy of the High C's

A & M Records v. Napster
284 F.3d 1091, U.S. App. LEXIS 4752 (2002)

Simple Facts

Napster is an online system that enables a computer owner to copy an audio CD onto the hard drive into compressed (MP3) files that facilitate rapid transmission between users. In 2000, the recording industry brought suit against Napster for copyright violations. Although Napster did not literally copy the recordings, the plaintiffs alleged contributory and vicarious copyright infringement, asking that Napster be permanently enjoined from enabling the swapping of copyrighted songs. Napster claimed that MP3 file exchange is a "noncommercial use" that was actually encouraged by the plaintiffs.

Details

Shawn Fanning spent the fall semester of 1998 as a computer science major at Northeastern University. During that time, he worked on a program that would enable him to exchange MP3 music files with his friends. The result was a "peer-to-peer" file-sharing system that streamlined sophisticated searches for music files on the hard drives of millions of other users. Napster began operations six months later; by year's end, upwards of 50 million subscribers were exchanging copyrighted material at a rate of 10,000 files per second. Scores of universities were banning Napster, as massive student usage threatened to cripple their computer systems.

At the same time universities were fighting to protect their computer systems, the Recording Industry Association of America (RIAA) was scrambling to protect its members' copyrights. In June of 2000, A & M Records was joined by 18 other recording corporations in seeking an injunction to block the exchange of all major-label songs through Napster. A month later, a U.S. district court granted the injunction, ordering Napster not to allow the swapping of copyrighted material over its network.

The basis for RIAA's claims was that Napster was a secondary infringer of the copyrighted material. That is, Napster did not directly use the material, but its subscribers did. In providing an efficient venue for its subscribers, Napster was guilty of **contributory infringement**. Essentially, Napster knew, or *should have known*, that it was *materially contributing* to acts of direct infringement by its subscribers. Plaintiffs also claimed **vicarious infringement**, that Napster had the right and *ability to control* acts of **direct infringement** and derived a direct *financial benefit* from the infringement.

Napster unleashed the renowned David Boies to nit-pick every element of the charges. For starters, the company denied that its subscribers were infringers, holding that they were engaged in constitutionally protected "fair use" of the material. As examples of fair use, Napster pointed to sampling and space-shifting, as well as to the permissible distribution of the works of both new and established performers. Two key factors ran against Napster here. First, downloading MP3 files necessarily entailed copying the works in their entirety. Second, over Napster's objections, RIAA provided expert testimony documenting significant reductions in sales to college students. Inasmuch as fair use is limited to copying that does not "materially impair marketability," the extent of the sales reductions was compelling.

Against the charge of contributory infringement, Napster relied heavily on the 1984 precedent of *Sony v. Universal City Studios.*[14] In that case, Sony was found not to be liable for infringements of copyrighted TV shows, in spite of clear evidence that video recorders were used to infringe copyrights. In finding for Sony, the court emphasized the abundance of noninfringing uses. A general awareness that the machines *could* be used to infringe copyrights fell short of the requisite level of knowledge for contributory infringement. The district court made a sharp distinction between Sony and Napster, holding that Napster could not show that the system generated commercially significant noninfringing uses. The circuit court rejected that line of reasoning; unless noninfringing uses were highly unlikely, one cannot automatically impute knowledge of infringement to Napster:

> We agree that if a computer system operator learns of specific infringing material available on his system and fails to purge such material from the system, the operator knows of and contributes to direct infringement. . . . Conversely, absent any specific information which identifies infringing activity, a computer system operator cannot be liable for contributory infringement merely because the structure of the system allows for the exchange of copyrighted material. . . . To enjoin simply because a computer network allows for infringing use would, in our opinion, violate Sony and potentially restrict activity unrelated to infringing use.[15]

Instead, the higher court relied on more direct evidence. A Napster document mentioned a need to remain ignorant of users' identities because they were exchanging "pirated music," and the RIAA had directly informed Napster of more than 12,000 infringing files:

> We nevertheless conclude that sufficient knowledge exists to impose contributory liability when linked to demonstrated infringing use of the Napster system. . . . The record supports the district court's finding that Napster has actual knowledge that specific infringing material is available using its system, that it could block access to the system by suppliers of the infringing material, and that it failed to remove the material.[16]

The latter essentially covered half of the vicarious infringement charge. Napster could have controlled the infringement, but failed to do so. The defense against direct financial benefit also rang hollow. Although Napster did not directly charge its subscribers, the ready access to copyrighted material attracts subscribers. At the time, the company had an estimated financial value in the neighborhood of $1 billion and that value drew almost entirely from expected future revenue, which was a direct function of its user base.

In addition to its specific defenses, Napster sought refuge under the "safe harbor" provisions of the 1998 Digital Millennium Copyright Act. The purpose of these provisions was to afford some protection to libraries, educational institutions, and online service providers (OSPs). However, the safe harbor provisions limit infringement liability of an OSP only if, upon notification from the copyright owner, it promptly removes or blocks access to the infringing material. While these provisions did not apply to Napster, they did suggest a way to forge a compromise.

On remand, the district court modified the injunction on March 5, 2001. The modified preliminary injunction called for cooperation between RIAA and Napster, so that Napster could continue to operate if it could effectively police the copyright infringements. Under the terms, Napster was enjoined from "facilitating" others in the copying, transmitting, or distribution of copyrighted sound recordings. The recording companies were required to notify Napster of titles, artists' names, and the names of Napster files containing the works in question. The order also imposed an additional duty upon Napster to search its files for copyright violations independently of notification by the recording companies.

In an attempt to comply with the injunction, Napster installed a file filtering system designed to block users from downloading specific files. The district court monitored the process over a three-month period. Although Napster was able to prevent the exchange of much of the works noticed by the recording companies, RIAA presented evidence that infringement of noticed works continued to occur. Accordingly, the district court determined that Napster was not in satisfactory compliance with the modified injunction and ordered the company to disable its file transferring service until it could take appropriate steps to ensure maximum compliance. Despite Napster's claim that the shut down order effectively required 100% policing, the ninth circuit upheld the decision:

> The district court ordered Napster to keep the file transferring service disabled until Napster satisfied the court "that when the new system goes back up it will be able to block out or screen out copyrighted works that have been noticed . . . and do it with [a] sufficient degree of reliability and sufficient percentage [of success]. . . . It's not good enough until every effort has been made to, in fact, get zero tolerance. . . . The standard is, to get it down to zero."[17]

Economic Analysis

1. Musical lyricists and performers have been giving away music for the better part of a millennium. Although it began to get complicated with the invention of the phonograph, tape recorder, radio, and TV, the economic problem has not changed all that much. The problem is to increase value by reaching expansive audiences while limiting access to free riders. In medieval times, wandering minstrels were the medium of transmission, and the free rider problem compelled minstrels to subsist on voluntary contributions or to draw support from wealthy patrons.

2. Enterprising teens of the 1950s swapped tape recordings of radio broadcasts of their favorite tunes, the main limitation being quality of transmission and networking the communications. It is ironic that the process has become illegal now that it has reached near perfection. Without question, the Napster technology of transmitting music from performer to audience is a vast improvement over records, tapes, and CDs. Like records and tapes, CDs will ultimately be replaced by MP3 technology. The only economic reason to maintain the present distribution system is to combat the free rider problem in order to enable recording companies to collect revenues.

3. In its initial form, Napster provided a clear contrast with Sony. Casual observation revealed that the vast majority of consumers used video recorders for the noninfringing purpose of time shifting. Just the opposite was true of Napster subscribers, the vast

majority of whom were direct infringers. Whereas the RIAA members were clearly harmed by the operation of Napster, the widespread use of video recorders very likely benefited, on balance, the producers of TV programming. Legal niceties aside, these simple facts provide the economic rationale for siding with Sony and against Napster. Translating these economic principles into law proved somewhat difficult, however.

4. As long as infringing uses exist, it is a statistical certainty that the seller (Sony or Napster) is materially contributing to direct infringement by some of its customers. The circuit court made it clear that this sort of *inferential* knowledge falls short of the standard for contributory infringement. The criterion that the court adopted—evidence that Napster had actual knowledge that specific infringing material was available on the system—suggests that the proportions of infringing and noninfringing uses are irrelevant. Napster had the ability to identify infringing material and the ability to block or remove it. The zero tolerance approach wiped out all legal protection of peer-to-peer service providers. Since the continuous policing of the activities of millions of members is impossible, the file *sharing* aspect of Napster was essentially shut down.

5. While the legal arguments underlying the zero tolerance approach are clear (Napster's knowledge of abuse and the ability to prevent it), it is hard to square such a hard-line approach with principles of efficiency. In light of the prohibitive exclusion costs at the margin, some tolerance of free riding must be economically justifiable, even in the narrow sense of promoting RIAA profit. Two important factors weigh in here. The first relates to control. Ideally, the decision to permit free downloading of any piece of music lies not with Napster, or even the RIAA, but with the individual holder of the copyright. Napster might claim to be exerting its best efforts, but its incentives clearly diverge from those of either the record companies or the performing artists. The second relates to the dynamics of technological change. The legal acceptance of Napster's current efforts as "tolerable" would remove incentives for improvement, not only from Napster, *but also from actual and potential competitors*. Why should any company seek to develop and implement a technology that would place it at a disadvantage relative to its competitors?

6. In the meantime, the short-run effects of this decision unquestionably uphold monopoly profit at the expense of potential economic surplus. More importantly, the prospect of reaping offsetting long-run gains through the promotion of creative activity is far from clear. The clear winners are the middlemen (recording companies), who are empowered to maintain monopoly profit by suppression of technology. The good news is that, while the court's decision empowers the suppression of *technology*, it does not empower the suppression of *technological progress*. Evaluating the full effects would require considerable speculation about the future of the industry in terms of (a) an efficient course of events and (b) how, or to what extent, the legal environment moves actual events off of that course.

7. Some food for thought is probably better than wild speculation:
   a. The basic economic transaction is between creative artists (song writers and performers) and the consuming public.
   b. Assuming that online file sharing is a more efficient medium of transmission than recording products (CDs), assigning rights to the recording industry necessitates

some potentially costly transactions. The industry is not just an agent for the interests of creative artists; it also has vested interests to protect.

c. A workable system of online file sharing is already in motion. Napster and its imitators are providing copious menus of downloadable music, some of which is copyrighted. The provider pays negotiated royalties to the copyright holders. In light of the enormous potential for cutting distribution costs, revenue from subscription fees and indirect sources rates to provide strong incentives for creative works.
d. Unrestrained peer-to-peer file sharing almost certainly goes too far in promoting the rights of free riders at the expense of copyright holders. Without the right to exclude material from the system, the process of negotiated royalties cannot operate. The Napster experience underscores the costs of monitoring the system for unauthorized materials.

CHAPTER 7

CONTRACT FORMATION

In its simplest economic form, a **contract** specifies the terms of a voluntary exchange. As long as the parties to the exchange are rational and fully informed, mutual benefit is the expected outcome. Indeed, the mutual benefit from exchange is the cornerstone of free market economics. Along with exchange and mutual benefit, the key words are voluntary, rational, informed, and expected. Ironically, the economic purpose of enforcing contracts by the rule of law is not to ensure mutual benefits. The mutual benefits generally flow automatically from the process. Accordingly, the role of the law is to uphold the integrity of the process.

Incentive Structures

Just as in economic theory, the law proceeds from the presumption that contracting parties are rational and informed and that they voluntarily accepted the terms. Given those presumptions, the primary economic reason to enforce contracts is that both parties *want* them to be enforced. In a typical contract scenario, a buyer offers a sum of money in exchange for a commodity or service provided by a seller, but the exchange is not simultaneous. The seller expects a profit, and the buyer expects consumer surplus. The seller needs the money to buy the materials, but the buyer fears that the seller will take the money and run.

The nonsimultaneous game is depicted in Figure 7.1. Imagine that the buyer expects \$100 worth of value from an addition to her home. A contractor can do the job at a cost of \$25 and offers a price of \$50. During construction, the buyer would have to rent a motel room at a price of \$25. At point A in Figure 7.1, the buyer chooses between "contract" and "no contract." If she chooses contract, the game moves to point B, where the seller gets to choose between "perform" and "not perform." Payoffs for the three possible outcomes are in parentheses, with the buyer's payoffs first. If no contract is made, neither party gains nor loses. If there is a contract and the seller performs, both gain \$25. If not, the seller gains \$50, but the buyer loses \$75.

Clearly, the buyer's choice depends upon her expectation of the seller's choice at point B. Both parties want the seller's promise to be enforced, but for different reasons. The buyer wants enforcement to induce the seller to choose "Perform." The seller wants enforcement to induce the buyer to choose contract. There is a well-known game played in "Peanuts," in which Lucy promises to hold the football, but always pulls it away at the last moment. One player chooses contract, expecting the other to perform, but the other chooses not perform. This endearing and fanciful story borders on economic absurdity because it seems that a rational Charlie Brown would choose "no contract" on the expectation of Lucy's choosing "not perform." However, *Brown v. Van Pelt* might make interesting economic fodder because (a) the payoffs are wholly subjective and (b) the game always produced the same outcome in spite of countless repetitions.[1]

FIGURE 7.1 If buyers expect sellers not to perform, they will forego contracts that would otherwise be mutually beneficial.

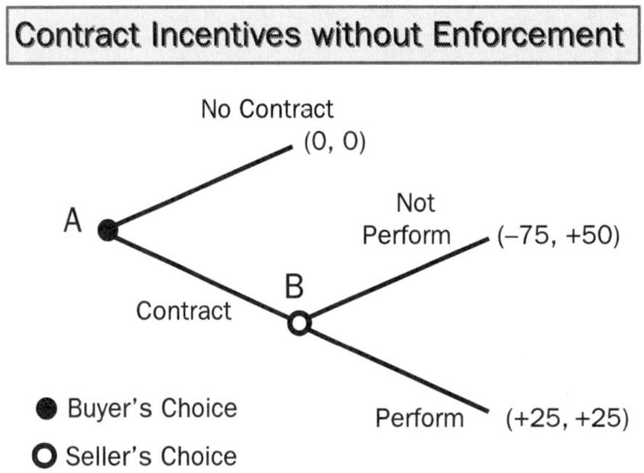

Subjective Considerations

Given the countless repetitions, the only reasonable economic conclusion is that the game produces mutual benefits; therefore, neither Lucy nor Charlie Brown would want the literal terms of the contract to be enforced. Lucy clearly gets a positive payoff from nonperformance and probably a negative payoff from performance. By his choices, Charlie Brown has revealed his preference for nonperformance over no contract. Whether he prefers performance over nonperformance is solely a matter of conjecture, but his success rate at other athletic endeavors would be admissible evidence. If he expected to miss the field goal, he might well prefer not to attempt it.

The lesson of *Brown v. Van Pelt* is that it is dangerous for a court to second-guess the terms of a contract. Even with considerable evidence about the circumstances leading to the formation of a contract, jurists cannot get into the hearts and minds of the litigants. From a pure economic perspective, it is important to keep in mind that the individual benefits and costs are subjective. Even when the terms of the contract appear to be unfair or harmful to one of the parties, it is the *process* that the law is evaluating, not the *substance* of the terms.

The really interesting issues in contracts arise when things do not turn out as expected or were not as they seemed in the first place. Here is where our old nemesis, the cost of transacting, comes into play. If transactions costs were zero or negligible, contracting parties could engage in perfect research (and always be perfectly informed), ask every conceivable question of each other, and then identify every possible future contingency of events and make appropriate provisions in the contract to allow for them. That having been said, mistakes and miscalculations occur, and vital circumstances change. The classic case of mutual mistake concerned the sale of Rose II of Aberlone.[2] Rose, a cow thought to be barren, was found to be pregnant between the sale agreement and actual delivery. Pregnancy and future fertility increased her value about tenfold. The seller repudiated the contract and prevailed in court, but the real issue was not who should have the cow. Because the contract was formed without a vital piece of information, the usually routine inference of mutual benefit ceases to be valid.

Basic Problems of Formation

In order to utilize economic principles, it is important to bridge the (sometimes enormous) gap between theory and reality. The smooth transition from initial positions to final outcomes is like a roadmap or a game plan. We know in advance that things may not work out perfectly, and the law makes allowances for imperfections in the process. Accordingly, the law proceeds on a number of working hypotheses. The underlying markets are essentially competitive. Information is less than perfect, but there are no grave impediments to the flow of information. Since transactions costs preclude the formation of perfect contracts, the standard of efficiency is the formation of contracts wherein both parties expect to benefit.

In this chapter, we examine basic issues of contract formation—whether an enforceable contract exists. We are looking for evidence that the agreement was an actual exchange, that both parties entered the agreement voluntarily, and that there were no major imperfections in information. In legal terminology, the three broad issues are **consideration, mutual assent,** and **volition**; the single unifying factor underlying all three is whether or not both parties *want* their promises to be enforced.

1. *Consideration.* In plain economics, each party gives up something in expectation of receiving something in return. This is the literal meaning of the Latin phrase, *quid pro quo*. An 1875 English decision defined consideration as "some right, interest, profit or benefit accruing to the one party, or some forbearance, detriment, loss or responsibility given, suffered or undertaken by the other." The term was an outgrowth of courts' reluctance to enforce gratuitous promises (e.g., Lucy's promise to hold the football).

2. *Mutual assent.* The key phrase is a "meeting of the minds." Simple mistakes and misunderstandings are grounds for rescinding a contract, provided that the nonoffending party was not substantially harmed. Nonetheless, understanding is an important part of rationality. Both parties are generally responsible for knowing what the terms of the contract are. A particularly important economic issue pertains to asymmetries of information—situations in which one party has private information that the other cannot reasonably be expected to possess. There are fine lines between duties to disclose and property rights to useful information.

3. *Volition.* There can be no expectation of mutual benefit unless both parties accept the terms voluntarily. The main event is duress, but there are less obvious forms besides threats of physical or economic violence. Fraud has the same effect as duress; its purpose is to induce a person to accept unfavorable terms. The first cousin of fraud is intentional suppression of information, and the second cousin is concerned with duty to disclose.

4. *Public policy.* Even if both parties want their promises to be enforced, contracts may be set aside if there is significant harm to third parties or to the public at large. Similarly, contracts that might otherwise be unenforceable may be enforced

if there are substantial external benefits to the public. Examples from this chapter include inducements for fathers to pay child support and the protection of sources of information.

The first case in this chapter (*Fiege v. Boehm*) involves virtually all of the fundamental issues of contract formation. The other three are more specialized, stretching to their limits a few key dimensions of formation. The sale of a haunted house (*Stambovsky v. Ackley*) strongly suggests an asymmetry of information, but the credibility of the information is open to serious question. The legal and economic approaches to gratuitous promises are sharply contrasted when political mud is exchanged for confidentiality (*Cohen v. Cowles*). Finally, the temptation to evaluate the terms themselves will become irresistible when "fine print" results in the repossession of a welfare mother's furniture (*Williams v. Walker-Thomas*).

Broehm Hilda

Fiege v. Boehm
210 Md. 352 (1956)

Simple Facts

A 1951 child-support agreement between Louis Fiege and Hilda Louise Boehm called for monthly support payments, plus compensation for medical expenses and lost wages. The agreement was voluntary in a strict legal sense—Fiege accepted the terms in exchange for "forbearance." Boehm agreed not to bring charges against him for the crime of bastardy. After discovering that he was not the father of the child, Fiege discontinued the payments. Boehm sought to enforce the terms of the verbal contract.

Details

Early common law cases held that a putative father had no legal liability to contribute to the support of his illegitimate child and that a promise to do so was unenforceable because it is based on a purely moral obligation. Motivations such as moral obligation or natural affection for the child were deemed insufficient consideration for the formation of a legal contract. The 1955 Maryland Bastardy Act compelled a person found guilty of bastardy to pay for the support of the child. Prosecutions for bastardy were treated as criminal proceedings, but the prime objective was to protect the public from the burden of maintaining illegitimate children. Upon conviction, the putative father was given a choice between payment of 18 years' child support or as much as two years in jail.

On September 29, 1951, Hilda Louise Boehm gave birth to a female child. At the time, she was 30 years of age and employed as a typist in Washington, D.C. During the following two years, Louis Gail Fiege paid Boehm the sum of $480 according to the terms of a verbal child support agreement. In May 1953, Fiege went to Boehm's physician to make inquiry about blood tests and discovered that he could not have been the father of the child. Accordingly, Fiege stopped payments. Boehm responded by instituting bastardy proceedings, but Fiege was acquitted.

Despite the acquittal on the criminal charges, there was a tab to settle. Boehm itemized out-of pocket expenses for doctor, hospital, and pharmaceutical care, plus a stint in the home for unwed mothers. The two large items included over $1,000 for six months' foregone wages and $1,400 for the 21 years of child support. In an effort to recover the balance, Boehm brought suit against Fiege for breach of the oral contract.

The Baltimore Superior Court found for Boehm on grounds that forebearance to sue for a lawful claim is sufficient consideration for a promise to pay child support. The only additional requirement was that the forbearing party have an *honest intention* to prosecute litigation *believed* to be well-founded. The court added that:

> The fact that a man accused of bastardy is forced to enter into a contract to pay for the support of his bastard child from fear of exposure and the shame that might be cast upon him as a result, as well as a sense of justice to render some compensation for the injury he inflicted upon the mother, does not lessen the merit of the contract, but greatly increases it.[3]

For the record, both parties testified to dinner and dancing after a movie in January 21, 1951. Fiege denied having sexual relations and contended that the payments were not for child support, but to prevent his mother from learning the details of his behavior. Of course, his defense relied mainly on his prior acquittal and upon the scientific findings from the blood tests. The appeals court dismissed the blood evidence for the simple reason that it was immaterial whether Fiege was or was not the father of the child. The court cited prior cases upholding similar contracts where the expectant mother did not even deliver. In one case, the plaintiff had died before coming to term; in another, she turned out not to be pregnant.

Economic Analysis

1. The Maryland court system's pre-*Days-of-Our-Lives* version of the shotgun wedding underscores the importance of property rights. What might appear to be duress is affirmed as valid consideration for a contract. Nonetheless, it is necessary to stretch the model to get the terms of the contract into Figure 7.1. At point A, Boehm offers forbearance (something Fiege wants) in exchange for money. It is easy to see why Boehm wants the contract enforced. Fiege wants enforcement to avoid the *prospect* of jail. That prospect does not have to be a certainty. The reduction or elimination of the *probability* of jail has economic value.
2. Fiege's gain from the exchange is mainly the avoidance of an *expected cost. Ex ante*, he considers the probability of conviction and the expected duration of jail time. The probability of conviction is a subjective calculation, as is the Hedonic calculus of incarceration, as is his marginal utility of money. Although the circumstances of the case are extreme, they give emphasis to the law's reliance on individual rationality.
3. The fact that Fiege began the payments implies an acceptance of the terms and suggests that he believed that he was the father of the child. A part of rationality is seeking information. If Fiege had any significant doubt about the paternity, it was largely his responsibility to gather facts pertaining to probability. On the basis of economic inferences drawn from his behavior ("revealed preference"), it is inconceivable that there had been no sexual liaison.
4. The blood evidence (the union of a Type O and a Type B cannot produce a Type A) and relatively short length of term (January 21–September 29) suggest that Boehm was not certain of Fiege's paternity. However, "not certain" translates into a subjective belief that the probability was something less than one. At one extreme, the blood tests may have been erroneous; at the other, Boehm could have been virtually certain that Fiege was not the father. The court held that good faith was to be presumed as long as the paternity claim was not "frivolous, vexatious, or unlawful."
5. For the sake of argument, assume that the blood evidence was accurate. Fiege was not the father, but Boehm *knew* only that Fiege *might not be* the father. This information does not compromise "good faith" because she also knew that he might be the father. In economic jargon, there is some "asymmetry of information." Had the issue of plaintiff's duty to disclose the information arisen, the court almost certainly would have sided with Boehm. For starters, Fiege also "knew" (as a participant in the Washington singles scene) that he might not be the father.

6. More importantly, however, parties to a contract are entitled to bargain "at arm's length." The simple economic reason is that the motivation for contracting is the expectation of gain. Having to divulge private information undermines a person's ability to secure favorable terms. The subjective costs to Boehm of revealing information that would further damage her reputation outweighed the value of the information itself.
7. There is also an element of public policy involved in affirming this contract. The legislative intent of the bastardy law was to create a means of enforcing child support to internalize the external costs imposed upon women and, indirectly, upon the state. In addition, the law was necessary to facilitate the enforcement of truly voluntary contracts, rendered unenforceable by the somewhat archaic notion of consideration.

Poltergeist IV

Stambovsky v. Ackley
72 N.Y.S. 2d 672 (1993)

Simple Facts

Jeffrey and Patrice Stambovsky made an offer to purchase Helen Ackley's Victorian mansion on the Hudson River. It was a standard real estate transaction except that the house was reputed to be haunted. Pleading ignorance of the local folklore, the couple sought to rescind the offer. Ackley denied that the house was actually haunted, despite prior claims in national publications. Rescission was granted, in part for Ackley's failure to disclose a material fact.

Details

The Village of Nyack is a charming multicultural community situated on the west shore of the Hudson River, about 25 miles north of New York City. Renown for its antiques, fine restaurants, and rich architectural styles, Nyack provides a true village atmosphere and an attractive retreat for Manhattan residents like Jeffrey and Patrice Stambovsky. The Stambovskys were particularly enamored with the charms of an old Victorian mansion. In 1990, the couple made a down payment of $32,000 to purchase the mansion for $650,000. In spite of its spooky veneer, the couple was taken aback when a local architect remarked that they were buying a haunted house!

For years, Helen Ackley had touted her home as one of the premier poltergeist pads in the country. Ackley vividly described her many encounters with ghosts and spirits in local and national publications, including a 1977 article in the *Reader's Digest.* In November 1989, the house was included in a five-home walking tour of Nyack and described in a newspaper article as "a riverfront Victorian (with ghost)." When the Stambovskys became aware of the home's reputation, they attempted to back out of the deal. When Ackley refused to cancel the sale, they brought suit to rescind the contract. Alleging unfamiliarity with the local folklore, Stambovsky sought to rescind the offer.

The lower court applied a strict rule of *caveat emptor*; New York law does not recognize any remedy for damages resulting from a seller's mere silence. The appellate court disagreed, in part because of Ackley's promotional efforts:

> Whether the source of the spectral apparitions seen by defendant seller is parapsychic or psychogenic, having reported their presence in both a national publication and the local press, defendant is estopped to deny their existence. . . .[4]

In simple economics, the house was ruled to be legally haunted! That unique designation was not sufficient to warrant rescission, however, and the New York rule of *caveat emptor* rendered "elusive" the theoretical basis for not enforcing the contract. The real estate broker was under no duty to disclose the "phantasmal reputation" of the premises to a potential buyer. Writing for the court, Judge Rubin remarked that "in his pursuit of a legal remedy for fraudulent misrepresentation against the seller, plaintiff hasn't a ghost of a chance. . . ."[5] Accordingly, the court looked for something more than mere failure to disclose.

ILLUSTRATION 7.1 Let the realtors beware: You may no longer sell haunted houses in New York without informing the buyer.

© Susan Van Etten

The court emphasized the fact that Ackley had deliberately fostered the public belief that the house was possessed. Having gone to extraordinary means to inform the local public, she owed at least that much to a contractual partner. Without explicitly saying so, the court implied that Ackley had crossed the line between passive silence and deliberate concealment of a material fact. As a practical matter, Rubin held (emphasis added) that:

> Applying the strict rule of *caveat emptor* to a contract involving a house possessed by poltergeists conjures up visions of a psychic or medium routinely accompanying the structural engineer and Terminix man on an inspection of every home subject to a contract of sale. . . . In the interest of *avoiding such untenable consequences*, the notion that a haunting is a condition which can and should be ascertained upon reasonable inspection of the premises is a hobgoblin which should be exorcised from the body of legal precedent and laid quietly to rest.[6]

The appellate court granted rescission by a narrow 3–2 majority.

Economic Analysis

1. In addition to being legally haunted, the house was economically haunted. Its reputation rated to have a significant effect upon resale value and, given its unique appeal to ghost seekers, upon the buyers' ability to enjoy their privacy. There can be little doubt that Stambovsky would not have offered to buy the house if he had known of its history.

2. Until she decided to sell the house, Ackley was proud of her poltergeist. Her sudden silence strongly implies an expectation that simple disclosure would adversely affect demand for the home. Accordingly, one may infer an active choice to take advantage of buyer ignorance. Without a meeting of the minds, the simple economic conclusion is that the presumption of mutual benefit falls by the wayside.

3. The case involves a classic asymmetry of information, analogous to the "lemons" model pertaining to the market for used cars. Asymmetries hamper the functioning of markets in two ways. First, under the principle of **adverse selection,** consumers come to expect a correlation between an owner's willingness to sell and the existence of a hidden defect. The effect of adverse selection is to induce potential buyers to underestimate value and thereby reduce the number of mutually beneficial exchanges.

4. The second adverse effect is to induce potential buyers to expend excessive effort in search of material information. While we cannot expect the routine employment of psychics to accompany the Terminix man, the accumulated costs of undue caution are significant.

Politics as Usual

Cohen v. Cowles Media Corp. 479 N.W.2d 387 (1992)

Simple Facts

Two Minnesota newspapers each published a story containing unfavorable publicity about a political candidate. In spite of promises of confidentiality, both newspapers revealed that Dan Cohen had supplied this information to them. Cohen was fired from his job and sued for breach of contract and fraudulent misrepresentation. The publishers defended their action on grounds that the source was an integral part of the story.

Details

On October 28, 1982, the *Minneapolis Star Tribune* and the *St. Paul Pioneer Press* each published a story on the gubernatorial election campaign, reporting that Marlene Johnson, a candidate for lieutenant governor, had been charged with three counts of unlawful assembly in 1969 and had been convicted of shoplifting in 1970. Both newspapers identified Dan Cohen, a political associate of the opposing gubernatorial candidate, as the source of the information. The story also named the advertising firm that employed Cohen.

Cohen had supplied the information in return for the reporters' promises of confidentiality. The editors overruled the promises, for a number of reasons revealed at trial. They contended that the source was newsworthy as part of the whole story of political intrigue and that failure to reveal the source might cast suspicion upon others. Moreover, since the *Star Tribune* had endorsed the Perpich-Johnson ticket in its opinion section, the editors feared that withholding Cohen's identity might be construed as an effort to protect its favored candidates. Whatever the reasons, Cohen was fired as soon as the stories were published.

Cohen brought suit against the publishers of the newspapers, alleging breach of contract and fraudulent misrepresentation. At trial, the jury awarded $200,000 compensatory damages for breach of contract and $250,000 punitive damages against each newspaper on the misrepresentation claim. The court of appeals overturned the verdict of fraudulent misrepresentation, but affirmed the damages for breach of contract. The Supreme Court of Minnesota also overruled the breach of contract damages, holding that the newspapers may have had a moral and ethical commitment, but "this was not a situation where the parties were thinking in terms of a legally binding contract."[7]

After considerable procedural wrangling, the court ultimately relied on the doctrine of **promissory estoppel**. In its simplest form, estoppel precludes a person from denying the truth of some prior statement, particularly when that statement was designed to induce action by another (e.g., as in *Stambovsky v. Ackley*). As applied here, promissory estoppel renders a promise binding if (a) the promise was designed to induce a particular action and did, in fact, induce the expected action and (b) injustice can be avoided only by enforcing the promise.

Part (a) was clearly satisfied. The reporters promised confidentiality to induce Cohen to provide the information, and Cohen provided the information, relying on the promise of confidentiality. With regard to the "injustice" part, the court emphasized that the newspapers themselves believed that they generally must keep promises of confidentiality given to a news source, and the reporters adamantly testified that their promises should have been honored:

> The editors who countermanded the promises conceded that never before or since have they reneged on a promise of confidentiality. A former *Minneapolis Star* managing editor testified that the newspapers had "hung Mr. Cohen out to dry because they didn't regard him very highly as a source. . . ." Other experts, too, stressed the ethical importance, except on rare occasions, of keeping promises of confidentiality. It was this long-standing journalistic tradition that Cohen, who has worked in journalism, relied upon in asking for and receiving a promise of anonymity.[8]

Accordingly, the court concluded that the harm requires a remedy to avoid an injustice and held the publishers liable in damages for the "broken promise" instead of the "breach of contract." Not surprisingly, Cohen was awarded the same amount ($200,000) as the jury had earlier awarded for the breach action.

The Minnesota court initially had rejected its own theory of promissory estoppel in favor of the publishers' First Amendment rights. That view was reversed and remanded by the U.S. Supreme Court (501 U.S. 663) in a 5–4 decision with two dissenting opinions. The procedural wrangling concerned the resurrection of an argument that had not originated with the plaintiffs.

Economic Analysis

1. Reading the multitude of transcripts concerning this case is like watching sausage being made. When the court speculated that "it is perhaps worth noting that the test is not whether the promise should be enforced to do justice, but whether enforcement is required to prevent an injustice," the sausage won out. Despite the barrage of double negatives and tortured phraseology, the court groped its way to the correct economic decision.

2. If this case were about justice, the Minnesota newspapers would be buried in six feet of mud and Dan Cohen would spend his eternity reading tabloids. In economics, even contracts between cockroaches merit enforcement. What made this case difficult for the law was that Cohen did not receive anything in exchange for the story. Strictly speaking, there was no "consideration." Cohen gave Cowles a story; Cowles gave nothing in return that Cohen did not already have. Interpreting a promise of confidentiality as "consideration" tortures the meaning of the term. What makes the case relatively easy economics is that, *ex ante*, both parties wanted the terms of the agreement to be enforceable.

3. Publishers empower their reporters to make promises of confidentiality as a tool for obtaining information. The gain to the publishers is a simple change in "x," an increase in information. That information may not be useful, but it may lead to a publishable article and therefore has an expected value. The same is true for the confidentiality that they are offering. Withholding the source of the information may be "doing nothing," but there is a reduction in "y" in the form of not publishing

a piece of information that the newspaper would otherwise have the right to publish.

4. Beyond the Cartesian coordinates, the agreement produces mutual benefit. The publishers get a potential story, and Cohen gets vicarious pleasure from smearing a political rival and/or a higher probability of his candidate's success. However, Cohen's prospective gain is more than offset by the consequences of having others know that he engaged in mud slinging. The reporters and the publishers wanted the promise enforceable in the sense that enforceability increases credibility and, in the long run, the flow of information to them.

5. Noneconomists are squeamish about the subject of trading rights. While economists may not be squeamish enough, the transfer of the property right to "y" from the newspaper to the source is the *quid* in the *quid pro quo*. The deliberations at the U.S. Supreme Court might have benefited from this framework. The First Amendment guarantees *freedom* of the press as a *means* of supporting the public's right to know. The right to trade a piece of that freedom does not diminish its value. Quite the contrary, its value is enhanced. In essence, the dissenters wanted to use the First Amendment as an excuse for blunting an instrument (enforceable promises) that increases the effectiveness of the press.

Life in the Shoe

Williams v. Walker-Thomas Furniture 350 F. 2d 445 (1965)

Simple Facts

A welfare mother made an installment purchase of a stereo system at a price of $514. She later defaulted, with a balance of $164. The credit agreement contained an "add-on" clause, which permitted the furniture company to repossess every item in Williams' past account. Williams claimed that the credit agreement was an unconscionable contract.

Details

During the period from 1957 to 1962, Ora Lee Williams purchased a number of household items from the Walker-Thomas retail furniture store in Washington, D.C. The terms were specified in a printed form contract, which provided for repossession in the event of a default in the payment of any monthly installment. In addition, the contract specified that "all payments now and hereafter made by [purchaser] shall be credited pro rata on all outstanding leases, bills and accounts due the company by [purchaser] at the time each such payment is made." This particular stipulation is known as an **add-on clause.** Its effect was to keep a balance due on *every* item purchased until the balance due on all items was paid off—regardless of when it was purchased.

In April 1962, Williams bought a stereo, priced at $514.95. She later defaulted, and Walker-Thomas sought to repossess all the items purchased since December 1957. When she bought the stereo, her account showed a balance of $164 owed on prior purchases. In all, she had paid $1,400 toward a total of $1,800 due.

Despite the obscure language of the contract, Williams did not claim to have misunderstood the terms of the contract. Her prime contention was that the terms were unconscionable and therefore not enforceable. This argument was rejected by both the trial court and the court of appeals. The Washington circuit court was more sympathetic. According to the court transcript, Walker-Thomas was aware of Williams' indigent financial position. In particular, the stereo contract listed the name of her social worker and indicated a monthly income of $218, a welfare stipend from the government. The court emphasized that the company sold Williams a $514 stereo "with full knowledge that appellant had to feed, clothe and support both herself and seven children on this amount. . . ."[9]

The court's rationale for applying the unconscionable label to this contract was not entirely specific. Judge Skelly Wright grasped for the collective effect of a set of conditions, none of which was determinative in and of itself:

> Unconscionability has generally been recognized to include an absence of meaningful choice on the part of one of the parties together with contract terms which are unreasonably favorable to the other party. Whether a meaningful choice is present in a particular case can only be determined by consideration of all the circumstances surrounding the transaction. In many cases the meaningfulness of the choice is negated by a gross inequality of bargaining power. The manner in which the contract was entered is also relevant to this consideration.[10]

Wright made further reference to Williams' lack of education and questioned whether she had "a reasonable opportunity to understand the terms of the contract," suggesting that the important terms might have been "hidden in a maze of fine print" or "minimized by deceptive sales practices."[11]

The dissenting jurist noted that the lower courts found no evidence that Walker-Thomas had actually engaged in sharp practices. He emphasized that many indigent consumers need credit and that businesses like Walker-Thomas will take long chances, expecting policies like the add-on clause to provide some financial protection commensurate with the risk. Citing the great latitude afforded by the law to contracting parties, he expressed concern about the effect that this decision would have upon thousands of installment credit transactions.

Economic Analysis

1. Printed form contracts, like the one used by Walker-Thomas, are generally known as **contracts of adhesion.** Consumers are presented with a set of nonnegotiable terms on a "take-it-or-leave-it" basis. The choice between accepting or rejecting the terms of the contract may not be meaningful, but it is economic. In defense of adhesion contracts, the ability of sellers to set unreasonable terms is limited by competition. If there exists a profitable set of alternative terms that are more favorable to them, many more consumers will "leave-it" than "take-it."

2. The dissenting opinion strikes a harmonic chord with traditional free market economics. Indeed, the unconscionability doctrine has been amply criticized for harming the very group of people that it was designed to protect. In terms of this particular case, the add-on clause appears to be the most efficient way of creating collateral to support loans to indigent customers. Used furniture is apt to be most valuable to the store that originally sold it. The problem is that used furniture depreciates rapidly, and no single item provides enough collateral to support its own financing. Therefore, the refusal to enforce add-on clauses harms the class of indigent customers by undermining their already meager credit opportunities.

3. At a more basic level, no rational, informed customer will accept truly unconscionable terms. The economic literature distinguishes between procedural and substantive unconscionability. **Procedural unconscionability** is based on inherent flaws in the process (e.g., fraud or duress), the point being that the flaws provide ample basis for enforcement without creating a new category. The substantive version is based on a subjective examination of the terms of the contract. **Substantive unconscionability** expands judicial prerogatives and paves the way for courts to interfere with voluntary contracts. The dissenting jurist remarked that the court should have looked for an appropriate remedy in laws dealing with "loan-sharking."

4. Beyond the simple efficiencies inherent in mutual gain from contracts, there is a larger efficiency issue involved here. In simple terms, do the benefits resulting from the existence of add-on clauses outweigh the costs? Banning them eliminates some economic surplus by creating a barrier to voluntary exchange, but also eliminates some costly mistakes if the market is not functioning perfectly. In more complex terms, how far should the law proceed in scrutinizing the terms of suspicious clauses—at what point do the marginal costs begin to outweigh the marginal benefits?

5. There is, in fact, some reason to doubt the effectiveness of competitive forces in this segment of the market. Add-on clauses exist for those who have few options. The number of competing firms may be small, and a "standard transaction" entails more complexity than at the upper end of the market (where credit cards or cash suffice). Even ignoring differences in education, acquiring information may be more difficult for the indigent, some of whom do not even have telephones. Of itself, this is a weak argument for banning add-on clauses, but the banning of add-on clauses is not what the unconscionability doctrine does.

6. The doctrine allows courts to oversee the machinations of contractual terms that superficially appear to be offensive. Add-on clauses—and any number of analogous market practices—are not offensive in and of themselves and invariably can be justified in theory. In practice, they may be administered in ways that prove to be offensive. In particular, it may be offensive that Walker-Thomas was so eager to repossess Williams' furniture. Instead of attempting to refinance the loan to enable her to pay the $164 balance, the company chose to act like a vulture.

7. In the final economic analysis, the unconscionability doctrine transfers some (a small amount) regulatory authority from the legislative and executive branches to the judiciary. It is worth considering whether this shift in authority makes economic sense. Statutory regulations are aimed at specific practices, with careful language spelling out the circumstances under which actions are legal or not. Part of the process involves anticipating mistakes and degrees of deviousness. In response, ethical businesses have to hire lawyers to keep abreast of current regulations. Accordingly, some reliance on the judiciary may be less costly and more effective.

8. In the (truly) final analysis, the logical foundation of this case may not be economic, except in the sense that society is willing to trade some of the potential gains from market exchanges for a heightened sense of social justice. In short, there is a larger tradeoff between efficiency and equity. Most economists are willing to pay lip service to this principle but still regard it as too subjective to form a basis for public policy.

CHAPTER 8

PERFORMANCE AND EXCUSE

The four cases discussed in the preceding chapter had one important feature in common: economic circumstances did not substantially change between the time of the initial agreement and the dispute over its enforceability. The paternity of Boehm's child did not change, and Ackley's house did not suddenly become haunted. The Minnesota newspaper did not uncover new facts, and Ora Lee Williams did not lose her job or suffer a major financial loss that caused her to default on her installment payments. In this chapter, our primary emphasis shifts from the question of *whether* a promise should be enforced to *how* it should be enforced.

When economic circumstances do change, it will generally be correct to modify the manner and/or extent of performance. The simple and straightforward remedy is to renegotiate the terms and bypass the courts entirely, but a wide range of legal procedures exists to encourage and promote flexibility. The legal remedies have the economic purpose of providing incentives with regard to two broad dimensions. One dimension (*ex post*) pertains to the completion or cessation of performance of the contract. For example, if costs of performance turn out to be substantially higher than expected, the correct economic decision may be to forego performance. Similarly, the value may turn out to be substantially lower than expected. Either way, it is inefficient to complete a contract once it is *known* to yield a net economic loss at the margin, even though both parties *expected* it to yield a net economic gain. The other dimension (*ex ante*) relates to precautionary behavior before the change in conditions. The most prominent precautions include research activity to anticipate the "unforeseeable" and productive effort to mitigate the adverse effects or increases in costs.

Ex Post Incentives

After a change has occurred, the simple objective is to maximize net value or minimize net loss from that point forward. In "either-or" terms, that means to perform contracts that yield a (positive) net marginal value and not to perform contracts that yield a net marginal loss. If only two parties are involved and they are in close communication, transactions costs rate to be low. In this context, it is useful to think about contract law as clarifying rights and duties of contracting parties so that contract disputes can be settled efficiently out of court. In Coasian terms, the law defines the property rights to set the initial position for the bargain.

To illustrate, we may return to the buyer-seller example developed in Chapter 7. The buyer incurs \$25 in motel expenses and pays \$50 for an addition to her home that is worth \$100 to her. The seller estimates the work to cost \$25 and anticipates a profit of \$25. While the buyer is resting comfortably in her motel room, the seller calls to explain that he cannot complete the job.

FIGURE 8.1 The consequences of economic breach impact upon the decisions to form contracts and to perform once the contract is formed.

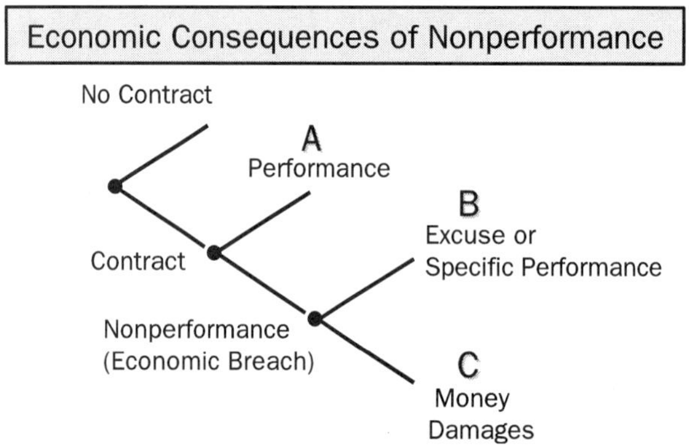

Of course, "cannot" is a strong word. The appropriate economic inference is that, for a variety of possible reasons, the contractor believes that nonperformance is in his best interests. In a perfect economic world of zero transactions costs, the buyer replies, "That's okay—send me a check for $100 and we will forget the contract" and the seller writes the check. The seller's economic obligation is fulfilled because the buyer is placed in an equal economic position to what she would have achieved had the contract been performed. In the real world, the probable result is that the seller offers to refund her $50 and the buyer has to search for another contractor (or worse). Let's now pretend that the matter goes to court.

In court, the buyer might ask for **specific performance** (force the seller to complete the job), and the seller might ask for **excuse** (nonperformance with a simple refund). Depending on various underlying circumstances, the court has the option of granting either of these extreme remedies or the pure economic remedy of a cash settlement.

These relatively simple alternatives are laid out in Figure 8.1. The economic breach occurs at the juncture where the seller announces his intention not to perform, choosing nonperformance over performance (outcome A in the figure). That choice does not entirely rule out performance because the court may impose specific performance (one of the two options at outcome B in the figure) as a remedy. The award of money damages lies at the end of the process (outcome C), but the anticipation of what the court will do at that juncture has ripple effects back through the whole set of choices and outcomes.

There are three theoretical bases for the case settlement, including reliance damages, expectations damages, and restitution. **Reliance damages** would cover the hotel expenses in addition to the refund. The term is almost self-explanatory; the buyer incurred the hotel expense because she relied on the contractor's performing the contract. **Expectations damages** compensate the buyer for the $100 in value lost as a result of the failure to perform (or $50 above the refund). The third option, **restitution**, should not be confused with the simple refund. Suppose that the seller breached the contract in order to accept a better offer, one that yielded a profit of $75. The remedy of restitution would transfer the $75 profit to the buyer (in addition to the refund). More generally:

- *Reliance damages* restore nonbreaching parties to the same economic position they would have achieved *if they had not entered into the contract.*
- *Expectations damages* restore nonbreaching parties to the same economic position they would have achieved *if the contract had been performed.*
- *Restitution damages* transfer "ill-gotten" gains from the breaching party to the nonbreaching party.

Of the three, the main focus of both law and economics is upon expectations damages. The presumption, or working hypothesis, is that breach is the result of unforeseen circumstances rather than bad faith or opportunism. Barring other complicating factors, the anticipation of having to pay "perfect" expectations damages induces the efficient choice between performance and nonperformance. To illustrate this all-important point, suppose the contractor breached the contract because the cost of performance had risen to $90 instead of the $25 on which he based the initial decision to enter the contract. By performing, the contractor stands to lose $40, but the buyer (still) stands to gain $50. On this basis, the contract should be performed and, if the contractor anticipates having to pay expectations damages, he will do so. Instead of losing $40 by performing, he loses $50 by paying expectations damages.

As long as we focus on marginal gains and losses associated with performance, the anticipated award of expectations damages always leads to the efficient outcome because the party who is contemplating breach treats the other party's benefits as his own. Nonetheless, it is useful to expound on the matter of the $25 hotel bill. In particular, suppose the contractor had notified the buyer of his intentions before going to the hotel (or irrevocably incurring the expense). If the court woodenly awarded reliance damages, the buyer might go anyway. More importantly, the contract now should not be performed because the buyer's net gain at the correct margin is only $25. Expectations damages now become $75, including the refund but not the hotel bill. Again, the contractor makes the correct decision, but that decision is not to perform. Instead of losing $40 by performing, the contractor loses $25 by breaching the contract.

Ex Ante Incentives and Risk Allocation

Expectations damages provide a simple solution to the simple economic problem of how to proceed after circumstances have changed "unexpectedly." The prospect of the unexpected raises additional economic questions of how to deal with risk. In relation to the example, hindsight reveals that the contract produced a net social loss. Even though the buyer was protected from the risk of the cost increase, she obtained something worth $100 at a real economic cost of $115.

A major part of the process of contracting involves the allocation of risk. This in turn involves speculation, research, or general information about states of nature (what possibly can go wrong), relative likelihoods (likely, possible, remote, unforeseeable), and contingency plans (what to do when bad things happen). To the extent that these things are anticipated and thought out, the contingencies, duties, and responsibilities will tend to get spelled out as explicit terms of the contract. Otherwise, the law has to impute terms to the contract.

Holding the seller responsible for the cost increase is an extremely simple example of imputing terms to a contract. The law assigned the risk to the seller—even though the possibility of a cost increase was not explicitly mentioned in the contract. Three important economic reasons point toward allocating risk to the producer or seller. Stated as general principles:

1. *Risk-bearing.* Assign the risk to the party who is in the better position to absorb it. The seller tends to be involved in a relatively large number of similar transactions. On average, the seller's price covers expected cost, plus a premium for risk.
2. *Information.* Assign risk to the party who is better informed about the potential pitfalls. The general problem of uncertainty is more complicated than rolling dice or flipping coins. Sellers tend to understand the risks better than the buyer as a natural result of specialization in a particular trade.
3. *Cost control.* Assign risk to the party who is in the better position to take the appropriate precautions. The risks of cost increases are not solely random. To the extent that costs are controllable, sellers are often better prepared to know how and when to exert the appropriate effort to minimize the expected costs.

Assigning risk "by default" to the seller reduces transactions costs by simplifying terms and avoiding unnecessary negotiations. It also reduces the likelihood of litigation and the costs of litigating those cases that do end up in court. Item (3) is particularly important because the allocation of risk tends to affect the seller's behavior. Assigning risk of cost increases to the buyer reduces the seller's incentives to avoid cost increases. The general problem, known as **moral hazard**, is commonly associated with insurance. If losses are fully ensured, there is no pure economic incentive to be cautious. Item (2) also has behavioral implications with regard to incentives to investigate and anticipate uncertain contingencies. It also relates to the problem of **asymmetry of information**. Assigning risks to the buyer would place a burden upon sellers to explain the consequences of risk, but the tendency would still remain for buyers not to believe them. The general problem, known as **adverse selection**, was addressed in Chapter 7 in context of the sale of Mrs. Ackley's haunted house. From the buyer's perspective, it becomes too risky to enter into a contract with a seller who would assign risk to the buyer!

Legal Doctrines and Remedies

The main options open to the court are to mandate or excuse performance, to assess damages, or to modify terms. The reasons for failing to perform contractual obligations range from simple bad faith to impossibility. Under the legal doctrine of impossibility, a party who fails to perform may be excused (without having to pay damages) if, *through no fault of his own*, performance is rendered impossible or totally impracticable. The related doctrine of impracticability excuses performance when unforeseeable events remove the premise upon which the contract was based (e.g., a fire destroys an auditorium leased for a theatrical performance). The symmetrical doctrine of **frustration of**

purpose applies to buyers (e.g., cancellation of the Super Bowl might warrant refund of a nonrefundable hotel room deposit).

It is important to note that these doctrines constitute exceptions to the general rule of enforcing contractual obligations, regardless of how burdensome they might become. As explained in section 454 of the Restatement of Contracts, "practical impossibility means that the result asked for is not possible within the basic objectives contemplated by the parties so as to amount to commercial senselessness." As an illustration of how rigid this standard can be, an 1874 Minnesota case[1] held a contractor responsible for expectations damages after attempting three times to construct a building on a lot later discovered to be composed of quicksand!

In this chapter, a wide range of circumstances between bad faith and impossibility bring real people to junctures like A, B, and C in Figure 8.1. We consider whether death (*INA v. Phoenix*) is a valid excuse for nonperformance and ponder an appropriate measure of damages when potential insolvency (*Walgreens v. Sara Creek*) prompts a shopping center to renege on an obligation. In the other cases, political upheaval (*Translantic Financing v. U.S.*) stretches the meaning of foreseeability, economic turmoil (*Eastern Airlines v. Gulf Oil*) undermines the intent of a carefully crafted contract, and matters of public policy (*Hopper v. All-Pet*) warrant an equitable adjustment of terms.

Modern Day Siddhartha

CNA International v. Phoenix 678 So. 2d 378 (1996)

Simple Facts

In 1993, actor River Phoenix was under contract to star in two films. As a result of his untimely death from a drug overdose, one of the films was cancelled, and the other was produced with a substitute actor. The insurance underwriters claimed that the estate was responsible for financial losses because Phoenix had breached the contracts by negligently causing his own death. The estate sought protection under the doctrine of impossibility.

Details

Born on the cusp of the '60s and '70s, River Jude Phoenix was the eldest of four children born to, but not raised by, a hippie "family." His name originated from Hermann Hess's *Siddhartha*, whose title character sat and listened to the river in the shade of a banyan tree. From the humble origins of singing for change with his siblings on street corners, River Phoenix found meaning in his life in a Hollywood acting career that included highly praised roles in films like *Stand By Me*, *The Mosquito Coast*, and a 1988 Oscar nomination for his performance in *Running on Empty*.

The youthful idol's career tragically ended from a heroin overdose in 1993. At the time, Phoenix was under contract to star in two films. One of them, *Dark Blood*, was never produced. The other, *Interview with the Vampire*, drew new life if not immortality from performances by Tom Cruise and Phoenix's substitute, Brad Pitt. CNA and American Casualty had written entertainment package insurance policies pertaining to the two productions. After paying off the policyholders, CNA and American Casualty became subrogated to claims against the estate.

The insurance companies, perhaps conditioned by a mindset against client destruction of their own health, were determined to establish that self-destruction is not the sort of conduct that will excuse contract performance. CNA's cause of action drew pranic energy from a collection of "actor loanout" agreements between the Phoenix-owned Jude Nile Corporation and various companies in the vertical chain of film production. One of them, which gave Geffen Pictures the right to lend Phoenix to Time Warner, contained the following provision (emphasis added):

> From the date two [2] weeks before the scheduled start date of principal photography until the completion of all services required of Employee hereunder, Employee will not ride in any aircraft other than as a passenger on a scheduled flight of a United States or other major international air carrier maintaining regularly published schedules, or *engage in any ultrahazardous activity* without Producer's written consent in each case.[2]

Without any precedents from case law, plaintiffs referred to some of the language in the Restatement of Contracts. Section 261 excuses a party's performance if it is made impracticable *without his fault* by the occurrence of an event, "the non-occurrence of which was a basic assumption on which the contract was made." The following section cites death or incapacity of a particular (critical) person as one such basic assumption. The law does not explicitly link the two sections with any suggestion that a person may be blamed for his own death.

Despite the lack of precedent with regard to self-induced *death*, there is an abundance of case law pertaining to destruction of one's *health*. For example, a Wisconsin speech therapist, with a history of hypertension, attempted to quit her job with one school district to take a higher paying position closer to her home. The school board's refusal to let her out of the contract so annoyed the therapist as to pump her blood pressure beyond safe levels. She again resigned her position (and got the other offer reinstated), this time on advice of her physician. The Supreme Court of Wisconsin held the therapist responsible for the salary increment paid to her replacement.[3]

As far as the insurance companies were concerned, the same reasoning should apply to death. Particularly in a society engaged in an accelerating struggle with problems created by illegal drug abuse, such conduct should not excuse the performance of the contract. To the circuit court judge for Alachua County, Florida, the argument was as transparently self-serving as that of the Wisconsin therapist. Subrogors and subrogees aside, the law is clear and unambiguous that death renders a personal services contract impossible to perform. The Florida court of appeals agreed, although mildly bothered by the clause about engaging in "ultrahazardous" activities:

> In [personal services] contracts, there is an implied condition that death shall dissolve the contract. With this implied condition in mind, we believe the parties to the agreements could have provided specifically for the contingency of loss due to the use of illegal drugs, as they provided for other hazardous or life threatening contingencies.[4]

The insurers had attempted to introduce an ambiguity, but the court refused to take the bait:

> [A]ny attempt to discern fault in a death case such as this one, or in a similar case, perhaps involving the use of tobacco or alcohol would create another case by case and hard to interpret rule of law. . . . [T]here are already too many of these in existence. . . .[5]

Reading between the lines, we see that the relative lack of ambiguity of the law trumps the somewhat subjective notion of ultrahazardous. To a super-successful scion of a family of flower children, the notion of ultrahazardous drugs was doubtless as foreign as the soothing sound of a river and the shade of banyans to the streets of Hollywood.

Economic Analysis

1. The primary economic issue underlying this case is moral hazard. Moral hazard was first diagnosed in connection with health care services. In theory, people with health care insurance will tend to overuse health care and/or fail to take adequate measures to prevent illness because they do not bear the full risks of getting sick. The "moral" implication came from physicians and other health care providers; economists tend to view the phenomenon as a simple manifestation of individual rationality.

2. The issue of adverse selection invariably arises hand in hand with moral hazard. First aligned with the sale of used cars, adverse selection is the direct consequence of asymmetrical information. By virtue of experience from operating the vehicle, the seller has information that is not available to the buyer. Awareness of this condition induces buyers to infer that any used car offered for sale is a lemon and the prophecy is self-fulfilling. As applied to insurance contracts, insurers infer that those who want insurance must have higher than normal risks.

3. Personal services contracts are routinely excused when death circumvents performance. The simple explanation is that death is an act of God, but as this case illustrates, death can be delayed by appropriate care. In relation to the moral hazard argument, it is more than just doubtful that the prospect of having to pay damages for breach of contract would induce a person to take additional precautions against dying, at least to an extent that would matter. Posner suggests an exception based on asymmetry of information (e.g., a lower than normal life expectancy), but does not provide any example from case law.[6] These considerations apply directly to both the drug-induced death and to the role of the insurance carrier.

4. As applied to the drug overdose, moral hazard is clearly an issue, but one of minor importance to the case. The reason for dismissing moral hazard as a major factor is that liability for contract damages is not likely to have affected River Phoenix's lifestyle. In other words, even an explicit disclaimer (that drug-induced death was not included in the coverage) would probably not have induced Phoenix to behave differently. However, the asymmetry of information advances the analysis to a higher level. If the employers (movie producers) had known about the drug abuse, they could have inserted a damage clause into the services contract itself. They also could have raised the issue with CNA, but that issue is clouded by adverse selection. Most importantly, insurance carriers ought to understand that these factors are part of the actuarial process.

5. To the insurance carrier, three probabilities matter with regard to drugs: (a) the probability that Phoenix was a substance abuser; (b) *given (a)*, the conditional probability that he would engage in drug use during the relevant time frame; (c) *given (b)*, the conditional probability that the drug abuse would result in his death or incapacity. It is only a small exaggeration to say that every insurance actuary ought to have these numbers in their "manuals." The main asymmetry of information is that, whereas Phoenix knows item (a) for a fact, the insurers "knew" it as a probability. The moral hazard applies to (b). The insurer hazards a guess about likelihood, while the actor makes a behavioral choice. The act of God determines the final outcome, but that probability is definitely in the manual. From a purely economic perspective, it is hard to take CNA seriously.

6. Moving away from death to matters of health, the court noted a range of cases, but that of the Wisconsin therapist provides an instructive contrast with the *Phoenix* case. The employee, Elaine Lukaszewski, had a history of hypertension (asymmetry of information) and allowed herself to get overwrought (moral hazard) over the employer's refusal to let her out of her contract. Although there is no evidence that she had any overt intent to pump up her blood pressure, the fact that she had a higher paying job with a shorter commute provided motive for her to do so. All of

the economic factors point to holding Lukaszewski responsible for the condition that impeded performance of the contract.

7. Finally, in a case involving "economic health," International Harvester Corporation was excused from performing a requirements contract (to provide farm machinery) with one of its franchisees. Performance was rendered commercially impracticable when International Harvester was forced into bankruptcy as the result of a dramatic downturn in the market for farm equipment.[7] The company had been in sound financial condition (no asymmetry of information), and the downturn was both unexpected and due to general market conditions beyond its control (no moral hazard).

Recipe for Efficiency

Walgreen v. Sara Creek Property 966 F.2d 273 (1992)

Simple Facts

A Walgreens drug store had a 30-year lease for space in a shopping mall owned by Sara Creek. The lease stipulated that Sara Creek would not lease to any competing retail drug outlet. With 10 years remaining on the lease, Sara Creek lost its anchor tenant and announced its intention to lease the space to a Phar-Mor store, which offered retail drugs among its product lines. Walgreens sought an injunction against the lease to Phar-Mor.

Details

Charles R. Walgreen, Sr., was nearly penniless when he arrived in Chicago in 1893. Undaunted, Walgreen tossed his last few coins into the Chicago River to symbolize a commitment to his pharmaceutical profession. Walgreen opened his first pharmacy in 1901 and began a series of innovations in merchandising. Each customer was personally greeted, aisles were widened, merchandise was broadened, prices were kept reasonable, and high pharmaceutical standards were maintained. By 1919, there were 20 stores in the chain, and that number climbed to 525 a decade later. The company claims to have

ILLUSTRATION 8.1 Charles Walgreen, Sr., opened the first Walgreens Pharmacy in 1901. Below, a ceremonial ribbon-cutting ceremony marks a 1954 grand opening in Greensboro, N.C.

Richard Posner: *If it is true that Walgreens' damages are smaller than the gain to Sara Creek, then there must be a price for dissolving the injunction that will make both parties better off. Thus, the effect of upholding the injunction would be to substitute for the costly processes of forensic fact determination the less costly processes of private negotiation.*

Courtesy, Judge Posner © Bettmann/CORBIS

invented the milkshake, a creation of Ivar "Pop" Coulson in 1922. Until then, malted milk drinks were a simple mixture of milk, chocolate syrup, and a spoonful of malt powder. Coulson added two scoops of vanilla ice cream and began a revolution! The chain, which remains in the Walgreen family, opened its 1,000th store in 1984 and plans to reach 6,000 by the year 2010.[8]

Phar-Mor opened its first store in 1982. The Phar-Mor concept merges the typical pharmacy with a department store, offering everyday discounts of up to 50%. By 2001, the chain was operating 73 stores under the motto of "Don't Pay Drugstore Prices!" Evidently, its customers took the motto too literally; Phar-Mor filed for Chapter 11 bankruptcy on September 24 of that year. The company planned to close 65 stores.

Walgreens opened a store in Milwaukee's Southgate Mall in 1951 and signed an extended 30-year lease in 1971. Both leases contained an exclusivity clause, whereby the landlord agreed not to lease space to another pharmacy. In 1990, Sara Creek Properties (the landlord) informed Walgreens of its intentions to buy out its anchor tenant and lease the space to Phar-Mor. The entrances to the two stores were to be within a few hundred feet of each other. As a remedy for breach of the exclusivity clause, Sara Creek proposed to pay liquidated damages.

A Wisconsin district court granted Walgreens a permanent injunction against letting the space to Phar-Mor until the expiration of the lease. Sara Creek's expert witness had testified that Walgreens' damages could be "readily estimated." Walgreens offered some evidence that damages would be difficult to compute, a prime reason being that damages included intangibles such as loss of good will. On appeal, Sara Creek emphasized the efficiency aspect of damages in lieu of specific performance. In particular, if the value of having Phar-Mor occupy the space exceeds the cost to Walgreens of facing increased competition, society would enjoy a net gain. This is why injunctions are granted only when the damages remedy is inadequate—and Sara Creek's appeal contended that Walgreens had failed to show that its proposed remedy was inadequate.

The circuit court opinion was delivered by Judge Richard Posner, author of a definitive text in the field of law and economics, along with scores of academic publications in the field. While conceding that Sara Creek made a "beguiling argument that contains much truth," Posner rejected the argument by balancing the "costs and benefits of the alternatives." He pointed out that, since damages are the norm, it was encumbent upon Walgreens to show that Sara Creek's proposal was inadequate. Posner's preference for the injunction was based on pragmatic economics:

> If it is true that Walgreens' damages are smaller than the gain to Sara Creek from allowing a second pharmacy into the shopping mall, then there must be a price for dissolving

> the injunction that will make both parties better off. Thus, the effect of upholding the injunction would be to substitute for the costly processes of forensic fact determination the less costly processes of private negotiation.[9]

He added that prices and costs are more accurately determined by the market than by government:

> A battle of experts is a less reliable method of determining the actual cost to Walgreens of facing new competition than negotiations between Walgreens and Sara Creek over the price at which Walgreens would feel adequately compensated for having to face that competition.[10]

Posner emphasized that an injunction at this stage creates a "bilateral monopoly" situation with potentially high negotiation costs and strategic advantages to Walgreens. With reference to bargaining ranges, assignment of rights, and the Coase Theorem, he held that the "weighing up of all these costs and benefits is the analytical procedure that is or at least should be employed by a judge asked to enter a permanent injunction."[11]

Despite the potential for high negotiation costs, Posner believed the alternative to be worse. In his words, "the determination of Walgreens' damages would have been costly in forensic resources and inescapably inaccurate."[12] Posner was highly sympathetic to Walgreens with regard to its burden of proof. The company would have had to project its sales revenues and costs over 10 years and then project the impact of Phar-Mor's competition. There was a serious question over whether the other malls were actually comparable to Southgate and there was a confidentiality issue with regard to Walgreens' internal cost and revenue data. Posner added that costs incurred in pretrial discovery and the complexity of a trial were themselves a part of the costs of the damages remedy that an injunction would save.

Economic Analysis

1. Those readers who are more engaged by Pop Coulson's milkshake recipe than by the court's recipe for efficiency may find the former on the plaintiff's Web site. Better still:

Old Fashioned Chocolate Malted Milk

1. Use a Frosted Malt Can
2. 1½ oz. Chocolate Syrup
3. 3 #16 Dips of Vanilla Ice Cream
4. 5½ oz. of Cold Milk
5. Malt Powder (One Heaping Tablespoonful)
6. Place on Mixer Only – Do Not Over Mix
7. Use a Generous Portion of Whipped Topping In a #1808 – 10 oz. Glass
8. Pour Malted Milk in Glass Approximately 2/3 Full
9. Serve Remainder of Malted in a Shaker Along With the Glass

2. Exclusivity clauses are commonly used in conjunction with shopping mall leases. Competition among malls, together with the free flow of information, renders unimportant the sort of hand-to-hand combat of adjacent location. The difference in the two companies' business philosophies underscores Walgreens' claims of intangible losses. Having to share the location with Phar-Mor would virtually force that particular Walgreens store to emphasize price. Having to move from a location that it had served for 40 years would tarnish a larger corporate image built over a century of tradition.

3. The court's analysis begins with an all-important principle, that if the right is worth more to Phar-Mor than to Walgreens, then there must exist a mutually acceptable price. In the absence of significant transactions costs, private negotiation will find a price if one exists. Whether private negotiation is necessarily less costly than court-administered forensic evaluation is debatable. This leads to the secondary condition, that courts should consider such matters as which *process* is apt to be less costly and/or more likely to produce the efficient outcome.

4. That courts "should" do this may be interpreted as either a positive or normative proposition. As a social scientist, Judge Posner is presenting a theory to explain how the law has evolved to deal with this type of issue. That theory is useful for the purpose of evaluating the precedential value of other shopping mall cases, where injunctions have sometimes been granted and sometimes not. As policy advocate, he is suggesting that other courts adopt similar criteria and methods.

5. The costs (or benefits) accruing to third parties, as applied to this case, might pertain to the social cost of monopoly. Even though Sara Creek did not pursue this angle, Posner mentioned and dismissed monopoly as a nonissue. Similarly, injunctions might require costly court supervision, but not in this case where the injunction is "negative." It would be an easy matter to ensure that Sara Creek did not lease the space to Phar-Mor.

6. The court indicates that the burden of proof (that Sara Creek's proposal is inadequate) lies with Walgreens, but then seems to relieve Walgreens of this responsibility largely because the burden would be too burdensome. The larger message is that forcing Walgreens to engage in number crunching would be tantamount to granting Sara Creek's proposal. What Sara Creek seeks to avoid is paying Walgreens' true reservation price, which almost certainly is more than Sara Creek is willing to pay. Walgreens is meeting its burden by addressing the issue on grounds of principle: (1) Walgreens' long-run corporate objective was to provide quality service and innovation at reasonable prices; (2) Phar-Mor's short-run objective was market penetration. The prospect of having to engage in hand-to-hand combat on a daily basis is wholly contrary to Walgreens' objectives and wholly compatible with Phar-Mor's.

3,000-Mile Detour

Transatlantic Financing Corp. v. United States 363 F. 2d 312 (1966)

Simple Facts

Transatlantic agreed to transport a shipment of wheat from Galveston to Iran for the U.S. government. While the shipment was en route to Iran, armed conflict resulted in the closure of the Suez Canal. In order to deliver the shipment, Transatlantic had to reroute the voyage around the Cape of Good Hope—a 3,000-mile detour. Transatlantic claimed that the contract was formed on the presumption that the voyage would take the "usual and customary route." That route having been rendered impossible by the closure of the canal, Transatlantic sought payment for the incremental costs of nearly $44,000.

Details

The idea of connecting the Red Sea with the Mediterranean dates back to the pharaohs. Pharaoh Necho began such a project in the sixth century B.C., and a canal was completed under the reign of King Darius I (522–486 B.C.) of Persia, linking the Red Sea with one branch of the Nile. That initial version of the Suez Canal served as a shortcut between Europe and India for over two centuries before falling into disrepair. The canal was periodically restored during the first millennium but was abandoned completely after the European discovery of the trade route around Africa. The modern version was opened on November 17, 1869.

In July 1952, Col. Gamal Abdul Nasser overthrew King Farouk of Egypt. Nasser sought to promote Arab objectives, in part by playing East and West against each other. After President Eisenhower retracted a promise of U.S. aid for construction of the Aswan Dam (July 1956), Nasser nationalized the canal, which had been under international control for 86 years. The move, which ultimately threatened to escalate into nuclear confrontation, took the world by surprise. British, French, and Israeli troops mobilized. On October 29, Israel launched an attack, seized the Gaza Strip, and blockaded the Gulf of Aqaba. The British and French issued an ultimatum and began bombing Egyptian airstrips when Nasser refused to capitulate. Egypt was invaded, and Russian Premier Nikolai Bulganin threatened to begin bombing European cities.

Three days before Israel invaded the Gaza, the *SS Christos* set sail from Galveston for Bandar Shapur, Iran, on a course that would have taken her through the Mediterranean and the Suez Canal. As British and French aircraft buzzed over Cairo, Nasser closed the canal. Accordingly, a representative of Transatlantic Financing Corporation (owner of the *Christos*) contacted an employee of the Department of Agriculture for instructions concerning disposition of the cargo of wheat. What Transatlantic really wanted was more money in compensation for a detour around the Cape of Good Hope. Without any official authorization, the employee advised Transatlantic to deliver the cargo and then later file a claim for additional payment, expressing doubts that such payment was warranted.

Like numerous shipping contracts executed at this time, this one ended up in court. Transatlantic contended that it had contracted for a voyage from a Gulf port to Iran. Based on the admiralty doctrine of deviation, Transatlantic asked the court to impute into the contract the term that the voyage was to be performed by the "usual and

ILLUSTRATION 8.2 Colonel Gamal Abdul Nasser rides triumphantly through Cairo streets (left) as the troopship Empire Ken arrives at Port Said during the 1956 Suez Crisis (right).

customary" route, via the Suez Canal, of course. When the Suez was closed, the contract became impossible to perform. By rerouting the cargo around the Cape, they were complying with the government's demand. In short, it had provided an incremental benefit to the United States (as customer), for which it is entitled to payment.

The Washington, D.C. circuit court addressed the doctrine of impossibility as an ever-shifting line, "drawn by courts hopefully responsive to commercial practices and mores," weighing public interest in contract enforcement with the "commercial senselessness of requiring performance."[13] The court focused on three conditions necessary to excuse performance: an *unexpected occurrence*, the risk of which was *not allocated by agreement or custom* and which renders *performance commercially impracticable.* The court accepted the first two planks, but balked at the impracticability argument. The detour added about 3,000 miles to a 10,000 voyage, resulting in an (alleged) incremental cost of $43,972 above the contract price of $305,842.92. The court paid special attention (emphasis added) to the issue of risk allocation:

> The vessel and crew were fit to proceed around the Cape. Transatlantic was no less able than the United States to purchase insurance to cover the contingency's occurrence. If anything, it is more reasonable to expect owner-operators of vessels to insure against the hazards of war. They are in the *best position to calculate the cost of performance by alternative routes* (and therefore to estimate the amount of insurance required), and are *undoubtedly sensitive to international troubles which uniquely affect the demand for and cost of their services.*[14]

In addition, the court was bothered by Transatlantic's theory of relief. If the contract were deemed impossible, the promissor should be relieved of performance. Transatlantic performed but then sought additional compensation, seemingly in contradiction of the premise of impossibility. Specifically, Transatlantic should have not simply sought compensation for incremental costs, but rather a *quantum meruit* adjustment based on the entire trip:

> When impracticability without fault occurs, the law seeks an equitable solution . . . and *quantum meruit* is one of its potent devices to achieve this end. There is no interest in casting the entire burden of commercial disaster on one party in order to preserve the other's profit. Apparently the contract price in this case was advantageous enough to deter appellant from taking a stance on damages consistent with its theory of liability.[15]

In effect, Transatlantic's failure to show a real economic loss cast doubt on the credibility of its entire claim. While a cost increase could conceivably constitute impracticability, this one was not large enough. By way of comparison, two other shipping companies were held to their contractual terms despite substantially larger proportionate cost increases. In one English case, the costs exactly doubled.[16] In another, a commercial vessel actually entered the war zone and was trapped there for two weeks.[17]

Economic Analysis

1. *Quantum meruit* literally translates to "as much as is deserved." The simple legal principle is that a person should not be obliged to pay, nor should another be allowed to receive, more than the value of the goods or services exchanged. From the perspective of Transatlantic, shipping the cargo around Africa was a more valuable service than the one specified in the contract. From the buyer's perspective, the service was simply delivering the cargo to Iran. Applying *quantum meruit* reduces transactions costs by substituting imputed terms for obscure contingencies.

2. All three elements of the court's stated criteria are somewhat subjective, both generally and as applied to this case. For example, Nasser's seizure of the canal may have taken the world by surprise, but once that event occurred, some form of trouble was foreseeable. Similarly, the doctrine of impossibility is continually shifting precisely because commercial impracticability is somewhat vague.

3. In principle, the economic meaning of commercial impracticability is that continued effort to complete the terms of the contract will result in an expected loss of economic surplus. As applied to this case, the overriding consideration is whether the incremental costs of delivering the cargo outweigh the incremental value. Transatlantic's options were to proceed around Africa, return to Galveston, or find an alternative destination. Applying simple marginal analysis: if delivery was worth over $300,000 before closure of the canal, it is almost certainly worth the incremental cost of $44,000 after closure.

4. Whether or not the possibility of closure was not considered by either of the two contracting parties, it is a near certainty that the market price included a premium for additional risk. The canal was seized in July, and troops were mobilizing.

While Transatlantic probably incurred a loss on this particular voyage, the market risk premium on other shipments covers this loss to some extent.

5. An important factor in transportation cases is that shippers are in control, and communication with the customer may be difficult or costly. Accordingly, they are largely responsible for making the key decision of whether or not to continue performance. If courts routinely awarded additional compensation, shippers would be encouraged to perform even when performance is uneconomical. By denying additional compensation, courts present shippers with a choice of either incurring the additional costs or paying damages for breaching the contract.

6. It follows that applying *quantum meruit* would make economic sense only if the shipper's prospective losses are large *and* performance is economically desirable. Otherwise, the expectation of getting reimbursed would be encouraging inefficient behavior. This provides a clean economic explanation of why the court was bothered by Transatlantic's theory of relief. If performance were commercially impracticable, the shipment should not be delivered and Transatlantic should not be encouraged to deliver.

7. The court may be correct that shippers are "in the best position to calculate the cost of performance by alternative routes" and "more sensitive to international troubles which uniquely affect the demand for and cost of their services." If so, imputing the risk to Transatlantic is "efficient" in the sense that future contracts will assign risks to those more capable of evaluating them. However, this criterion was not the deciding factor in this case. If the court had imputed the risk to Transatlantic, the claim of commercial impracticability would have been moot.

West Texas Sour Grapes

Eastern Air Lines v. Gulf Oil 415 F. Supp. 429 (1975)

Simple Facts

Eastern and Gulf had a long-standing requirements contract, whereby Gulf provided all of the jet fuel required by Eastern. The contract specified a particular fuel price index to ensure that cost increases were borne by the airline. Imperfections in the price index resulted in Gulf's having to provide fuel at prices that were significantly below cost. Gulf repudiated the contract, claiming that Eastern was acting in bad faith by exploiting the situation and that continued performance was commercially impracticable.

Details

It was in the aftermath of the Suez Crisis (1960) that Saudi Arabia, Kuwait, Iran, Iraq, and Venezuela formed the Organization of Petroleum Exporting Countries, now commonly known as OPEC. This little cartel initially failed to have a noticeable impact upon the market, as the real price of crude oil maintained a steady decline (from about $15 to $12 per barrel in 1996 prices) throughout the 1950s and 1960s. Six other nations had joined the group by the end of 1971, while Americans were buying gas at 38 cents a gallon. If anything, it seemed as though the cartel was a stabilizing force in the market and that the abundance of low-cost oil was a major factor in the downward march of prices at the pump. Except for the post-depression 1930s, oil and gas prices were at an all-time low, as illustrated in Figure 8.2. The chart also suggests that the world was unprepared for the use of fuel as a political weapon.

On October 4, 1973, Egypt and Syria attacked Israel, beginning the Yom Kippur War. Most Western countries, including the United States, sided with Israel. In retaliation, OPEC imposed an oil embargo upon all nations supporting Israel. Crude oil production in the Arab exporting countries declined by 5 million barrels per day, amounting to about 7% of world output. The government declared an "energy crisis" and implemented a series of price controls, designed to cushion the blow of the worldwide recession and to forestall "windfall profits" accruing to domestic oil companies. Prices at the pump more than doubled and, in part due to the price controls, long lines of cars wound around the block in major cities. By the end of 1974, crude oil prices had quadrupled, but Eastern Airlines made out like the proverbial bandit.

Eastern had maintained a business relationship with Gulf Oil Company for over 30 years. Gulf satisfied virtually all of Eastern's fuel requirements at contractual prices. Prior to 1970, a major feature of the contract was that Eastern absorb 50% of crude oil price increases. In 1972, several contracts were consolidated into one and Eastern agreed, in principle, to absorb 100% of crude prices. In order to implement the pricing formula, they chose a specific price index, "West Texas Sour." Although generally reliable, that index went haywire in response to the government price controls. The "two-tier" controls, aimed at the windfall profits, classified oil as "new" or "old." The new oil was released from price control. West Texas Sour was largely based on old oil, which remained subject to controls. As a result, the West Texas index vastly understated Gulf's costs.

FIGURE 8.2 Oil prices skyrocket in the 1970s as the world begins to experience the use of fuel as a political weapon.

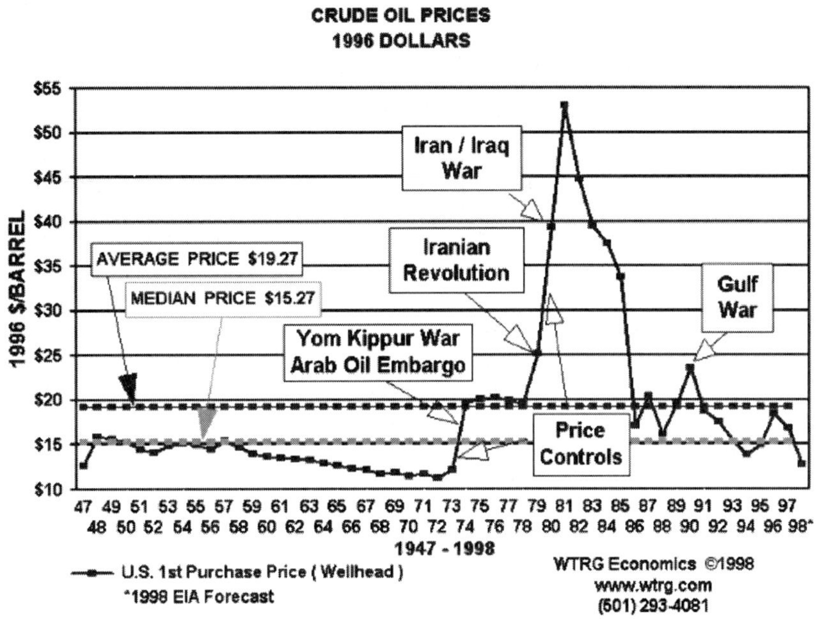

Eastern took full advantage of the relatively lower prices. When refueling at cities covered by the contract, Eastern "topped off the tank" to avoid having to pay the higher prices at destination cities. That practice, known as "fuel freighting," resulted in additional fuel consumption (due to the extra weight), but nevertheless saved Eastern money. On December 31, 1973, Gulf repudiated the contract. At trial, Gulf's main contentions were that Eastern had violated the contract by manipulating its requirements through fuel freighting and that the malfunctioning of the price index had rendered performance commercially impracticable. Eastern defended the fuel freighting as a customary practice within the industry and the justified price index as the product of mutual agreement.

The court did not consider the fuel freighting charge as serious enough to constitute a breach of good faith by Eastern. Gulf had never complained or refused to comply with Eastern's fuel demands before repudiating the contract. Gulf's witnesses pointed to various large swings in monthly consumption (over 50% from one year to the next at one station and 500,000 in a single month at another station), but the court concluded that fuel freighting was an established industry practice, "inherent in the nature of the business."[18] The sole purpose of a fuel contract, from the buyer's perspective, was to have an assured source of supply. Perhaps most importantly, the court observed (emphasis added) that Gulf had an alternative remedy:

> If a customer's demands under a requirements contract become excessive, [the Uniform Commercial Code] . . . would allow [the seller] to refuse to deliver unreasonable

> amounts demanded (but *without eliminating his basic contract obligation*); similarly. . . , the seller might be excused from performance if the buyer suddenly and without warning should descend upon him and demand his entire inventory. . . .[19]

Thus, Eastern had not breached the contract. Gulf fared no better on its claim of commercial impracticability. Citing the *Suez* cases, the court affirmed that even onerous cost increases are insufficient to establish impracticability. With particular reference to the price index:

> The short and dispositive answer . . . is that the language of the contract is clear and unambiguous. The contract does not require interpretation and requires no excursion into the subjective intention of the parties. The intent of the parties is clear from the four corners of the contract; they intended to be bound by the specified [price index]. . . .[20]

The court also made note of the fact that 1973 was Gulf's best year in the company's history, with after-tax profits exceeding $800 million. In 1974, profits topped a billion. In light of those numbers, it was not inclined toward sympathy with regard to Gulf's claim of economic hardship. The court also noted that Gulf was involved in ongoing lobbying efforts with the government over price controls. Accordingly, rule changes were foreseeable, even though the specifics of the changes might not be: "Gulf was well aware of and assumed the risk that the OPEC nations would do exactly what they have done."[21]

Economic Analysis

1. As a matter of principle, few things will bother an economist more than fuel freighting. Using up extra fuel merely to "save money" is a classic example of deadweight loss. It is comforting to know that the law would have at least leaned toward supporting Gulf if the seller had simply balked at Eastern's exploitation of the artificially low price.

2. The notion that fuel freighting was a "common industry practice" seems odd. On a small scale, topping the tank might be justified by the avoidance of refueling time. However, the testimony may have been directed more toward random variance in fuel requirements due to such factors as weather, schedule changes, and aircraft. In general, the opportunities for fuel freighting were regarded as limited; whatever inefficiencies may have resulted from the practice seem to have been relatively small. That being the case, excessive fuel freighting was not a matter to be resolved by the court.

3. The apparent increase in the incidence of fuel freighting suggests that Eastern was exploiting its insulation from the higher costs. It is therefore *possible* that Eastern was also operating some flights that would have been discontinued if the company were acting in response to prices that reflected actual costs. However, Gulf was not contending that Eastern should have been cancelling any flights (at least, Gulf offered no evidence to that effect). Except for the fuel freighting, the use of jet fuel to operate aircraft was part of an ongoing efficient use of resources. The faulty price index merely transferred income from one party to the other. If Eastern and Gulf had been two divisions of the same company, total enterprise profit would have been unaffected. On that score, the claim of impracticability necessarily fails.

4. In spite of the failure of the legal claim of impracticability, the reader should be bothered by the perverse incentive structure that enables Eastern to disregard the real cost increase. However, the perverse incentives need not persist once the legal issues are resolved. Had the court sided with Gulf, Eastern would then have been paying a correct price for its fuel. Once the court sided with Eastern, Gulf could have offered a lump-sum settlement in return for Eastern's acceptance of a higher price. Indeed, Eastern's absorption of cost increases was the intent of the contract, and the two parties very likely renegotiated that issue later on.

5. Assuming that such renegotiation was relatively costless, the economic issue narrows from the risk of cost increase to the risk of a flawed price index! Moreover, that particular risk is almost totally distributive because of the low cost of renegotiating the terms. The court did address the matter of which party was in the better position to evaluate that risk (of the flawed index), but only peripherally. Both Eastern and Gulf, as major buyer and seller, have an acute interest in oil market conditions. However, Gulf's share of the market as the seller was much larger than Eastern's share as the buyer—and this explains Gulf's lobbying interests and greater familiarity with the mechanics of price control.

6. Gulf's overall profitability was largely irrelevant. It *might* have had some relevance, however, *if* the claim of impracticability could have been taken with any seriousness. Specifically, Gulf would have been in a better position to bear the risk, and the success of the rest of the firm's activities bear witness to its ability to "insure itself."

7. The final irrelevance is the "spirit" of the contract, which translates into a clear intent that Eastern absorb fuel cost increases. The "four corners" of (what is printed in) the contract made it clear that both parties believed that the best way to enforce the spirit of the contract was to rely on the price index, rather than submit the matter to arbitration or court interpretation. Accepting "default" provisions imposed by law is an important alternative to incurring the transactions costs of detailed contractual terms. Courts tend to accept mutually accepted provisions for resolution of disputes, unless they are deemed excessively punitive.

Animal Farm

Hopper v. All-Pet Animal Clinic 861 P.2d 531 (1993)

Simple Facts

As part of her employment contract, Dr. Hopper accepted a noncompetition clause. The clause specified that she not practice small animal veterinary medicine in Laramie, Wyoming, for a period of three years after termination of her employment. Hopper was fired and then opened her own small animal practice. All-Pet sought compensation for loss of business attributable to Hopper's actions.

Details

Dr. Glenna Hopper earned a degree in veterinary medicine from Colorado State University in 1988. Shortly afterward, she accepted a part-time position with the All-Pet Animal Clinic in Laramie, Wyoming. All-Pet specialized in small animal care; Dr. Hopper practiced under the direction of Dr. Robert Bruce Johnson. In February of the following year, Johnson made an oral offer of full-time employment. In addition to salary and bonus potential, the offer was conditioned on Hopper's acceptance of a covenant not to compete.

The noncompetition covenant was not discussed in detail. Hopper relocated to Laramie and began full-time employment under the oral agreement. A written agreement was not formalized until December 1989. It was predated to March 3 and set forth the precise terms of the covenant:

> This agreement may be terminated by either party upon 30 days' notice to the other party. Upon termination, Dr. Hopper agrees that she will not practice small animal medicine for a period of three years from the date of termination within 5 miles of the corporate limits of the City of Laramie, Wyoming. Dr. Hopper agrees that the duration and geographic scope of that limitation is reasonable. [22]

Eventually, a second clinic (Alpine) was opened, Hopper's salary was increased, and bonus provisions were eliminated. Hopper and Johnson had a falling out in July 1991. In response to a rumor that Hopper was attempting to acquire a competing practice, Johnson fired off a letter demanding a $40,000 buyout of the noncompetition agreement. Hopper balked, and Johnson fired her. Hopper subsequently purchased the Gem City Veterinary Clinic and began a small and large animal practice, in violation of the covenant not to compete.

All-Pet and Alpine responded with a complaint seeking injunctive relief and damages for breach of the covenant. By the time a trial was held (September 1992), the list of Gem City's clients had expanded from 368 to approximately 950. A comparison of client lists revealed that 187 of Gem City's clients were also clients of All-Pet or Alpine. Some of the shared clients received permissible large animal services from Dr. Hopper. The district court held that the covenant was enforceable and enjoined Hopper from practicing small animal medicine for the duration of the three-year period. However, the court refused to award damages, finding that the alleged amount was speculative and unsupported by a preponderance of evidence.

On appeal, the Supreme Court of Wyoming applied a rule of reason to the noncompetition agreement. General guidelines relate to (minimum) protection of employer interests, hardship imposed upon the employee, and considerations of public policy (e.g., restraint of trade from reduced competition). Neither the court nor the plaintiff claimed any significant injury to competition or to consumers of veterinary services. Legitimate interests of the employer pertain to trade secrets, confidential information, and special influence by the employee obtained during the course of employment over the employer's customers. The "special influence" certainly applied to Hopper's interaction with clients. In matters of substance, the court sided with All-Pet:

> . . . As a professional, Dr. Hopper certainly realized the implications of agreeing to the terms of the covenant. While she may have doubted either her employer's desires to enforce the terms or the legality of the covenant, her actions in establishing a small animal practice violated the promise she made. . . . The public will not suffer injury from enforcement of the covenant. . . . While Dr. Hopper provided competent care to All-Pet's and Alpine's clients, her services there were neither unique nor uncommon. Furthermore, the services which Dr. Hopper provided in her new practice to small animal clients were available at several other veterinary clinics within Laramie.[23]

The court emphasized that Hopper could have sought a declaratory judgment before acquiring her own clinic. Accordingly, some restraint upon Hopper was warranted, due to her access to records and doctor/client relationships. Nonetheless, the court paid particular attention to the timing of the formation of terms. The oral terms were vague, inducing Hopper to relocate and get established. The three-year, five-mile condition was foisted upon her at a time when she was at somewhat of a bargaining disadvantage.

Ultimately (in October 1993), the court held the three-year time period to be unreasonable and reduced its duration to one year. That time period had already expired, and the court upheld the district court contention that damages were speculative and unsupported. The court harbored doubts with regard to All-Pet's application of a familiar economic principle:

> All three . . . methods of damage calculation were based on figures for *gross profits*. In his testimony, Dr. Johnson *speculated* that his net profits from the lost clients would be ninety percent of the gross. He based this figure on the *incredible assumption* that his only costs for servicing these clients would be drugs. Dr. Johnson . . . assumed that the profit margin from all clients lost to Dr. Hopper would be at a higher rate because the lost clients would be served at the clinics after all fixed costs were paid.[24]

Except for having to endure a legal battle, Hopper avoided her obligations with impunity. As the dissenting jurist proclaimed, Hopper had "beaten the system."[25]

Economic Analysis

1. Human capital theory suggests that employers who provide general training to employees must allow for the fact that they will have to pay higher wages in order to retain them after the training is completed. In the simplest scenario, the employer covers training costs by paying a lower wage or salary during the training period. Salary adjusts upward as the employee's productivity increases, but both employer and employee reap an economic surplus.

2. Professional services create special problems because portions of the employer's costs are incurred after employment is terminated. Inability to control these costs drives a wedge between willing employers and young professionals seeking internships.

Noncompetition clauses have economic justification as a way of addressing this problem, but they are very blunt instruments. In order to protect the employer's proprietary interest in vulnerable intangible assets (here, the list of clientele), the employee's skills go unutilized or underutilized. That misallocation of resources is a social loss as well as an individual loss. Thus, the state has an interest in such contracts whether or not they create monopoly power.

3. The state also has an interest in defining the property rights to clients, particularly when private contracts fail to do so. Conceptually, it would appear efficient to allow Hopper to maintain doctor/client relationships already established, but not to allow her to pirate clients away from All-Pet by accessing privileged records. However, such lines are difficult to establish and enforce in a contract. If they were, All-Pet might have been more amenable to looser restraints upon competition.

4. A harsh evaluation of the court's decision would characterize it as an open invitation for breach of contract. Hopper violated the noncompetition clause and got a slap on the wrist; All-Pet received no compensation. The court's excuse, that damages were vague and unsupported, seems untenable. Johnson documented 187 "shared clients." Even a cursory examination of the two clinics' records could surely produce a useful estimate. In relation to other things that courts and juries place numbers on, this item seems highly tangible and measurable.

5. A softer evaluation would focus on the division of proprietary rights. A reasonable application of the *legitimate purpose* of the noncompetition clause (along the lines of item 3) would permit Hopper to work if she did not steal clients. "Shared clients" are not the same as "stolen clients," and the term suggests that clients are exercising free choice of preferred alternatives. While evaluating the profit potential of 187 partial clients is a matter of elementary econometrics, establishing the proprietary rights is a matter for the law.

6. Of the remaining 700 or so clients of the Gem City clinic, some might have switched from All-Pet or Alpine, but Johnson did not even document a reduction in clients. The right to these clients is also open to interpretation. Protection from ordinary competition is not a legitimate purpose of the noncompetition clause. To the extent that providing training to Hopper is costly in terms of subsequent loss of business, All-Pet must capture these costs upfront in the form of reduced salary. If the market is competitive, Hopper's clinic rates to attract a small number of customers from each of a large number of existing firms. If the market is not competitive, the noncompetition clause fails on monopoly grounds.

7. Although the issue was not raised at trial, the circumstances leading to Hopper's termination warrant some attention. The noncompetition clause, which substantially reduced the costs to Johnson of losing Hopper's services, suggests an element of moral hazard. The contract, and its mutual benefits, might have been salvaged if Johnson had stronger incentive to make it work. Johnson also sowed the seeds of nonperformance by enticing Hopper to relocate to Laramie without a contract—or at least without informing Hopper of the nature of the contract that he had in mind. Once Hopper had accepted the position and relocated, she accepted a set of unfavorable terms that she might have rejected under more neutral circumstances.

CHAPTER 9

DAMAGES FOR BREACH OF CONTRACT

The simple approach to **breach of contract** is to say that expectations damages provide appropriate incentives to perform contracts. In principle, **expectations damages** place the innocent party in the same position that she would have been if the contract had been performed. However, performance issues (short-run) interact with formation issues (long-run) in a number of subtle ways.

As vividly illustrated in *Walgreens v. Sara Creek* in the preceding chapter, judges and juries are not mind readers. The more subjective the damages, the less likely they are to get them right. Accordingly, rational agents will form fewer mutually beneficial contracts if there is a general dissatisfaction with court assessments of damages. The law may guard against this problem by refusing to evaluate damages (as in *Walgreens*), but adhering to the principle of expectations damages rates to generate correct performance incentives as long as awards are not biased in one direction.

Even if damages are tangible and measurable, expectations damages—at least in their simplest form—may not be the correct theoretical standard. The general reason is that, in complex contractual situations, efficient performance often becomes a cooperative effort. To the extent that maximizing net gains (or net expected surplus) does require effort by both parties, it is not ideal to place the burden of performance solely upon one side or the other. The problem of eliciting cooperation is compounded by the possibility of externality. In the interest of theoretical purity, we will use "B" in reference to the breaching party and "A" in reference to the party who claims injury resulting from the breach.

The Problem of Excessive Reliance

If A is always paid expectations damages, she will be encouraged to rely excessively, that is, to act as though B will always perform. But sometimes performance becomes impossible or commercially impracticable or B's best effort just fails. Accordingly, there is a danger that a literal interpretation of expectations damages encourages B to try too hard and A to rely too much. In economic terms, B's best effort calls for a balancing of his own costs and the consequences of nonperformance upon his contracting partner.

The spirit of the law holds B responsible for treating these consequences as though they were his own. The ability to perform relates, in a multitude of possible ways, to the extent or quality of performance. However, the primary concern is with regard to the probability of being able to perform. For example, River Phoenix might have increased the probability of performing in *Interview with the Vampire* by abstaining from heroin. Although "effort" (x) may be hard to quantify, we may think about it in terms of 0–100%. At the lower end, $x = 0$ suggests bad faith or, at best, negligence. At the upper

FIGURE 9.1 If performance is uncertain, optimal reliance lies in between the extremes of "no reliance" (y_0) and "complete reliance" (y_1).

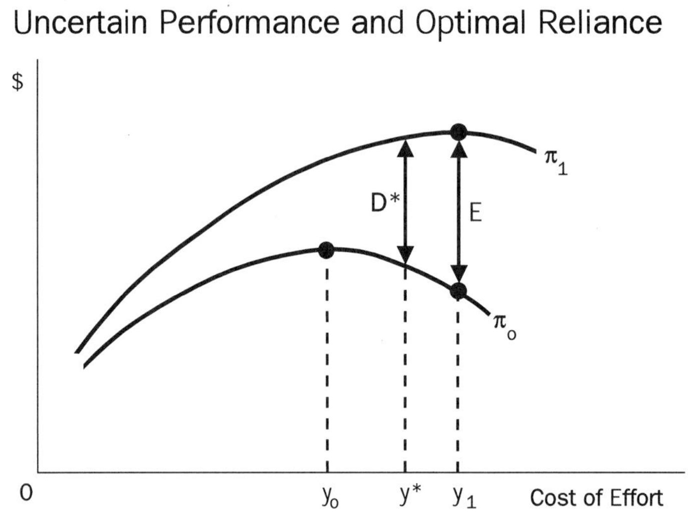

end, x = 100 would suggest trying too hard. The probability of performance (p) is a function of x. How hard B should try depends on the costs of effort and the incremental benefits of performance to A. From B's perspective, those consequences are measured by liquidated damages (D).

It does not follow that the nonbreaching party (A) is free of responsibility for the consequences of breach. Correct incentives foster a cooperative effort toward maximizing expected surplus. The crux of the matter is illustrated in Figure 9.1, which measures A's efforts (reliance) on the horizontal axis. The two profit curves, labeled π_0 and π_1, represent A's payoffs corresponding with the outcomes "not perform" and "perform," respectively. If B performs, A operates along the π_1 curve, implying that A gets the most from the contract by expending effort level y_1. However, if B does not perform, y_1 turns out to be excessive; A is worse off for having chosen y_1 instead of y_0.

The main problem is that A has to choose y before knowing whether or not B will be able to perform. In many contracting situations, performance may be regarded *ex ante* as a virtual certainty. It was reasonable, for example, to disregard the possibility of the 1956 closure of the Suez Canal. Accordingly, it would have been reasonable for buyers expecting shipments to act as though they knew that the shipments would arrive, more or less on time.

However, if there are significant indications that performance is uncertain, A should hedge a little on reliance. In terms of Figure 9.1, the optimal level of reliance effort (y^*) lies somewhere in between y_0 and y_1. Generally speaking, the greater the uncertainty and the costs of reliance, the greater the extent of caution that should be exercised. If the law woodenly adopts the rule of expectations damages, A is encouraged to act as though performance is a certainty. Specifically, the literal meaning of expectations damages is the vertical difference between π_0 and π_1. Wooden application does not question A's choice of y. Here, this would encourage A to choose y_1 independently of the risk of nonperformance because he knows that the law will award damages of (vertical distance) E for B's failure to perform. In theory, optimal effort *ex ante* is encouraged by awarding damages (vertical distance D*) that would have been incurred if A had relied optimally.

Excessive reliance manifests itself in a number of practical ways. While the diagram measures excessive reliance in terms of trying too hard (spending too much) in anticipation of performance, a more common mistake is spending too little to alleviate the adverse effects of a possible breach. The classic case of *Hadley v. Baxendale*[1] is largely based on excessive reliance. The plaintiff sought recovery of lost profits due to the forced closure of his mill resulting from the defendant's failure to repair the mill shaft and deliver it on time. The court found for the defendant on grounds that it was customary to have a spare shaft and that the plaintiff at least bore the burden of informing the defendant of the consequences of nonperformance. In effect, the plaintiff adversely affected both the costs of nonperformance (by not having a spare shaft) and the probability of performance (by failing to inform). Similarly, duties and responsibilities shift once it becomes known that breach has become inevitable. The breaching party has a duty to inform of its intent to breach (**anticipatory repudiation**) and the nonbreaching party has a duty to mitigate damages.

The Problem of Externality

Efficiency requires that the law pay attention to effects upon third parties, particularly large numbers of third parties. Public policy is seldom a deciding factor or even a major factor, but third-party considerations ought to have some impact at the margin. As applied to damages for breach, the presence of external benefits of performance suggests the use of stronger incentives than the nonbreaching party's expectations damages. In a perfect world, these incentives would come from sources outside of contract law itself; in the real world, the law makes allowances for the imperfections in the rest of the system.

In the perfect world, it would be absurd to use the promisor's cost of performance as a basis for damages. A major reason for not requiring specific performance is that costs become prohibitive. If the prospective damage award is cost of performance, breach and performance become equally attractive to the one who is making the decision. Accordingly, cost of performance tends to provide excessive incentives to perform. However, if external benefits point strongly toward performance as a matter of public policy, cost of performance becomes less unreasonable. Conversely, if the existence of external costs points toward nonenforcement, damages awards should err on the low side.

Bad faith is an externality of sorts. Those who enter into a contract with the intention of behaving opportunistically must have some expectation of "getting away with it." In any equilibrium, some offenders will not be apprehended. To make them pay for the expected costs of their actions, the right theoretical penalty would be actual damage, divided by the probability of apprehension. For this reason, cost of performance (if unusually high) is sometimes used in cases involving bad faith, serving partly as an *ex post* punishment and partly as an *ex ante* deterrent. Another remedy is restitution. In the context of bad faith, restitution involves transferring ill-gotten gains (**unjust enrichment**) back to the nonoffending party.

A second type of externality arises from interdependence of contracts. In the abstract, imagine that B has made contracts with two separate parties, A_1 and A_2 (assume identical terms, for simplicity). If B fulfills both contracts, each A gains \$35. But if B performs only one contract, then A_1 gains \$25 and A_2 gains zero (or vice versa). Accordingly, the correct measure of damages for one contract is \$25 or \$35, depending on whether B performs or breaches the other. Other things being equal, the correct measure of damages would be \$25 if the contract is viewed in isolation, \$35 if the fulfillment of the other contract is assumed, or \$45 if the external effects upon the other contract are considered. While the courts are not in the position to be calculating and imposing Pigouvian taxes to internalize these kinds of effects, the use of stronger performance incentives may be appropriate where public policy is otherwise inadequate.

Free Raisins

Allied Canners & Packers v. Victor Packing Co. 162 Cal. App. 3d 905 (1984)

Simple Facts

Allied Canners contracted to buy a shipment of raisins from the Victor Packing Company of Fresno, California. Rains severely reduced the Fresno raisin crop, causing Victor to breach. Victor sought to limit damages to a normal profit that Allied would have made from the resale through forward contracting. Allied sought damages based on the market price of raisins at the time of default.

Details

The San Joaquin Valley in central California stretches some 300 miles between the coastal ranges and the Sierra Nevada, from Sacramento in the north to the Tehachapi range bordering the Mojave Desert in the south. For the mindset that recognizes only city and wilderness as being meaningful, Visalia, Fresno, Madera, Modesto, and Stockton are just a string of homogeneous communities interrupting the dull, flat, utilitarian countryside along Highway 99. For the muckraker, the valley provides an enduring symbol of rampaging capitalism, the evils of large-scale, labor-intensive agriculture immortalized by the pens of Frank Norris, Carcy McWilliams, and John Steinbeck. In the words of noted geographer James Parsons, it is "the land of chicken-fried steaks, biscuits and gravy, black-eyed peas . . . , drag racing, southern country music, and religious revivals."[2] It is a lifestyle revolving around 4-H clubs, tule fog, and bountiful crops that have made California the agricultural wonder of the planet.

In 1875, grapes accidentally left to dry on the vines in a colony near Fresno spawned an industry that gave rise to towns called Reedley, Sanger, Clovis, and Selma, collectively known as the Raisin Capital of the World. Over half of the world supply is grown there in a labor-intensive, year-round effort of tending and irrigating vineyards to produce luscious grapes and then shrivel them to a tenth of their initial weight. Handpicked grapes, arranged carefully on paper trays next to the vines, dry naturally in the sun for two to three weeks.

By 1975, the factors of an arid climate, subsidized water, cheap labor, and economies of scale combined to yield staggering annual volumes at average prices of about 30 cents per pound. The Raisin Administrative Committee (RAC), which regulates international distribution, determines quantities that may be sold as "free" and "reserve" raisins. The former may be sold anywhere, but market forces usually direct them to domestic and Canadian destinations. The reserve raisins may be sold only outside the Western Hemisphere, the major destination being Japan. Annual RAC estimates of free tonnage hovered around 180,000 during the 1980s, and reserve tonnage varied from 15%–40% of that figure during any calendar year.

Packer members could purchase reserve raisins from the RAC, but exporters are not eligible for membership. In early September 1976, one such member (Victor Packing Company) entered into two separate contracts with a fruit exporter (Allied Canners & Packers). The contracts called for the delivery of 375,000 pounds of raisins. At that

ILLUSTRATION 9.1 Promotional collage for California Raisins portrays the various phases of raisin production.

Courtesy, California Raisins

time, members could obtain raisins at 22 cents per pound, well below market price. Victor intended to sell the raisins at 29.75 cents per pound with a discount of 4%. RAC records revealed that Allied had a forward contract with a Japanese importer (Shoei), apparently at a net price of 29.75 cents per pound. The discount from Victor implied an expected profit of $4,462.50.

On September 9, heavy rains rehydrated the raisin crop drying on the ground, drastically reducing supply in the Fresno area; about 50% of the new crop was lost. Together with the lack of a substantial carryover of 1975 raisins, the crop loss caused a severe increase in market prices. On September 10, the RAC withdrew its offer to release reserve raisins to members who had not already made the necessary commitments. Victor was one of those members left out in the rain, so to speak. The raisins that had been in the reserve pool were released into free tonnage, and Victor conceded to Allied that it was forced to breach the contracts. Neither party could acquire raisins on the open market until October 18; by that time, the price had risen to 87 cents per pound.

At both trial and appeal, Allied contended that it was entitled to damages based on the October price of 87 cents, rather than the expected profit of $4,462.50 inferred from the contracts with Victor and Shoei. The basis for that theory lay in section 2713 of the Commercial Code:

> Subject to the provisions of this division with respect to proof of market price, the measure of damages for nondelivery or repudiation by the seller is the difference between the market price at the time when the buyer learned of the breach and the contract price. . . .[3]

The trial court refused to apply section 2713 because Allied was a "broker," rather than a "buyer." Therefore, Allied did not qualify for remedies applying to buyers. As a broker, Allied was damaged only to the extent of its foregone commission. The appellate court rejected that interpretation as a narrow technicality. There was no mention of Shoei in the contract, which called for delivery to Allied and for payment from Allied. Accordingly, the proper framework was that Allied was indeed a buyer, but the court still had to grapple with conflicting language found in the Commercial Code. At odds with the market price differential approach was an alternative clause providing that remedies should be "liberally administered" so as to place the nonbreaching party in "as good a position as if the other party had performed:"

> Certainly it is not uncommon for an exporter to have "back-to-back" contracts, one to buy and the other to sell. . . . [Given that] the seller knew that the buyer had a resale contract . . . , the buyer has not been able to show that it will be liable in damages to the buyer on its forward contract, and there has been no finding of bad faith on the part of the seller, [the policy that] the aggrieved party be put in as good a position as if the other party had performed requires that the award of damages to the buyer be limited to its actual loss, the amount it expected to make on the transaction.[4]

Ultimately, the court limited the damages to the $4,462.50 inferred from the contracts, but not simply because that figure was a foregone commission. The contract with Shoei specifically exempted Allied from liability for damages due to "developments beyond its control." Shoei never brought suit, and there was no evidence that Allied voluntarily paid damages to Shoei.

Economic Analysis

1. The possibility of "disastrous" rain damage to the 1976 raisin crop was foreseeable. The pattern of rainfall in the San Joaquin Valley is well chronicled and subject to statistical analysis and experience over time. Raisin packers understand the risks inherent in contracting to sell raisins at a fixed price. Knowledge of the risk afforded Victor an opportunity to hedge its bets through access to the RAC reserves.

2. Given the extent of the crop damage, the rise in price was readily predictable. Agricultural commodities are well known for inelastic demand, and price elasticity estimates lie in the 0.2 to 0.5 range for raisins. The volatility of prices placed exporters like Allied in particularly risky positions because they did not have access to the RAC reserves. It is therefore not surprising that Allied expressly limited its liability in its forward contracts. Importers, in turn, covered their risks either by

insurance or by diversification. Although the record does not reveal fully Shoei's position in the market, it ought to have had other contracts with other exporters.

3. If Allied had been vulnerable to market risks, the formula based on price differential would have been a correct measure of expectations damages, equivalent to what was necessary for Victor to put Allied in the same position as if the contract had been fulfilled. In a related case also involving Victor, Sun-Maid contracted for a significantly larger quantity (610 tons) and had to cover for the default in the open market. Victor was held responsible for the difference.[5]

4. As it was, the measure based on the 4% discount fully covered the loss in profit incurred by Allied. However, it is important to note the asymmetry of Victor's position. The court's ruling placed a cap upon the downside risk, but Victor stood to profit from any reduction of market price between the times of formation and delivery. The behavioral effects are subtle, but the "Victors" of the world are encouraged toward excessive risk taking. In fact, the issue of Victor's bad faith was raised in the *Sun-Maid* case.

5. The fact that all of the litigants are involved in a large number of contracts adds an important dimension to the resolution of cases like this one. What appears to be substantial risk may well be a biased look at the downside. In other words, the complete economic picture entails many upsides and downsides that tend to offset each other. Since the market environment underlying *Tongish v. Thomas* (see next case) raises similar issues, we shall reserve their analysis until the post mortem of that case.

Noxious Weed, Noxious Deed

Tongish v. Thomas and Decatur Coop Assn. 251 Kan. 728 (1992)

Simple Facts

Denis Tongish contracted with the Decatur Coop Association to grow and deliver 160 acres of sunflower seeds in three separate installments. A minor dispute over docking procedure arose over the first delivery, but was apparently resolved. Tongish later refused to deliver the remainder of the sunflower seeds, selling them instead to another buyer at a substantially higher price.

Details

Legend has it that Kansas' first sunflower seeds hitch-hiked from New Mexico, over the Santa Fe Trail, buried in the mud clinging to the wagon wheels. In any event, settlers noticed that sunflowers sprang up along wagon trails and generally appeared wherever the sod was disturbed. In 1895, the Kansas legislature branded it a "noxious weed," mandating its destruction. To the great frustration of farmers, the weed was too tough to destroy. In a grand reversal of fortune, the populace came to admire its tenacity and, in 1903, the legislature unanimously adopted the sunflower as Kansas' official state flower!

Sunflower seeds became an important crop in the 1950s in North Dakota and Minnesota. The confection variety with the black-and-white stripes is the one that people eat before spewing hulls all over creation. Prices vary considerably with size, the largest being earmarked for the shell market. The medium-sized seeds are usually hulled for the kernel market (for packaging without the shell), and the smallest sizes go to the bird and pet feeding market. The contractual squabble involved in this case originated from the process of sorting and pricing of tons of sunflower seeds.

In April 1988, Denis Tongish contracted with the Decatur Coop Association to grow and deliver 160 acres of sunflower seeds. Delivery was to be in three equal installments on or before the last day of December, March, and May. Payment was based on size distribution, with separate prices of $13 and $8 per hundredweight, for "large" and "small" seeds, respectively. Coop had an oral agreement with Bambino Bean & Seed, whereby Coop merely charged a 55-cent per hundredweight handling fee.

Tongish was one of a number of growers who sold sunflower seeds to Coop. The procedure for delivery and payment was to comingle the seeds, determine one size distribution by statistical sampling, and then pay all growers the same average price, based on the sample. Because his seeds were evidently of higher-than-average quality, Tongish felt disadvantaged by Coop's procedures. A dispute arose in January with regard to the first deliveries, but this was apparently resolved when Coop issued an additional check to Tongish. In the meantime, a combination of bad weather and short crops drove the market price close to twice that of the Tongish/Coop contract.

On January 13, Tongish announced that he would not deliver any more sunflower seeds to Coop. Later that year, Tongish sold over 80,000 pounds of sunflower seeds to Danny Thomas at an average price of $20 per hundredweight. Tongish was to net over

$14,000, but had to sue Thomas to collect a balance $7,359.61. Thomas paid this amount to the court, at which time Coop intervened seeking damages for Tongish's breach of contract.

Coop sought damages based on the market price differential, but the lower court awarded damages based on the 55-cent handling fee. As Tongish contended, covering the expected profit from the deal with Bambino placed Coop in the same position he would have obtained if the contract had been performed. As in *Allied Canners*, both damage theories had some support via conflicting passages of the Commercial Code. Noting the similarities between the two cases (the buyer had a resale contract known to the seller), the Kansas Supreme Court chose to emphasize the differences:

> Victor had no raisins to sell to any buyer, while Tongish took advantage of the doubling price of sunflower seeds and sold to Danny Thomas. Although the trial court had no need to find whether Tongish breached the contract in bad faith, it did find there was no valid reason for the breach.[6]

The court skated around the issue of bad faith, justifying the decision on market efficiency grounds. Pointing to Coop's *obligation to buy* at the fixed contractual prices, the court noted that a decision in favor of Tongish would enable him to use contracts to establish a price floor and then take advantage of escalating prices by selling to the highest bidder. Accordingly, the award based on the price differential was essential to "encourage the honoring of contracts and market stability."

Economic Analysis

1. The static version of the events and participants of this case are modeled in Figure 9.2. Tongish agreed to supply seeds to Coop at P_0, and Coop agreed to sell the same seeds to Bambino at $P_0 + F$. Thomas was not involved in the contract. When the

FIGURE 9.2

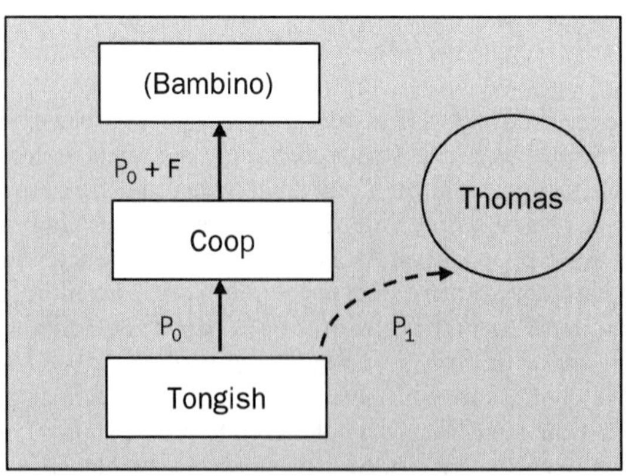

market price increased from P_0 to P_1, Tongish found a better deal. Economics aside, this is noxious behavior, an affront to the integrity of contract.

2. Even though Bambino is not a part of the contract as narrowly construed, Tongish knew about the secondary arrangement. Taken together, the two agreements fully allocated market risk. Tongish and Coop were insulated from price fluctuations, and Bambino was not. From a pure economic viewpoint, the contract is between Tongish and the Coop/Bambino "partnership." The damage to the partnership, correctly measured by the price differential, is the loss of profit opportunity.
3. From an ethical viewpoint, Tongish owes compensation to Bambino. The law cannot solve that problem because Bambino has no legal standing in the contract, but the court did swat down Tongish's claim that the decision would result in the unjust enrichment of Coop. Focusing on the hypothetical Coop/Bambino partnership gets right to the economics of the matter, bypassing alternative legal procedures. For example, suppose the court bought the Tongish argument about Coop's unjust enrichment. The foreseeable legal result is that Bambino would sue Coop for contract damages, forcing Coop to file another claim against Tongish. Awarding full damages to Coop eliminates two unnecessary and potentially costly lawsuits.
4. Treating the Coop/Bambino contract as an economic partnership bypasses the ethical question of whether Coop or Bambino is entitled to profit from the price increase. It also avoids creating the inference (that might be drawn from the court's reference to encouraging the honoring of contracts) that the ruling is punitive in nature. Forcing Tongish to pay the costs of his breach is deterrence, not punishment.
5. Together with *Allied Canners*, this case directs our attention to the two simple elements of market risk on the supply side of commodities markets. In both cases, bad weather induced a rapid decrease in supply, illustrated by a shift from S_0 to S_1 in Figure 9.3. The downside risk associated with bad weather is the value of the

FIGURE 9.3 If demand is relatively inelastic, the sellers' total gains (B) from higher prices outweigh losses (A) from crop destruction.

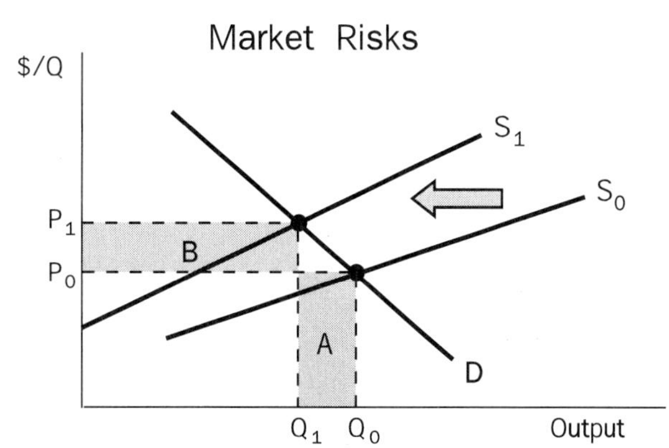

crop destruction (illustrated by area A), earmarked to producers (e.g., Tongish, Victor) and middlemen (e.g., Coop, Bambino, Thomas, Allied, Shoei). In *Allied Canners*, neither Allied nor Shoei could obtain raisins that they expected to buy at P_0, and lost their portion of A. The upside is the gain from the price increase that accrues to those whose purchase orders get filled. In the present case, Bambino (through Coop) was entitled to delivery of goods at P_0, which it could have sold at a price of P_1.

6. Analogous risks are associated with an increase in supply; the main point is that the cases reveal only one side of the participants' risks. Shoei's losses were not covered by law, but they were (or should have been) covered by diversification. Some contracts were fulfilled at prices in the neighborhood of P_0, enabling Shoei to earn offsetting profits. Similarly, Bambino may have contracted for sunflower seeds that actually were destroyed by weather. The two decisions are wholly consistent with each other and with Sun-Maid, which was entitled to raisins at P_0 but had to cover at P_1 because Victor was playing fast and loose in raisin futures. These risks pertain to crop destruction by weather, not to intentional breach. The court's reference to maintaining stability in the market refers to the subtle rules that collectively comprise the incentive structure underlying the production and distribution of commodities.

Terms of Estrangement

Parker v. Twentieth Century Fox
3 Cal. 3d 176 (1970)

Simple Facts

Actress Shirley MacLaine signed a contract with 20th Century Fox to star in Fox's proposed musical adaptation of "Bloomer Girl." Fox subsequently cancelled the film and repudiated the contract with MacLaine. In order to avoid contract damages, Fox offered her the leading female role in a Western film entitled "Big Country, Big Man"—to be produced in Australia. MacLaine refused the offer, contending that the substitute role was inferior.

Details

Amelia Jenks Bloomer (1818–1894) was a nineteenth-century feminist and abolitionist. As founder and editor-publisher of a monthly periodical, *The Lily*, Bloomer campaigned against sexual discrimination and advocated causes of temperance, women's suffrage, and dress reform. On lecture tours during the 1850s, Bloomer became renowned for wearing trousers, gathered at the ankle, under a short skirt. These trousers later came to be known as bloomers. "Bloomer Girl," a biographical story of the women's reform movement and struggle for civil rights, was adapted for the stage and opened in New York in 1944.

In 1965, 20th Century Fox planned to produce a motion picture version and chose Mrs. Parker (Shirley MacLaine) to play the leading role of Amelia Bloomer. The contract guaranteed MacLaine a minimum salary of $750,000. Six weeks before production was scheduled to begin, Fox decided not to produce the picture and notified MacLaine that it would not honor the salary guarantee. In order to avoid contractual damages, Fox offered a substitute role.

The role that Fox offered was as leading actress in a western that was tentatively entitled "Big Country, Big Man." Whereas "Bloomer Girl" was to be produced in California, "Big Country" was slated for Australia. That film never materialized because MacLaine refused to accept the substitute role. In her estimation, the proposed substitute was both different from and inferior to the one in the original contract. The mere fact that "Bloomer Girl" was to be a musical review utilizing her talents as a dancer was significant. The stark contrast between that image and a western story framed around an opal mine in Australia underscored a difference in kind between the two employments.

In Fox's defense, musicals were waning in popularity at the time and the prospect of a "bomb" was risky to MacLaine as well as to the studio. The salary offer was identical, as were 31 of the 34 provisions of the original contract. Be that as it may, MacLaine's complaint asked for damages resulting from a breach of contract, in addition to the salary stipulated in the contract. The Los Angeles County Superior Court granted a summary judgment, which was appealed by Fox. In upholding that judgment, the California Supreme Court cited the general rule that placed the burden of an affirmative defense upon the employer:

> The general rule is that the measure of recovery by a wrongfully discharged employee is the amount of salary agreed upon for the period of service, less the amount which

ILLUSTRATION 9.2 A biography of abolitionist Amelia Jenks Bloomer (1818–1894) inspired the screenplay for "Bloomer Girl."

> the employer affirmatively proves the employee has earned or with reasonable effort might have earned from other employment. . . . [T]he employer must show that the other employment was comparable, or substantially similar, to that of which the employee has been deprived. . . .[7]

MacLaine's affidavits claimed that the substitute role was inferior, and Fox merely claimed that she was being unreasonable in failing to mitigate damages. The court specifically distinguished between a discharged employee's effort to seek alternative employment and the acceptance or rejection of a particular option (deemed to be inferior). Fox did not raise the issue of reasonableness of effort, merely reasonableness of rejecting the substitute.

A dissenting jurist decried the narrow interpretation of reasonableness as a subversion of the doctrine of mitigation of damages:

> The values of the doctrine of mitigation of damages in this context are that it minimizes the unnecessary personal and social (e.g., nonproductive use of labor, litigation)

> costs of contractual failure. If a wrongfully discharged employee can, through his own action and without suffering financial or psychological loss in the process, reduce the damages accruing from the breach of contract, the most sensible policy is to require him to do so.[8]

If the court had adopted this broader view as reasonable, the appropriate ruling would have been to reverse the superior court, to set aside the summary judgment, and to remand the case back for trial on the merits.

The studio had, in fact, offered some declaratory evidence in support of its position. In one declaration, Frank Ferguson (Fox's chief resident counsel) affirmed that "Big Country" would have been filmed if MacLaine had accepted the offer and that the terms were not inferior to those of the first offer. Even though it was to have been produced in Australia, it was common for films to be shot on location and MacLaine was, in fact, accustomed to such arrangements. In another, Richard Zanuck (vice-president for production) claimed familiarity with her ability and previous artistic history and stated that she had previously appeared in dramatic and western roles. Accordingly, Zanuck opined that she would not have suffered any detriment to her image or reputation by appearing in this film.

Economic Analysis

1. The relationship between a film studio and a performing artist is a prime example of a contract that requires cooperative effort to maximize net benefits. Fox was in the best position to evaluate the financial risks and benefits and chose to cancel the film. With regard to the personal services contract, the legal term is anticipatory repudiation and the appropriate remedy is payment of compensatory damages. If the issue were solely one of foregone wages, MacLaine would have suffered no damage.

2. The duty to mitigate damages, if properly administered, discourages inefficient actions by both employer and employee. Without that duty, wrongfully discharged employees would have the option of working for wages or not working for the same wages. Similarly, not excusing the employers from payment would lead them to overestimate the costs of breaching the contract, thus interfering with correct evaluation of marginal costs and benefits of continued performance.

3. The declarations by Fox executives fail to get to the heart of the matter and, indeed, do not go much beyond the issue of foregone wages. The reference to location in Australia is interesting, however. Since actors and actresses are accustomed to such arrangements, a simple "fair market adjustment" could have handled that aspect of the dispute. Zanuck's statement, that the role in "Big Country" would not have been a *detriment* to her image or reputation, misses the point that the role in "Bloomer Girl" might have been a significant *asset* to her image and reputation.

4. The court's distinction with regard to reasonableness of activities may be more substantive than the dissenting opinion gives it credit for. Whereas there are objective means of evaluating a person's effort in seeking alternative work, the evaluation of intensity of feelings for alternative jobs is highly subjective. As applied to performing artists in general and MacLaine in particular, the reference to "psychological loss" might have opened a Pandora's Box if the case had actually been brought to trial.

5. The practical limits on Fox's liability are a lower bound of zero and an upper bound of \$750,000. Picking a number within those limits is arbitrary, but that is why juries are impaneled. As a matter of law and economics, however, the theoretical limits are much wider. For this reason, it is critical that the role in "Big Country" be held to a minimum threshold of comparability. On one hand, Zanuck was probably correct in his assessment that the role would not harm MacLaine's career. In 1970, she voluntarily performed in a western, co-starring with Clint Eastwood in the highly publicized "Two Mules for Sister Sara."

6. At the other end, the tangible and intangible differences between the two roles could be enormous. The court opinion makes no mention of the potential impact that "Bloomer Girl" might have had at a time when the women's movement was gaining serious momentum in the United States. At a more visceral level, people are entitled to freedom of choice and expression. Who knows? Given the plaintiff's more recent inclinations toward the bizarre, she might have thought that she was the reincarnation of Amelia Bloomer.

A Fine Time to Strip Mine, Lucille

Peevyhouse v. Garland Coal & Mining 382 P. 2d 109 (1962)

Simple Facts

In 1954, Willie and Lucille Peevyhouse agreed to a five-year lease of their farm to the Garland Coal Company. The land was to be strip-mined, but on the expressed condition that Garland restore the land to useable condition after the mining activity was concluded. When Garland defaulted on its obligations, the landowners sought contract damages based on what it would have cost to restore the land. The mining company sought to limit its liability to what the restoration would have added to the market value of the land.

Details

Mountaintop strip-mining in Kentucky and West Virginia regularly ignites explosions with 10 to 100 times the force of the 1995 Oklahoma City bombing. They shake and crack homes, destroy wells, and roll huge rocks into yards and public roads. The rolling hills of southeastern Oklahoma are more compliant, as were the many landowners who passively adhered to standard lease contracts. Mining drained the land of its soul, but the contracts provided upfront compensation for surface damage and advance royalties

ILLUSTRATION 9.3 Abandoned pit from strip-mining operation in Owensboro, Kentucky, fills with floodwater.

Courtesy, Adjusters International

for the coal. The damage allotments alone covered current market values, and the vast majority let the coal companies have their way with the land. There were no laws requiring reclamation, nor did the typical landowner bargain for it.

In many respects, Willie and Lucille Peevyhouse were typical property owners whose family roots in Haskell County, Oklahoma, traced back to the 1890s. They owned a 120-acre farm, just below Cedar Creek on the outskirts of the town of Stigler, with a house, a garden, and pasture for cattle grazing. The 60 acres eventually leased to the Garland Coal Company in 1954 bore a large stand of trees and fertile soil suitable for farming.

In one respect, Willie and Lucille were atypical; they stood up to the mining companies. They were opposed to any mining on their land, and the overburden from an earlier mining operation came to a screeching halt at their property line. But Garland had a special interest in diverting the creek to facilitate mining of adjacent properties. When the Peevyhouses finally sat down at the bargaining table, they were prepared. They rejected many of the standard terms, including the advance payment for surface damage (amounting to $3,000), because they wanted the land restored to usable condition after the mining. In their view, it was simply "not right" to take money for allowing land to be raped. They obtained a higher royalty rate and denied customary rights of passage over the 60 acres where the home, pasture, and garden were located.

The contract granted Garland broad authority to alter the property without damage liability, but contained several addenda enumerating remedial obligations. Advance royalties amounted to $2,000, but Garland was not obligated to extract any specific minimum quantity and the company eventually paid only $500 in additional royalties. In comparison with neighboring properties, the royalty/damage ratio was quite low. The reason for this anomaly was never fully established. Garland contended that the coal deposits were relatively deeper and thinner on the Peevyhouse land; Willie maintained that Garland's apparent intentions to mine were merely a facade to obtain rights to divert the creek.

It is important to emphasize that the contract certainly did not require Garland to restore the land to its initial condition. It was not until Garland was quitting the site that Willie discussed the remedial work with the company's negotiator. A tentative agreement was reached with regard to stabilizing the highwall, redirecting the creek, and leveling a diversionary channel. A bulldozer spent one day on the project, but heavy rains caused unstable conditions, and Garland ceased all remedial efforts. Willie then offered to accept $500 so he could hire his own bulldozer and level the ground himself! Garland refused and matters escalated. Willie kept upping the ante, and Garland eventually agreed to settle for $3,000, conditioned on the Peevyhouses signing a release. Willie turned down the settlement offer, apparently on advice of counsel who warned that signing the release might leave him open to liability for damage to neighboring property.

Virtually none of this background material, chronicled by Judith Maute,[9] appeared in the court opinion. Law school folklore abounds of country bumpkins exploited by the same industry that introduced company towns, company stores, and a trail of environmental holocaust from sea to shining sea. A pair of creative Minnesota law students crafted a parody (copyright, Todd Lowrey and William Blodgett) set to the tune of a Kenny Rogers classic:

We picked a fine time to strip mine, Lucille.
It sure looks to me like we got a raw deal.
That smooth city-slicker

said we'd all get rich quicker
I should have known it warn't real.
We picked a fine time to strip mine, Lucille.

During the course of the trial, the plaintiffs introduced expert testimony as to the amount and nature of the work. The remedial work that was to be done involved the moving of many thousands of cubic yards of dirt. An expert witness estimated the cost at about $29,000. Much of Willie's testimony about the formation of the contract and the nature of the work was excluded from the record. Garland stipulated that it failed to perform its obligations, but maintained that the cost estimates were excessive, in part because much of the proposed work would serve no useful purpose.

The company's main line of defense, however, was with regard to the theoretical basis for assessing damages. Whereas the Peevyhouses asked for $25,000 based on a "cost of performance" theory of damages, Garland argued for application of the "value" rule. That is, if the remedial work were to be performed, the market value of the land would increase by only $300. Hence, performing the remedial work was unreasonable and unrealistic. The jury was allowed to choose between the competing theories and returned a damage award of $5,000.

Both sides appealed to the Oklahoma Supreme Court. Peevyhouse relied heavily on a 1939 Minnesota precedent, in which plaintiffs recovered a $60,000 "cost of performance" award for a property with an appraised value of $12,000, if restored.[10] The Oklahoma court gave little weight to this decision because the restoration had been the plaintiff's prime motivation for the contract. The court adopted a practical approach:

> It is highly unlikely that the ordinary property owner would agree to pay $29,000 [for improvements] that would increase its value only about ($300) three hundred dollars. The result is that we are called upon to apply principles of law theoretically based upon reason and reality to a situation which is basically unreasonable and unrealistic.[11]

In context, an award based on the exorbitant damages (even if accurate) would be tantamount to granting specific performance of a grossly inefficient contract. In siding with Garland, the court paid lip-service to the cost-of-performance theory, but the bottom line for Willie and Lucille was harsh indeed:

> [W]here the contract provision breached was merely incidental to the main purpose in view, and where the economic benefit which would result to lessor by full performance of the work is grossly disproportionate to the cost of performance, the damages which lessor may recover are limited to the diminution in value resulting to the premises because of the non-performance. . . . Under the most liberal view of the evidence herein, the diminution in value . . . was $300.[12]

Accordingly, a 5–4 majority reduced the jury award from $5,000 down to $300. The dissenters pointed to the negotiations prior to the agreement, particularly the Peevyhouses' insistence on the remedial work and the fact that the cost of performance could have been reasonably approximated. The opinion emphasized that Garland knew that the cost might be disproportionate to value received and, therefore, the breach was willful and not in good faith:

> [If] the value of the performance of a contract should be considered in determining the measure of damages..., the value of the benefits received under the contract by a party who breaches a contract should also be considered.[13]

The thrust of the dissenters' conclusion was that Garland was not entitled to benefit from the intentional breach, so that Peevyhouse was entitled to the cost equivalent of specific performance. A motion for rehearing was denied.

According to Maute, Willie and Lucille remained on the farm, but the land was never repaired. Half of the leased acreage was unusable, the diversion of Cedar Creek caused long-run harm, and at least one drowning incident (a man and his horse) occurred in the unfilled pit. By 1995, the estimated cost of the reclamation, given modern environmental standards, was $50,000 to $100,000. The land, if repaired, would be worth $200–$375 per acre. Labor problems forced Garland into involuntary bankruptcy in 1984, and the owner emerged with $1.4 million. Five years after *Peevyhouse*, Oklahoma adopted its first reclamation statute. Public policy over strip-mining remains an ongoing national headache. There is no truth to the rumor that 20th Century Fox offered Shirley MacLaine the role of Lucille Peevyhouse as a substitute for the gig in "Bloomer Girl."

Economic Analysis

1. The argument in support of damages based on cost of performance is twofold. First, defendants accepted the remedial work as part of the contract. Since no unforeseeable factors significantly altered those costs, we may presume that they benefited from the contract in spite of having to bear the reconstruction costs. Second, performance was possible, and they chose not to do so. Accordingly, the dissenting jurist interpreted the breach as willful (bad faith) and held that the plaintiffs were entitled to specific performance or its equivalent. Any award less than the cost of performance provides incentives for the Garland Coals of the world to disregard their contractual obligations for personal gain.

2. As long as the contracting parties can renegotiate terms, awarding cost of performance does not encourage performance of inefficient contracts. However, renegotiation is not always feasible or costless. For this reason, courts are reluctant to enforce damage awards (even when liquidated damages are explicitly specified in the contract) that are substantially out of proportion to tangible, measurable costs. Therein lay the problem from the court's perspective: the $25,000 to $29,000 cost of performance wildly exceeded the $300 measure of tangible loss to the plaintiffs.

3. At best, the realtors' estimates of diminution of value and the engineers' estimates of cost of performance provide imperfect indices of the contracting parties' subjective reservation prices. The $300 award was abysmally low; the remedial work was obviously worth something beyond the tangible effect upon market value. Although Peevyhouse was later willing to settle for the $500 to rent a bulldozer, that willingness may have been more a reflection of what he thought he could get than what the restoration was actually worth to him. The fact that the Peevyhouses rejected

the standard $3,000 restoration fee implies that this figure was a lower limit, and the $5,000 jury award at trial seems like an eminently reasonable estimate of expectations damages. As a practical matter, judges cannot divine subjective valuations, and this particular court was poorly informed about the underlying facts—a situation that Maute attributes to a variety of factors ranging from inadequate counsel to subtle matters of strategic choices made by both sides.

4. Whatever the reasons for bad information, the potential for judicial error raises interactive strategic considerations at every step of the way from formation through performance and trial. At the outset, the Peevyhouses knew that rerouting the creek was especially important to Garland. Accordingly, the restoration clause might have been a ploy to extract higher royalties. Knowing that the cost of restoration would greatly exceed its marginal value, Garland was willing to call their bluff, expecting the court not to enforce specific performance or to award cost-of-performance damages. This sort of game playing imposes a burden upon the court. Ayres and Gertner suggest that the court's unreasonably low number provides an important incentive for contracting parties to negotiate liquidated damage clauses.[14]

5. The game playing continued at trial. The plaintiffs chose a strategy to seek damages based on cost of performance. They could have gone for specific performance or sought expectations damages based on intensity of subjective value of the land. Because of the cost-of-performance strategy, some of the subjective value testimony became inadmissible, and the part that survived was not given much weight by the jurists. The defendants could have adopted a strategy based on commercial impracticability instead of conceding breach and offering to pay expectations damage. The risk inherent in that strategy would be exposure to a claim of material breach which might ultimately entitle plaintiffs to restitution for unjust enrichment. At a minimum, they could recover the $3,000 compensation that was initially given up (as consideration) for the promise of remedial work. At the other, they might get the net market value of the coal (estimated at $55,000), on grounds of fraud and wrongful conversion of property.

6. Given the strategies that were chosen by the plaintiff and the defendant, the court was presented with a choice between the two simple damage theories. The cost-of-performance strategy was a huge gamble. Given the lack of credibility of wanting specific performance, a precedent of awarding costs runs the risk of inducing future contractors to incur excessive costs to avoid a breach that would be efficient. Accordingly, some convincing evidence of bad faith was necessary for this strategy to succeed. In spite of a weak presentation by Peevyhouse's counsel, the decision was a skinny 5–4 majority. This vote, coupled with the speculation that the Supreme Court almost granted the motion for rehearing, suggests that the *ex ante* odds were about even. In context, the expected value of the case was about $12,000. The risk and uncertainty to which the law exposes the litigants might seem like an imperfection in the law. Indeed, it might be. More broadly conceived, however, it is a reflection of the uncertainty faced by courts, which lack the omniscience that textbooks too often presume them to have.

7. The uncertainties with regard to court settlements also create strategic situations during performance. An expectation of an unrealistically high settlement (the

$29,000 figure in this case) induces the contractor to incur excessive costs to avoid default. As applied to Garland, this consideration might have impacted upon Garland's decision to cut short its mining efforts on the Peevyhouse property. Garland's mining engineer testified that the last vein of coal was "too thin" to warrant an additional pit. When pressed, he admitted that the remedial provisions in the contract could have been performed without difficulty, involving little additional cost, if Garland had made the additional cut as expected.[15] As obscure as this might appear, Garland may have foregone an incremental profit in order to raise the costs of restoration as a means of increasing the likelihood that the court would not enforce performance or award cost-of-performance damages.

8. The main reason why fixing the land would add so little to its market value was that the rest of the "neighborhood" was a shambles as the collective result of the strip-mining contracts. That outcome was not caused by bad contracts. The typical contract between landowner and mining company generated mutual benefits at terms that were driven by competitive forces. Garland was one of a number of coal companies that facilitated royalties for landowners and employment for the general citizenry. The collective effect of the individually rational contracts was a classic tragedy of the commons. Whatever measures the law might have taken to adjudicate one disputed contract would not have had any effect upon the incidence of strip mining.

CHAPTER 10

LIABILITY RULES

Common law theory stresses three conditions that have to be met in order for plaintiffs to recover tort damages. The plaintiff must incur harm, the harm must be caused by the defendant's action or inaction, and most importantly, the action or inaction must constitute a breach of duty. In other words, the law must establish three standards: (1) what constitutes harm, (2) in what sense does an action cause damage, and (3) under what circumstances shall a person be held liable for the damages that he or she caused. Except for allowances for duties owed by plaintiffs, the general approach has not substantially changed over the past 200 years. However, the application of the law has become more expansive with regard to all three standards. For example, the meaning of "harm" has broadened from property damage and personal injury to now include pain and suffering and emotional stress. The first two requirements are universal; the third (breach of duty) has given way to the doctrine of **strict liability** in extreme cases.

The fulcrum of economic analysis of tort law is the internalizing of the external costs of accidents. This broad goal translates into something a little more specific: to minimize the expected social costs of accidents. The main components of the social cost (S) equation are precaution (B) and loss (L). Since the L is incurred only if an accident occurs, it is appropriate to discount the loss according to the probability (p) of occurrence. Thus, the broad social objective is to minimize the social costs of accidents: $S = B + pL$. This objective is the essential message of the Hand Formula, the rule enunciated in 1947 by Learned Hand in *U.S. v. Carroll Towing,*[1] to be discussed later.

Modern economics has expanded the Hand Formula in two directions. The first is to specify the objective as a continuous function. As applied to potential defendants, the probability of the accident is a decreasing function of the level of caution (x). Since costs of prevention increase with x, there exists a point M in Figure 10.1 where social costs are minimized. In theory, the rule of negligence holds defendants (culprits) liable for damages if they chose an x below x^*. Under the negligence rule, the culprit's private cost curve has a discontinuity at x^*. That is, it coincides with the S(x) curve for $x < x^*$, but coincides with B(x) for $x \geq x^*$. As a result, the rule induces the rational culprit to choose x^*.

The second extension is to consider the level of caution (y) on the part of potential plaintiffs (victims). The full equation becomes: $S = B(x) + C(y) + E(x, y)$. The C(y) term covers precautionary costs on the part of potential victims, and the E(x, y) component generalizes the expected damages from accidents. The latter term is frequently simplified to p(x, y)L, the case in which both parties can affect the probability of an accident, but the actual costs of the accident are random. If caution, or lack thereof, does affect the severity of an accident, L becomes a function of x and/or y as well. Depending on particular circumstances, the E(x, y) component can be expanded in innumerable ways, but the social objective remains the same—to induce the "players" to choose the x^* and y^* that minimize S.

FIGURE 10.1 By holding a defendent liable for damages (L) whenever $x < x^*$, the negligence rule provides incentives for efficient behavior.

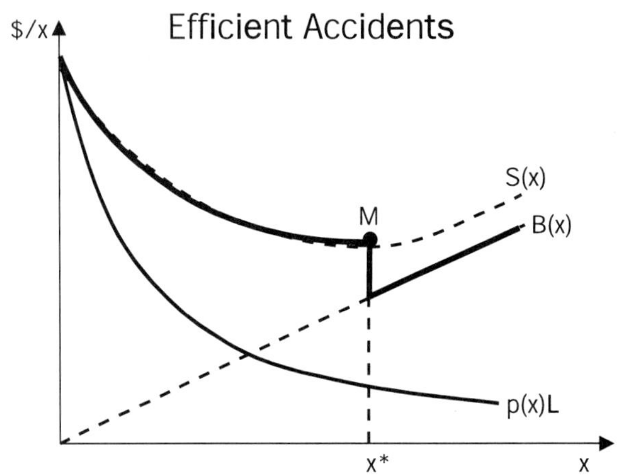

It should be emphasized that this formula has virtually no practical value. Every element in the equation is highly subjective, and the nature of the costs and probabilities tends to vary considerably from one situation to another. However, the analysis neatly formalizes the legal concept of the "reasonable man." Every person is a potential culprit and a potential victim. Accordingly, everyone has a duty to behave responsibly, as well as the right to act on the presumption that others are behaving responsibly. Translated into economics, "responsibly" means "efficiently." Assuming that courts can sort out the facts and ascertain the efficient levels of x and y, a number of alternative liability rules induce efficient behavior:

- *Negligence:* Hold defendants liable for breach of duty ($x < x^*$), whether or not plaintiff behaved responsibly.
- *Strict liability:* Hold defendants liable for damages, even if they behave efficiently.
- *Contributory negligence:* Apply standard of negligence to defendants, but bar recovery if the plaintiff behaves irresponsibly. In effect, the defendant is liable if $x < x^*$, unless $y < y^*$. Equivalently, the defendant is liable if $x < x^*$ *and* $y \geq y^*$.
- *Comparative negligence:* If both parties fall short of the standard for care ($x < x^*$ *and* $y < y^*$), apportion the costs in accordance with relative fault.

On the surface, both negligence and strict liability would seem to encourage recklessness on the part of potential victims. In the case of negligence, however, potential victims will expect to bear their own costs because they expect defendants to behave responsibly ($x = x^*$). Given that expectation, victims' best option is to behave efficiently. Strict liability does encourage victim irresponsibility and tends to be applied only to cases where victim behavior is irrelevant and the costs of accidents are extraordinarily large.

The other two rules operate like classic two-person noncooperative games. Under both scenarios, the only equilibrium is for both parties to behave efficiently.

Even strict liability would generally promote efficiency if (as it sometimes is) accompanied by a defense of contributory negligence. Despite the fact that a wide range of theoretical rules is amenable to promoting efficiency, the choice of rules does matter in practice. The simple reasons are that laws are not perfectly enforced and administered and that people do not always behave rationally. The list of possible imperfections in the process is virtually endless. For example, forensic evidence may not reveal the *ex ante* connections between behavior and probability of accident. Similarly, trials are costly, and the adversarial system encourages excessive effort in establishing fault. In the face of random error by the system, simple negligence tends to encourage excessive caution, but comparative negligence tends to encourage excessive squabbling after the fact.

Our case analysis begins with the classic enunciation of the Hand Formula in a case (*U.S. v. Carroll Towing*) involving multiple victims and culprits. The "production function" underlying that particular accident is actually quite complicated. The second case (*Trimarco v. Klein*) involves a much simpler accident technology, but matters are complicated by the existence of a contractual relationship between the plaintiff and the defendant. The third case involves the rule of strict liability as applied to ultrahazardous activities (*Yukon Equipment v. Fireman's Fund*). The chapter concludes with a social issue of epic proportions (in *Hymowitz v. Eli Lilly*), as the reckless promotion of a "miracle drug" precipitates intergenerational disaster.

The Hand Formula

United States v. Carroll Towing 159 F. 2d 169 (1947)

Simple Facts

A series of events combined to release a barge, the *Anna C*, from its moorings. The runaway barge careened into a tanker, spilled its cargo, and sank. The barge was unattended, but would not have broken loose were it not for the activities of a tugboat owned by the Carroll Towing Company. The sinking could have been prevented if the tugboat operators had been aware of a pre-existing leak. Since the leak went undetected, the bargee's absence was a contributing factor to the sinking of the *Anna C*.

Details

On the afternoon of January 4, 1944, a tier of six barges, headed by the *Anna C,* broke loose from Pier 52 in New York's North River. The wind and tide carried the six barges down river until the *Anna C* crashed into a tanker moored to Pier 51. Two other tugs, the *Grace* and the *Carroll* came to her rescue, but the rescue attempt failed. The *Anna C* dumped her cargo and sank. Ships, of course, do not sink themselves. The accident was the product of human hands combined by a compound-complex production function.

To unravel the production function, we need to turn back the clock to June 1943, when the Connors Marine Company chartered the *Anna C* to the Pennsylvania Railroad Company. The charter agreement included the services of a bargee to be on board continuously between the hours of 8 AM and 4 PM. It was determined at trial that the bargee left the *Anna C* at 5 PM on the evening of January 3 and did not return the following day. It was apparently during that time period that the *Anna C* developed a leak that contributed to her sinking after the collision.

On the afternoon of the accident, the tugboat *Carroll* set out to retrieve ("drill out") one of four barges tiered to a public pier adjacent to Pier 52. The *Carroll* was owned by Carroll Towing and chartered to Grace Lines, Inc. Access to the slip between the two tiers of barges was obstructed by a line that was attached between the fourth barge in each tier. In order to drill out the barge, the *Carroll* had to disconnect the line. Before doing so, the captain of the *Carroll* dispatched a deckhand (employed by Carroll) and a harbormaster (employed by Grace) to inspect the moorings of the *Anna C* and the five barges that were attached to her.

As soon as the crew disconnected the line, the *Anna C* broke loose and careened into the tanker. Carroll Towing and Grace were held jointly liable for the collision damages (50% each). A minor issue concerned Grace's liability. Grace contended that its harbormaster was simply acting on orders issued by the captain of the *Carroll.* However, the court held that the harbormaster was delegated discretionary authority and, consequently, was acting as Grace's employee rather than Carroll's.

The bargee's absence was held not to be a contributing factor to the collision:

> [T]he deckhand and the "harbormaster" jointly undertook to pass upon the "Anna C's" fasts to the pier; and even though we assume that the bargee was responsible for his fasts after the other barges were added outside, there is not the slightest ground for

Learned Hand: *The owner's duty, as in other similar situations, to provide against resulting injuries is a function of three variables:*
(1) the probability that she will break away
(2) the gravity of the resulting injury
(3) the burden of adequate precautions.
Possibly it serves to bring this notion into relief to state it in algebraic terms. . . .

> saying that the deckhand and the "harbormaster" would have paid any attention to any protest which he might have made, had he been there. We do not therefore attribute it as in any degree a fault of the "Anna C" that the flotilla broke adrift.[2]

The major issue concerned Connors' responsibility for the sinking of its own barge. The bargee's absence was directly responsible for failure to notice that the *Anna C* had developed a leak. Testimony revealed that the *Carroll* and the *Grace* could have prevented the sinking. Both tugs had syphon pumps aboard and could have kept the *Anna C* afloat if they had had timely knowledge of the leaks.

It was with regard to Grace's contributory negligence that Judge Learned Hand articulated his famed formula. Hand cited a long list of precedents relating to absences on the part of bargees or engineers under a variety of circumstances, where court findings ranged from gross negligence to full exoneration. At the end of this discourse, he commented on the lack of a general rule:

> It becomes apparent why there can be no such general rule, when we consider the grounds for such a liability. Since there are occasions when every vessel will break from her moorings, and since, if she does, she becomes a menace to those about her; the owner's duty . . . to provide against resulting injuries is a function of three variables: (1) the probability that she will break away; (2) the gravity of the resulting injury . . . ; (3) the burden of adequate precautions.[3]

Hand then assigned the algebraic symbols of P, L, and B, respectively, to the three variables. As a matter of principle, there is a breach of duty if $PL > B$. Applying the principle to the bargee's absence, Hand first noted that P and L vary with circumstances. Potential danger (PL) is greater under crowded conditions or inclement weather and, therefore, B should ebb and flow with changes in PL:

> We need not say whether, even in such crowded waters as New York Harbor a bargee must be aboard at night at all; it may be that the custom is otherwise . . . and that, if so, the situation is one where custom should control. We leave that question open; but we hold that it is not in all cases sufficient to a bargee's absence without excuse, during working hours, that he has properly made fast his barge to a pier, when he leaves her. In the case at bar the bargee [was absent for twenty-one hours] and we hold that his fabricated story was affirmative evidence that he had no excuse for his absence.[4]

Accordingly, Hand concluded that Connors Marine, through its bargee, was guilty of (contributory) negligence. Subject to limitations on individual liabilities, Carroll, Grace, and Connors were each held responsible for one-third of the sinking damages.

Economic Analysis

1. As noted in the introduction, *U.S. v. Carroll Towing* is the springboard for all economic discussions of accident liability rules. The case provides a prime example of how the Hand Formula serves as an analytical framework, but not as a practical guideline. As the learned judge observed, all accidents are different, so that the only general rule is that there are no general rules. The components of the formula (P, L, and B) are fundamental to unraveling the incentives to prevent accidents from occurring.

2. Judge Hand's version of the formula is to find negligence if it is determined that B was, *ex ante*, less than PL. Modern theorists regard Hand's version as relatively crude because it does not explicitly embody marginal analysis and because it fails to consider both plaintiffs and defendants as potential "producers" of the accident. However, the judge's application of the underlying principles reflects considerable economic sophistication. The crux of the analysis is that the one accident involves two events, the collision and the sinking. Accordingly, there are two *ex ante* probabilities, a P_c (probability of collision) and a P_s (conditional probability of sinking, given the collision).

3. The expected cost of the accident is $E = P_c(L_c + P_sL_s)$. The two "L" components are largely random variables, so the analysis focused mainly on the determinants of the two probabilities. The behavioral variables (levels of caution) include an x_1 (for Carroll, via the captain and deckhand), an x_2 (for Grace, via the harbormaster), and a y (for Connors, via the bargee). With regard to the collision, Carroll and Grace were equally responsible, but Connors was not. Thus, by the Court's judgment, $P_c = P_c(x_1, x_2)$. Carroll's deckhand and Grace's harbormaster were supposed to check and adjust the moorings and evidently failed to adjust them properly. Connors' bargee might have been negligent by his absence, but his negligence did not cause the accident.

4. With regard to the sinking, the court imposed a burden upon all three parties. The sinking parlayed collision and ignorance of the leak. The joint probability is $P = P_c(x_1, x_2)\, P_s(y)$. Clearly, $P = 0$ if either $P_c = 0$ or $P_s = 0$. Arguably, efficient behavior on either side would have avoided the accident, reducing P to zero, for all practical purposes. Judge Hand intimated that the bargee could be excused of negligence even if absent for a short time during working hours. Given the particular circumstances of this case, a short absence was not a barrier to discovering the leak.

Customary Practice

Trimarco v. Klein et al. 56 N.Y.S. 2d 98 (1982)

Simple Facts

Plaintiff Vincent Trimarco was severely injured in 1976 when he fell through the glass door that enclosed his tub in the defendants' apartment building. The door turned out to be ordinary thin glass that looked the same as the tempered glass that Trimarco thought it was. Although the door did not conform to 1976 accepted safety standards, the apartment was built in 1953. Since 1965, it had been the customary practice to install tempered glass when replacing broken glass or to comply with the request of a tenant.

Details

New York's General Business Law was enacted in 1972 and became effective on July 1, 1973. Section 389-o of that law states that "it shall be unlawful within the state of New York to knowingly . . . install, consent or cause to be installed glazing materials other than safety glazing materials in or for use in, any 'hazardous locations.'" Specifically included as "hazardous locations" were shower doors and bathtub enclosures. This particular section of the law reflected a growing concern, voiced by consumer organizations and in official government publications. Indeed, it had been common practice since the mid-1960s for landlords to install safety glass whenever replacing cracked or broken items or in response to accidents or tenant complaints.

The shower door in Vincent Trimarco's apartment was made of ordinary glass, and its appearance was no different from that of tempered safety glass. Trimarco became aware of the potential hazard by accident—his own accident. By the time he slipped and fell through the untempered glass door in 1974, it was too late to register a complaint. Trimarco suffered very severe lacerations from his fall and brought suit against the owners of the apartment building, alleging negligence. At trial, both Trimarco and his wife testified that they assumed the door to have been made of tempered safety glass. The owners, Irving Klein and others, took refuge in the fact that the apartment building was constructed in 1953, so that they were under no legal obligation to replace the door prior to the accident. No similar accident had occurred in the building, and the Trimarcos had not complained of any danger. However, there was no indication that Klein had ever called their attention to the true nature of the glass.

Trimarco's case relied upon the existence of a "customary practice" to install shatterproof glass at the time the accident occurred. The relatively low cost and ready availability of safety glass, together with the expanding custom to use it for bathroom enclosures, had transformed what once was a reasonably safe part of the apartment into a potentially hazardous one. Indeed, the defendants' managing agent admitted that, since at least 1965, it was customary for landlords to utilize safety glass whenever they "had occasion" to install glass for shower enclosures, either to replace broken glass or to comply with the request of a tenant. As further evidence of the growing custom, Trimarco's lawyer cited the 1972 Business Law statute, including section 389-m, which provided for criminal sanctions.

The jury sided with Trimarco and found damages of $400,000, but reduced the award to $260,000 for contributory negligence. The Appellate Division dismissed the jury verdict. The majority reasoned that, even if customary usage called for shatterproof glass, the owners were under no common law duty to replace the glass unless they had "prior notice of the danger" either from the plaintiffs or by inference from a similar accident in the building. The court added that, even if it were not dismissing the verdict, it would have ordered a new trial because the pertinent sections of the General Business Law should not have been admitted into evidence.

The New York Supreme Court addressed both the merits of the complaint and the admissibility of the statute. A key issue was the applicability of section 78 of the Multiple Dwelling Law, which specifically required that every part of every multiple dwelling be kept in good repair. Whereas the appellate court held that this requirement did not apply to the issue of safety glass, the higher court brought the quality of the glass within its reach:

> From early on, it was understood that this statute was enacted in recognition of the reality that occupants of tenements in apartment houses, notwithstanding their control of the rented premises, as a practical matter looked to their landlords for the safe maintenance of the tenanted quarters as well. The result was that, if responsibility for keeping "every part thereof in good repair" was not placed on the landlords, defects would remain unremedied.[5]

Whether a failure to provide safety glass amounted to a breach of this duty reduced to the matter of customary practice. The court emphasized that proof of a common practice aids in the formulation of "the general expectation of society as to how individuals will act in the course of their undertakings" and thus a guide to judging particular conduct under particular circumstances. While not a conclusive standard for negligence, custom reflects "the judgment and experience and conduct of many" and provides an opportunity for others to learn the better and safer ways of doing things.

The court concluded that, even without the insertion of the sections of the General Business Law, the evidence was sufficient to send the case to jury and to sustain the verdict:

> The expert testimony, the admissions of the defendant's manager, the data on which the professional and governmental bulletins were based, the evidence of how replacements were handled by at least the local building industry for the better part of two decades, these in the aggregate easily filled that bill. Whether [the weight of custom warrants a finding against the defendants] was also for the jury to decide.[6]

While reversing the appellate court on the merits, the court affirmed the inadmissability of the General Business Law sections:

> Without belaboring the point, it cannot be said that the statutes, once injected into the adversarial conflict, did not prejudice the defendants. Nor is it any answer to suggest that balancing the risk of prejudice against the asserted relevancy of the statutes here was a supportable discretionary judicial act. Unlike hearsay, which at times may be rendered admissible by necessity, the other proof of custom here eliminates the possibility of this justification.[7]

The case was remanded back to the trial court for a second trial.

Economic Analysis

1. The contractual relationship between Trimarco and Klein moves the analysis to a different plane. While transactions costs of negotiating appropriate levels of caution rate to be prohibitive between strangers, contracting parties ought to be able to bargain to efficient outcomes. As applied to this case, if safety glass was cost-effective, Trimarco would be (at least hypothetically) willing to pay for its installation. The fact that the appearance of the ordinary glass was no different from that of safety glass contributed to Trimarco's unawareness, which became an impediment to a bargain.

2. Trimarco's claim that he thought the door was made of tempered glass raises three interrelated economic issues. First, the fact that Trimarco acted under misinformation implies an inefficiently low level of caution by the victim ($y < y^*$). Second, there is an obvious asymmetry of information that could have been resolved if Trimarco had inquired about the glass or if Klein had volunteered the information. The third issue, whether the tempered glass should have been installed ($x^* > x$) is clouded by the first two. Trimarco's claim of unawareness does not imply that he would have paid a premium for the superior glass. Indeed, if safety glass (or safety features in general) was important, he could have inquired. By the same token, a simple reason for Klein not to offer the information as a general practice is to avoid a confrontation over who has to pay for the additional safety feature. The contract principle that permits each party to deal at arm's length supports Klein.

3. Ignoring these sorts of transactions costs, the law requiring safety glass would be inefficient because it tends to remove the option of trading off one potential cost (severity of accident) for another (cheaper shower doors). A simple economic way to justify the law is to argue that the vast majority of tenants would opt for safety glass and that the uniform requirement reduces transactions costs by avoiding costly game playing between landlords and tenants.

4. Analogous considerations apply to customary practice. The fact that a large majority of landlords adopt various safety features does not imply that all should do so. Indeed, a competitive marketplace will tend to generate an appropriate set of choices that cater to the variety of consumer wants and needs. A key component of a competitive marketplace, however, is information. As the court opinion stressed, customary practice shapes "the general expectation of society as to how individuals will act in the course of their undertakings." If an industry practice becomes so widespread as to become a part of consumer expectations, it becomes counterproductive to place the burden on consumers to ask about conformity.

5. Accordingly, the efficiency argument against Klein reduces mainly to an asymmetry of information: (a) customary practice induced Trimarco to expect safety glass; (b) the ordinary glass appeared to be no different from safety glass; (c) therefore, it is less costly to impose the burden of providing information upon the landlord. It should be emphasized that the court did not explicitly acknowledge the information angle as a driving force underlying the opinion, though it was implied in the plaintiff's argument.

6. Translating the court opinion into the advanced Hand Formula, Trimarco's behavior (y) directly affects the probability of the accident, while Klein's behavior (x) directly affects the costs of the accident. So, the expected cost of the accident simplifies to $p(y)L(x)$. The comparative negligence award, holding Trimarco responsible for 40% of the costs, implied negligence on both sides. Trimarco slipped and fell, suggesting a y below y^*. Klein's choice of x was negligently below the x^* implied by customary practice.

7. Resolving the issues on that basis seems excessively shallow. In theory, Trimarco might have behaved differently had he known that Klein had chosen an x below x^*. If so, Klein's negligence induced Trimarco's complacency. If not (as many would suppose), Klein's duty to install safety glass implies Trimarco's *right* to be complacent. Either way, simple economics exonerates Trimarco. It is only when the information issue resurfaces that comparative negligence makes easy economic sense. Klein had a duty to inform, and Trimarco had a duty to ask. Law and custom were in transition, so that a generally informed Trimarco would have entertained the notion that the probability of shatterproof glass was less than 1.

Yukon Equipment v. Fireman's Fund 585 P. 2d 1206 (1978)

Simple Facts

An explosion occurred at a storage magazine operated by Yukon under lease from the federal government. The magazine, which stored 80,000 pounds of explosives, was located 3,820 feet from the nearest building not used to store explosives and 4,330 feet from the nearest public highway. Nonetheless, property damage extended beyond a two-mile radius of the facility. The explosion was caused by thieves who had set off the explosion in an effort to conceal their earlier theft of explosives.

Details

In the wee hours of the morning of December 7, 1973, residents of north Anchorage experienced a stark remembrance of the bombing of Pearl Harbor. A massive explosion caused a ground concussion that registered 1.8 on the Richter scale 30 miles away, at the Palmer earthquake observation station. The blast originated at a storage magazine, operated by the Yukon Equipment Company and leased from the federal government by E. I. Du Pont de Nemours and Company.

The explosion was not an accident. Four young men had broken into the facility to steal some explosives and then set off a prepared charge in an effort to conceal their crime. The charge ignited some 80,000 pounds of explosives, and the resulting property damage extended over a two-mile radius and beyond. The resulting lawsuit involved more than 60 claimants, including 41 homeowners and 25 insurance companies. Their claims were based on a wide range of liability theories, from nuisance to absolute liability. In granting summary judgment of liability, the lower court did not rely on any particular theory.

Other than the mere fact that Yukon stored explosives on the premises, the company did nothing to cause the damage. Largely on that basis, Yukon appealed the summary judgment to the Alaska Supreme Court. Specifically, the petitioners contended that they were not guilty of negligence, that the mere storage of explosives did not constitute a nuisance, and that strict liability theories did not apply because their location had been specifically designated by the U.S. Department of Interior for the purpose of storing explosives. Respondents maintained that strict liability did apply because the storage of explosives was an "ultrahazardous" activity.

The Restatement (Second) of Torts (1977) identifies six factors for consideration in determining whether an activity is "abnormally dangerous." The first three pertain to risk and reduce to a significant probability of great harm, which cannot be eliminated by the "exercise of reasonable care." The last three pertain to circumstances, all matters of degree: common usage, appropriateness of the activity relative to its location, and social value relative to dangerous attributes. Yukon's initial jab was to impute a theory of absolute liability to the superior court's summary judgment. On that basis, they sought, and were granted, an independent judgment from the higher court.

The first three factors were obviously present, and the court also found that the activity was not "a matter of common usage." Although necessary for many public and private works, the actual storage and use of high explosives are carried on by a relatively small number of persons or businesses. Yukon based its argument almost entirely on the fifth factor. The activity was not "inappropriate" relative to its location because the location was actually designated by the government for the express purpose of storing explosives! The court conceded that this factor was "arguably not present," but emphasized that the designation took place when the area was less densely populated. Moreover, the explosion caused damage well outside the designated boundaries. The facility was located only 3,820 feet from the nearest building (that was not used to store explosives) and 4,330 feet from the nearest public highway.

Holding that this factor was "debatable" and the other five were clearly met, the court concluded that it *would* impose absolute liability *if* it were to use the approach specified in the Restatement. The court went on to reject that approach:

> Instead, we adhere to the rule of *Exner v. Sherman Power Constr. Co.* [54 F.2d 510, 1931] and its progeny imposing absolute liability in such cases. . . . The six-factor analysis may well be necessary where damage is caused by unique hazards and the question is whether the general rule of absolute liability applies, but in cases involving the storage and use of explosives we take that question to have been resolved by more than a century of judicial decisions.[8]

As applied to the specific issue of "locational appropriateness," the court added:

> We see no reason for making a distinction between the right of a homesteader to recover when his property has been damaged by a blast set off in a remote corner of the state, and the right to compensation of an urban resident whose home is destroyed by an explosion originating in a settled area. In each case, the loss is properly to be regarded as a cost of the business of storing or using explosives. Every incentive remains to conduct such activities in locations which are as safe as possible, because there the damages resulting from an accident will be kept to a minimum.[9]

A concurring opinion expressed a preference for using the six-factor analysis as a "sounder rule of law" and a "rational solution to the problem of determining whether a particular activity is abnormally dangerous."

Yukon's last stand was to brand the intentional detonation by thieves as a superceding cause of the damage. The court snuffed out that argument by noting six prior break-ins to Yukon's magazines:

> The incendiary destruction of premises by thieves to cover evidence of theft is not so uncommon an occurrence that it can be regarded as highly extraordinary. . . . Absolute liability is imposed on those who store or use explosives because they have created an unusual risk to others.[10]

The burden of foreseeing the possibility of incendiary destruction was especially applicable to Yukon because of its extraordinary vulnerability to fire.

Economic Analysis

1. The major efficiency argument against a rule of strict liability is that it discourages caution by would-be victims. The problem is then compounded by the injurer's reaction to the rule. In anticipation of insufficient caution by victims, injurers take

FIGURE 10.2 Strict liability without contributory negligence defense induces inefficient choices (B) by both parties.

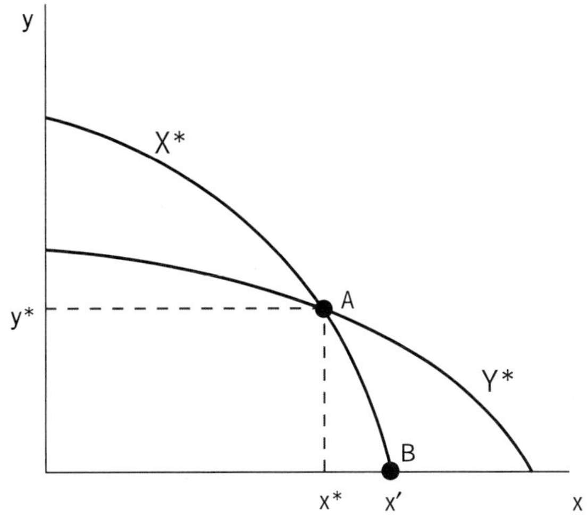

excessive caution. This point is obscure, but worthy of amplification. Recall that the problem of minimizing social costs (S) requires cooperation by potential injurers (x) and victims (y). Figure 10.2 illustrates the social optimum point (x^*, y^*) in relation to "second-best" positions. The X* curve illustrates the best level of x for alternative levels of y (not necessarily y^*). The Y* curve illustrates analogous positions of levels of y. The social optimum lies at point A, where the two curves intersect. Our concern is that a simple rule of strict liability drives the solution to point B: victims choose $y = 0$, inducing injurers to choose $x' > x^*$.

2. This argument loses its teeth if strict liability is tempered by a rule of contributory negligence. That is, "strict liability" merely implies that behaving reasonably or efficiently does not excuse plaintiffs from responsibility for accidents that they *cause*. On that score, contributory negligence merely makes appropriate allowances for joint causation. In relation to Figure 10.2, the rule induces victims to y^* and injurers respond by choosing x^*—the best level of x, given the victim choice of y^*.

3. That having been said, contributory negligence is generally not a defense to strict liability for ultrahazardous or "abnormally dangerous" activities. One reason may be simple expediency. Activities such as blasting or fumigation get classified as abnormally dangerous because extreme caution is warranted and the determination of how to exercise caution requires a certain level of expertise. Figure 10.3 illustrates the circumstances. The shape of Y* indicates that there is not much that victims can do and, at least in the neighborhood of the optimal point, the efficient level of victim care is negligible. The shape of X* (highly inelastic) indicates that the best x is virtually independent of y. The contributory negligence issue becomes economically irrelevant.

FIGURE 10.3 In the case of ultrahazardous activities, optimal care by potential victims is largely irrelevant.

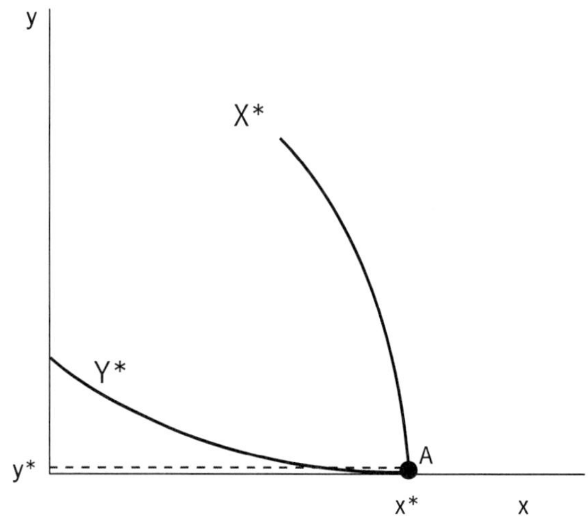

Accordingly, the ultrahazardous label simplifies the proceedings, allowing courts to bypass the issues of negligence and contributory or comparative negligence.

4. The Alaska court seems to have engaged in a bizarre exercise to emphasize the premium that it placed upon simple expediency. First, it subjected Yukon's activities to the six-point analysis laid out in the Restatement of Torts. Second, it concluded that the storage of dynamite was ultrahazardous under those standards. Third, it maintained that the application of such standards amounted to a rule of negligence, which is not appropriate to ultrahazardous activities! Ironically, in taking this stand, the court opened the door for applying judgment in its analysis of "locational appropriateness." By insisting that those storing explosives have a responsibility to isolate themselves, the court implied that some threshhold quantity was necessary to qualify for ultrahazardous status.

5. The quantity of dynamite involved raises another, perhaps more important, reason for invoking strict liability (without contributory negligence). Holding injurers to only a standard of reasonable caution may encourage them to engage in the hazardous activity at excessive *levels*. As applied to Yukon, "level" means the quantity of dynamite. The storage of explosives—even applying optimal standards of care—entails a cost to neighboring households unless they are always fully compensated for their losses. If the neighbors have to incur *any* precautionary costs to ensure compensation, those costs are the result of the hazardous activity. The extent of the precautionary costs increases with the quantity of explosives stored on the premises. As the case suggests, the radius (2+ miles) of the damage is a function of the quantity of explosives (80,000 pounds).

6. In context, the level of the activity was the driving force in the court's decision, but timing and location issues surfaced as well. The federal government's designation of Yukon's location for storage of explosives took place when the area was less densely populated and, moreover, the explosion caused damage well outside the designated boundaries. The level of the activity determines a radius of vulnerability. The radius could have been reduced by storing a smaller quantity of explosives or, perhaps, by distributing the same quantity over more buildings (e.g., four magazines, each storing 20,000 pounds). Although the court insisted that the same principle of strict liability should apply to the storage of explosives (independently of circumstances), the majority might have been swayed to consider the other factors if substantially smaller quantities were involved.

7. Three years later, an Indiana court considered another case involving the theft of dynamite. In *Bridges v. Kentucky Stone*,[11] a thief used dynamite (taken from Kentucky Stone's storage facility) to blow up Bridges' home, killing one son and injuring Bridges and another son. Ultimately, the Indiana Supreme Court held that whether the *storage* of dynamite (as distinct from the actual *use* of dynamite) was ultrahazardous must be determined on a case-by-case basis. In addition to the ultrahazardous designation, this case raises a series of interrelated issues about causality and adverse selection. The main economic issue is this: if Yukon's thieves were not an "intervening cause," why should Kentucky Stone's thief be? If there is an economic answer here, it is that the quantity of dynamite stored by Kentucky Stone had no effect upon the extent of damage. The irrelevance of quantity (at the margin) argues against invoking strict liability. Once the ultrahazardous label is dropped, no additional weight is attached to the fact that the thief stole dynamite. The lone dissenter hinted at a subtle matter of "adverse selection," suggesting that anyone who steals dynamite is very likely to use it for sinister purposes.

Synthetic Liability

Hymowitz et al. v. Eli Lilly et al. 73 N.Y.2d 487 (1989)

Simple Facts

Four plaintiffs filed independent suits against drug manufacturers, seeking damages for injuries resulting from a drug taken by their mothers during pregnancy. The FDA had approved the drug in 1947, but banned its use in 1971 after studies revealed its harmful effects upon offsprings. Because of inadequate records, the plaintiffs could not determine which (of over 300) manufacturers had supplied the drugs that actually caused the damage.

Details

Millions of women are "DES mothers," and more millions of women and men are DES daughters and sons. Many of the DES grandchildren arrive unnoticed because their deformities are hidden. Their parents may not even be aware that they are at risk for a

ILLUSTRATION 10.1 A 1957 ad in a major medical journal claimed that women who took DES would have bigger and stronger babies without side effects.

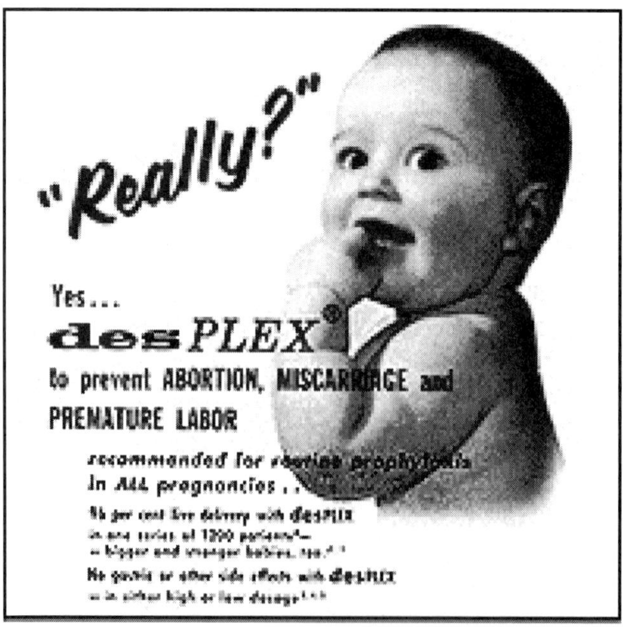

Courtesy, DES Action USA

variety of cancers because their grandmothers were given DES for experimental purposes without their knowledge.

The 1937 brainchild of two British scientists, diethylstilbestrol (DES) was the first synthetic estrogen ever created. While experimental mice and rats were developing breast cancer and deformed reproductory organs in 1938, Eli Lilly and Company was developing its marketing plans. While the regulatory authorities were analyzing copies of the lab results, 267 American drug manufacturers were preparing to copy the formula for the unpatented product. While DES daughters began giving birth to a new generation, the medical community was giving its blessings in the form of advertising space in its journals.

The Food and Drug Administration approved limited use of DES by humans in 1941. The drug was not to be taken during pregnancy, but that restriction was largely ignored. Approval for use during pregnancy was granted in 1947 and recommended for women with diabetes or for those at risk of miscarriage. It was soon touted as a wonder drug and prescribed, with little restraint, for healthy pregnant women. By the early 1950s, scientists began to question its efficacy, and there was some evidence linking the drug with infant mortality and premature birth.

The FDA finally decided in 1959 that DES was unfit—for lambs and chickens. It was only in 1971, after unprecedented numbers of young women began showing up with rare cancers, that the FDA issued a medical alert. Physicians continued prescribing DES in the United States for a few more years, and the drug was still being sold outside the United States and Europe in the late 1980s.

Mindy Hymowitz was 25 years of age when her cancer appeared in 1979. Under the prevailing statute of limitations, her time for filing suit had expired on her 24th birthday. Jane Dolan, Barbara Hanfling, and Elizabeth Tigue found themselves in similar predicaments. In 1975, Max Bichler filed suit on behalf of his daughter, Joyce. Their day in court was put on hold for seven years, while New York courts fenced with the pharmaceutical companies. The initial line of defense was that the drug was properly tested and approved by the FDA. When that line wore thin, they contended that the plaintiffs could not prove which company had, in fact, supplied the pills that caused the specific injuries.

In 1986, the New York legislature enacted a comprehensive tort reform package, which included a provision for revival of actions based on the latent effects of exposure to five substances, including asbestos and DES. The defendant drug companies then challenged the revival statute on equal protection and due process grounds, arguing that it was the result of an "arbitrary and irrational political arrangement." That challenge was overcome in a series of rulings, opening the door for the onslaught of an estimated 800 actions seeking damages for personal injury and wrongful death. The claims of Hymowitz, Dolan, Hanfling, and Tigue were combined not as class actions, but as representative of the other impending claims.

The primary issue before the New York Supreme Court was left over from *Bichler v. Lilly & Company*: whether the inability to identify the specific manufacturer precludes plaintiffs from recovering for injuries caused by DES.[12] In product liability actions, identification of the exact defendant is generally required. The court first examined the doctrine of **alternative liability**. As typified by the case of *Summers v. Tice*[13] (a hunting accident in which two defendants fired at the same victim), this theory applies if two defendants breach a duty to the plaintiff, but there is uncertainty as to which actually caused the injury. The court pointed out that the underlying rationale of holding both defendants liable was to induce them to speak, ultimately revealing the identity of the guilty party. That rationale embodies the presumption that the defendants have superior information and, therefore, could not be applied to the DES cases. Another reason was based on the large number of drug companies involved, many of which were very unlikely to have caused the injuries, due to their minute market shares.

For similar reasons, the court rejected the doctrine of **concerted action**, which provides for joint and several liability to a group of defendants if they have an explicit or tacit understanding to participate in "a common plan or design" to commit a tortious act. That doctrine, which was commonly applied to drag racing, provided the basis for Bichler's successful action in 1982. However, it did not generally apply to the pharmaceutical companies. They each pursued profit independently and competitively, with no evidence of any collusion or conspiracy. Their individual actions were "parallel," but not the result of any mutual understanding. Upon reaching this conclusion, the court lamented that:

> [E]xtant common-law doctrines, unmodified, provide no relief for the DES plaintiff unable to identify the manufacturer of the drug that injured her. This is not a novel conclusion; in the last decade a number of courts in other jurisdictions also have concluded that present theories do not support a cause of action in DES cases. Some courts, upon reaching this conclusion, have declined to find any judicial remedy for the DES plaintiffs who cannot identify the particular manufacturer of the DES ingested by their mothers.[14]

However, the court also expressed a strong motivation for modifying extant doctrines to fit the circumstances of the situation:

> Indeed, it would be inconsistent with the reasonable expectations of a modern society to say to these plaintiffs that because of the insidious nature of an injury that long remains dormant, and because so many manufacturers, each behind a curtain, contributed to the devastation, the cost of injury should be borne by the innocent and not the wrongdoers.[15]

Ironically, the court created a "synthetic" liability rule, patterned after a number of related cases in other jurisdictions. The court adopted a market share theory, based on the national market for DES. The liability was *several* only (not *joint and several*), meaning that those included in the national market were not responsible for the shares of others in the group. Recognizing a number of possible imperfections associated with the application of this rule, the court placed the burden of proof upon each individual manufacturer to show, if possible, that its product was explicitly not marketed for use during pregnancy:

> We understand that, as a practical matter, this will prevent some plaintiffs from recovering 100% of their damages. However, we eschewed exculpation to prevent the fortuitous avoidance of liability, and thus, equitably, we decline to unleash the same forces to increase a defendant's liability beyond its fair share of responsibility. . . . We are confronted here with an unprecedented identification problem, and have provided a solution that rationally apportions liability. We have heeded the practical lessons learned by other jurisdictions, resulting in our adoption of a national market theory

with full knowledge that it concedes the lack of a logical link between liability and causation in a single case.[16]

The obvious imperfections in this scheme were that (1) national market shares are generally different from New York market shares and (2) not marketing the drug for use during pregnancy was only one of a number of possible exculpating factors. The dissenting jurist agreed in principle with the majority but argued for joint and several liability to ensure 100% recovery for plaintiffs' injuries. He also urged more latitude in allowing individual firms to exculpate themselves. For example, if a firm produced pills of a memorable size or shape, careful screening of victims could establish that that firm was not responsible for at least some of the particular injuries. The majority was sensitive to these issues but held its ground:

> The dissent ignores these lessons, and, endeavoring to articulate a theory it perceives to be closer to traditional law, sets out a construct in which liability is based upon chance, not upon the fair assessment of the acts of defendants. Under the dissent's theory, a manufacturer with a large market share may avoid liability in many cases just because it manufactured a memorably shaped pill. Conversely, a small manufacturer can be held jointly liable for the full amount of every DES injury in this State simply because the shape of its product was not remarkable, even though the odds, realistically, are exceedingly long that the small manufacturer caused the injury in any one particular case.[17]

Mindy Hymowitz Cella graduated from the Brooklyn Law School in 1991 and practiced law for six years. A scholarship fund was established in memory of her courageous battle with the disease that claimed her life at the age of 43.

Economic Analysis

1. In principle, the market share liability rule provides an unbiased estimate of the *expected number* of victims attributable to an individual manufacturer. On average, the firm's exposure to claims would be the same as it would if it were possible to match customers with specific firms. For example, if Firm X had a 20% share of the market, its *ex ante* expected number of victims would be 20% of the total. Even on grounds of simple equity, it is hard to quibble with this formula. In theory, it fully internalizes the costs (at least to surviving firms) as long as it is not woodenly applied. That is, the administration of the formula must make allowances for differences in probabilities across firms (see item 3).

2. The dissenting jurist was particularly bothered by the fact that compensation was less than 100%. Because the court imposed only *several liability* (rather than joint and several), surviving firms were not held liable for the costs attributable to those firms that were no longer operating. If the objective of tort law was simply to compensate victims, several liability is a glaring inequity. On efficiency grounds, neither rule is perfect. Several liability allows the nonsurviving firms to avoid the (expected) costs of their actions. Joint and several liability requires surviving firms to bear more than the costs of their actions. In choosing between the two, several liability rates to be the lesser of two evils because it provides correct incentives to the more stable and durable elements of the market.

3. The issue of exculpation has very strong efficiency implications. If individual manufacturers are denied the opportunity to show that they could not have caused the injuries, the incentive to take extra caution is highly compromised. For example, suppose that 10 manufacturers have equal market shares, so that each expects to bear 10% of the expected costs of injury. If this share is etched in granite, each firm reaps only 10% of the benefits of product improvement. The exculpation of firms whose product was explicitly not marketed for use during pregnancy removes an important bias from a woodenly applied market share rule. The pills of "memorable" size or shape are a different matter, and their presence in the market raises subtle economic and statistical issues.

4. As the majority emphasized, it is counter-productive to exculpate a manufacturer solely because it happened to produce a memorable pill. Memorability does not change the expected number of customers harmed by them. Size and shape are merely superficial characteristics that provide no *ex ante* expectation that the pill would be more or less injurious than any other. Relying on casual evidence introduces a bias into the statistical estimates. Relying on scientific or exhaustive sampling will not generate useful information. The statistical issues are somewhat arcane, but perhaps worth pursuing (and perhaps not—if "not", ignore item 5).

5. Suppose firms A, B, and C each sell a million pills and that 3,000 customers are harmed. The numbers suggest an *ex ante* probability of 0.001 that any individual customer would be harmed—independent of which pill the customer actually ingested. If firm C produces a red pill and the other two produce white pills, what purpose is served by asking customers to recall the color of the pill? We "expect" the survey to reveal that 1,000 victims took the red pill, but that estimate is subject to statistical error. Firm C might be responsible for only 950, but 1,050 is just as likely. If the actual number is 950, then firms A and B would be responsible for an extra 25 each; if it is 1,050, then A and B would each be responsible for 25 fewer injuries. The effects of the survey are to incur additional costs and to increase financial risk without changing the *ex ante* expectations of harm.

6. The counter-argument is that adverse selection theory suggests that firms use recognizable pills because they want their customers to know who they are—because they have taken special precautions to reduce customer harm.

CHAPTER 11

LIABILITY: RIGHTS AND DUTIES

The major theme of Chapter 10 was to establish the connection between liability rules and efficient levels of caution by so-called victims and culprits. The hypothesis that the purpose of tort law is to internalize the costs of accidents is the common perception among theorists in the field, and the bulk of economic analysis in the professional literature proceeds in that direction. However, the efficiency hypothesis is far from universally accepted, and is relatively more controversial as applied to torts than to property or contract law. As an exercise in positive economics, a major deficiency is that the analysis (to the extent developed in Chapter 10) provides no rational explanation for choice among the rules of negligence, comparative negligence, or contributory negligence. Because each rule induces the theoretically correct levels of caution, the hypothesis does not explain why courts adopt different rules under different circumstances. The same deficiency applies to exercises in normative economics—it is hard to advocate one rule over another in the context of a theory which proves that each is as good as the other.

There are basically two ways to get more substance out of the theory. One is to add more detail to the "production function" for accidents, that is, to modify p(x, y) to allow for a variety of different circumstances. This is easier said than done. The cases covered in the preceding chapter dealt with one barge crashing into another in a crowded public harbor, a household accident with the litigants involved in a rental contract, a massive explosion on private property damaging neighboring property, and the overzealous marketing of a miracle drug with multigenerational implications. It would seem that the only way to add realism to the model is to have a different model for each situation.

The alternative is to leave the model alone and use it as a guide for evaluating important factors not in the model. The circumstances of the cases already discussed illustrate that tort law does not operate in a vacuum; these cases involved strong elements of property and contract law. Unraveling the production function in *Carroll Towing* was aimed at the simple purpose of deterring inefficient behavior. However, if deterrence were the sole objective, there would be little point in compensating victims at all! It is therefore useful to seek a firmer foundation for the well-established norm of awarding compensation. In context of *Carroll Towing*, we do not have to search very hard. Even though a harbor is a public place, custom assigns rights and duties to those who utilize the facilities. Holding the negligent parties liable for damages served as a police action to promote a safe environment. While there is no denying that awarding compensation is partly a matter of distributive justice, it is also an imperfect means of enforcing the rights of the passive victim. It is the assurance of compensation that enables a society to function without paranoia and the prospect of denied compensation (through contributory or comparative negligence) that guards against the excesses of complacency.

The Hand Formula notwithstanding, Richard Epstein maintains that the dominant objective of tort law was to compensate victims for harm caused by others.[1] Even in *Carroll Towing*, compensating the owner of the barge into which the *Anna C* collided was never in question. In Epstein's terms: A hit B, A *caused harm* to B, therefore B is entitled to compensation. In this regard, liability and compensation imperfectly enforce rights that are already in place, either by custom, ownership (private property), or agreement (contract). The "A hit B" theory is the guiding principle of nuisance law, and the same principle spilled over to *Yukon Equipment.*

The process of clarifying and affirming property rights points toward comparative negligence as the dominant rule of tort law. Rules of simple negligence and contributory negligence as complete bars to recovery are blunt instruments that treat rights as all-or-nothing concepts. The comparative negligence principle is more flexible and also allows for the all-or-nothing outcomes when they are appropriate. The fine-tuning of property rights is consistent with not only generally accepted principles of equity, but also long-run efficiency objectives of maintaining expectations of stability. Finally, there is reason to believe that the extreme rules are not efficient in practice. Simple negligence does not distort victim behavior in theory, because victims expect rational culprits to act rationally and behave efficiently. That being the case, victims expect to bear their own costs and respond rationally with socially efficient behavior. The logical fallacy is that real culprits sometimes behave inefficiently and real victims will be conditioned to expect compensation some of the time.

An extreme interpretation of negligence or comparative negligence is that applying the Hand Formula is tantamount to assigning property rights. A softer version is that the courts clarify and interpret property rights *at the margin*, while engaging in the process of enforcing rights that are already established. The cases developed in this chapter are designed to illustrate this process. A passing train creates sparks that cause a fire on private property (*Leroy Fibre v. Chicago, Milwaukee & St. Paul Railway*). The first legal and economic inclination is to award compensation for damages as a means of affirming a private property right. The Hand Formula kicks in at the margin and pertains to the property owner's duties to mitigate damages or to reduce the probability of damage. An offshore oil platform experiences a blowout, causing a massive oil slick that severely damages the surrounding ocean fishery (*Union Oil v. Oppen*). The oil company accepts responsibility for property damage but not for harm done to birds and fish. Fishermen seek compensation, but the oil company claims that no one owns the fish. These cases explore the boundaries between torts and *private* property rights and between torts and *common* property rights. The other two examine links between torts and contracts (*General Foods v. Valley Lea Dairies*) and between torts and criminal law (*Tarasoff v. UC Regents*).

Milwaukee Road

Leroy Fibre v. Chicago, Milwaukee & St. Paul Railway 232 U.S. 340 (1914)

Simple Facts

A Minnesota factory used flax straw in the manufacture of fibers and stored the straw 75 feet from the railroad tracks adjacent to the property. The straw caught fire when a passing train emitted sparks and live cinders. Evidence at trial indicated negligence on the part of the engineer. The railway contended that the factory owner was guilty of contributory negligence for storing the straw so close to the tracks.

ILLUSTRATION 11.1 Locomotive engines produced sparks from "steel-on-steel" friction between wheel and track and cinders from the burning of wood or coal.

Public Domain

Details

The "Milwaukee Road," as the Chicago, Milwaukee & St. Paul Railroad came to be known, was a major innovator in the latter half of the nineteenth century. By turn of the century, the railroad had a respectable presence throughout the Midwest, linking Chicago with Minneapolis, Omaha, and Kansas City. In 1905, the Milwaukee Road began its expansion into the Pacific Northwest. The route, which eventually connected the Great Lakes with Puget Sound, passed through Wisconsin and the Twin Cities, then across the grain belt of Minnesota and South Dakota.

Shortly after the railway began operating through Grand Meadow, Minnesota, the Leroy Fiber Company established a factory for the manufacture of tow, a mixture of fibre used to produce paper products. The primary material input in the production of tow is flax straw. Adjacent to the factory premises and abutting upon the railroad right of way, Leroy owned a small tract of land (250 × 400 feet) upon which it stored flax straw. More than 200 three-ton stacks were arranged in two rows parallel with the right of way. The closer of the two rows lay about 75 feet from the center of the track and 25 feet from the fence. On April 2, 1907, during a high wind, a fire started in one of the stacks in the second row. The entire inventory was consumed.

Evidence at the trial indicated that the fire was the result of the negligent emission of large quantities of sparks and live cinders by the operators of the passing locomotive. The railway's main line of defense was contributory negligence. The only evidence that the plaintiff had been negligent lay in the fact that it had placed the highly inflammable straw so close to the railroad tracks. Inasmuch as the potential fire hazard was well understood, the character of the property and its proximity to an operated railroad added up to a failure to exercise due caution. Accordingly, the trial court also submitted two questions to the jury—essentially whether the fibre company and the engineer had failed to exercise the degree of care that a person of ordinary prudence would have used under like circumstances.

The jury verdict in favor of the railroad was appealed to the U.S. Supreme Court. In reversing the verdict, the majority held that the issue of contributory negligence should not even have been submitted to a jury. Writing for the Court, Justice McKenna's opening salvo addressed the anomaly of a servitude for wrongful use:

> That one's uses of his property may be subject to the servitude of the wrongful use by another of his property seems an anomaly. It upsets the presumptions of law and takes from him the assumption and the freedom which comes from the assumption, that the other will obey the law, not violate it. It casts upon him the duty of not only using his own property so as not to injure another, but so to use his own property that it may not be injured by the wrongs of another. How far can this subjection be carried?[2]

McKenna proceeded to point out that crops and houses are also flammable. While flammability is a matter of degree, limiting property rights by wrongs is a matter of principle. Justice Holmes concurred with the reversal; Leroy Fibre was found not guilty of contributory negligence. However, he maintained that the issue was one for jury consideration. Focusing on the distance, Holmes argued that the manufacturer should not be allowed to recover damages if the flax were stacked so close to the tracks as to be in danger of a prudently managed train:

> I do not suppose that any one would call it prudent to stack flax within five feet of the engines or imprudent to do it at a distance of half a mile, and it would not be absurd if the law ultimately should formulate an exact measure.[3]

Of course, it would be absurd for a *legislature* to establish an exact measure, because the optimal distance would vary according to a range of circumstances. Nonetheless, the public interest is sometimes served by assigning rights to inflict various inconveniences upon neighboring lands. Holmes conceded that many such rules are absolute under the common law (e.g., the right to build or maintain a barn does not depend upon the speculations of a jury), but he characterized the distinction between "the inevitable and the negligent escape of sparks" as "one of the most refined in the world." That being the case, the issue of negligence is inseparable from that of contributory negligence.

Economic Analysis

1. In the first edition of *Wealth and Welfare*, Arthur Pigou made a casual reference to the emission of sparks by railroad trains. In particular, the "uncompensated" damage that would accrue under a "natural" state of affairs was an example of a divergence (externality) that might be improved upon by governmental action.[4] Nearly half a century later, Ronald Coase leapt upon the statement to launch his critique of Pigouvian externality theory.[5] Focusing on the words, "uncompensated" and "natural," Coase inferred that Pigou was advocating government intervention and insisting that railways should be forced to compensate those whose property was damaged by fire. That inference may or may not have been accurate, but the story of the railroad sparks has become a classic paradigm in law and economics.
2. The issue of what is, or is not, a "natural" state of affairs is more than just semantic quibbling. In pure economic theory, institutions are exogenous and competitive equilibria are achieved by the formation of market prices without the explicit aid of government. Coase maintained that a real price mechanism cannot operate without cost and, therefore, "transactions costs" shape the development of institutions. In particular, property rights are endogenous to the economic system. As applied to the problem of railroad sparks, the natural state was to enforce the property rights of the passive manufacturer from intrusion.
3. Locomotive technology provided two sources of fire hazard. One was the "steel-on-steel" friction between wheel and track that produced sparks. The other was the burning of wood or coal that produced flying cinders. As Holmes noted, the distinction between inevitable and negligent is a fine one, but elementary statistics can determine how far sparks fly at alternative train velocities. The 50-foot right of way, owned by the railway, ought to have been sufficient to contain the sparks, but the cinder that started the fire evidently flew beyond the second stack of flax. Given the high wind conditions, extra caution was warranted.

4. The storage of two billion pounds of straw adjacent to a fire hazard seems inefficient. However, the risk of destruction must be balanced with the costs of moving such a high-bulk, low-value substance. All things considered, the actual choice made by Leroy Fibre is consistent with an optimal one. The court opinion does not explicitly say so, but the straw was probably delivered by the Milwaukee Road. That being the case, transactions costs rate to have been low, so that the distance might have been increased if it were efficient to do so.

5. Holmes' analysis of distance, though economically reasonable, misses the point that the railway owned the 50-foot buffer zone. By ruling out absurdly low distances, a different economic margin kicks in. The size of the buffer zone becomes a choice variable for the railroad. That decision is compounded by the fact that the railroad was constructed prior to development. Indeed, since the construction of facilities like the fibre factory tends naturally to follow the railroad, buffer zones must be acquired before the nature of the neighboring activity becomes known to the railroad.

6. At the time this case was heard, Minnesota did not recognize a rule of comparative negligence. At the legal margin, the alternative property rights were strict liability, negligence, and negligence with contributory negligence. Strict liability would essentially affirm the absolute right of the manufacturer to use his property as if there was no railroad there. If the railway could continuously adjust the buffer zone to suit the nature of the neighboring activity, strict liability would make sense. Given the reality of the situation, however, strict liability would induce the railroad to buy up too much land. Allowing for a defense of contributory negligence has the opposite effect, largely eliminating the railroad's need for buying up a buffer zone at all.

7. The size of a buffer zone, along with the obscure issue of who should pay for it, underscores two important Coasian themes. One is the idea that social costs are reciprocal. Given that railroads operate and throw out sparks, efficiency requires that neighboring activities maintain some distance. If the law creates an environment in which railroads find it necessary to buy up the extra land, the neighbor's presence is essentially imposing a cost upon the railway. If the neighbors are held responsible for a vacant easement adjacent to the tracks, the railway is imposing a cost upon its neighbors. The possibility of contributory negligence (or comparative negligence) establishes joint responsibility without being too specific. Accordingly, each party has incentives to take actions that increase value or reduce cost.

8. The second theme is that economists frequently get carried away with marginal conditions. For example, Posner and Landes express a general concern that contributory negligence might result in excessive levels of the (damage-generating) activity:

> If (the courts) fail to consider the possibility that it might be "negligent" for a marginal railroad to exist because the costs of its ceasing operations might be lower than the costs of crop damage to the farmers along its right of way, a socially excessive amount of railroading may result . . . [and conversely for the neighbors] if they fail to consider the possibility that a farmer might be "contributorily negligent" by remaining in business, the amount of farming may exceed the socially efficient level under a standard of strict liability with a defense of contributory negligence. [6]

To some extent, this reasoning is circular and begs the question that the railway is the source of the damage. If rights and duties are enforced in ways that induce each existing party to make efficient choices, costs are allocated efficiently. That being the case, the market rather than the law will determine whether marginal firms should or should not exist. Coase's larger point is that problems like this one have practical solutions, but not ideal solutions.

A Few Birds

Union Oil v. Oppen 501 F.2d 558 (1974)

Simple Facts

In the aftermath of an environmentally disastrous oil spill, a group of commercial fisherman sought to recover damages for loss of livelihood from the diminution of the fishing potential of the Santa Barbara Channel. Union Oil Company had already stipulated negligence in return for a waiver of liability for punitive or environmental damages. Union contended that the diminution of the stock of fish was included in the "environmental damage."

Details

On the afternoon of January 29, 1969, a Union Oil platform stationed six miles off the coast of Santa Barbara, California, suffered a "blowout." An initial effort to cap the hole was successful, but the resulting buildup of pressure created five breaks in an east-west fault on the ocean floor. Oil and gas poured forth from depths of more

ILLUSTRATION 11.2 Oil gushes from beneath a platform near Santa Barbara, as sea animals and birds wash onto beaches and volunteers work at damage control.

than 3,500 feet beneath the ocean floor. An unprecedented environmental disaster was underway.

Oil workers struggled for two weeks in an effort to contain the spill, as the oil gushed to the surface and spread into a massive slick encompassing approximately 800 square miles. The incoming tides carried the residue ashore, ravaging over thirty miles of coastline and pristine beaches on the Channel Islands. Animals that depended on the sea suffered horrible deaths. Shorebirds fled the scene, but diving birds like seagulls, pelicans, and cormorants washed onto the beaches, their feathers coated with tar. Volunteers were recruited to bathe the birds in solvent, but the survival rate was low, even for those that were captured and treated. Thousands of birds died of suffocation.

In the aftermath, Earth Day was created, environmental consciousness became a reality, and economics curricula began paying serious attention to the problem of externality. Thomas More Storke, editor of the conservative Santa Barbara *News Press*, remarked that he had never seen such an aroused populace at the grassroots level. The oil spill "united citizens of all political persuasions in a truly nonpartisan cause." Union Oil's president, Fred Hartley, saw things a little differently: "I don't like to call it a disaster, because there has been no loss of human life. . . . I am amazed at the publicity for the loss of a few birds." The law of torts was about to give Fred a lesson in political correctness. [7]

Fifteen months after the blowout, a stipulation was approved by the district court, whereby a number of the cases were consolidated. Under the stipulation, Union Oil admitted negligence in return for certain limitations upon its liability. The company agreed to pay "all legally compensable damages arising from a *legally cognizable injury*" caused by the oil spill. The wording was intended to avert further liability and explicitly ruled out punitive or exemplary damages.

Two years later (May 1972), Union moved for a partial summary judgment to strike the claim of Oppen and others for "ecological damage." Specifically, the oil company sought to eliminate damages consisting of profits lost as a result of the reduction in the commercial fishing potential of the Santa Barbara Channel. From Union's perspective, such long-term ecological damage was not compensable under the law. The motion was denied by the district court. The district judge held that such damages were compensable, independently of any proprietary interest in, or ownership of, the sea life in the Santa Barbara Channel.

After a lengthy evaluation of the relative forces of California, federal, and admiralty law, the appellate court honed in on the substance of Union's argument. The motion relied on the principle that no cause of action lies against a defendant whose negligence prevents the plaintiff from obtaining a prospective pecuniary advantage. The strength of the argument lay in the notion that awarding damages to the fishermen (who lack direct ownership of the marine life) opens up claims for ancillary damages by those who profit from servicing the fishing industry. The logic could be extended indefinitely to third and fourth classes of remoteness. A major precedent was the 1945 case of *Rickards v. Sun Oil Company*,[8] involving the negligent destruction of a bridge connecting the mainland with an island, which caused a loss of business to merchants on the island. The merchants were denied recovery.

On the other side, the Court found a number of precedents, which it grouped under the right to recover for economic losses that are "parasitic to an injury occurring to person or property." Examples included use of a company airplane and lost cargo from a sunken vessel, where compensation was paid to individuals other than the direct owners of the plane or vessel. A 1926 precedent applied to a polluted stream, where downstream riparian owners of businesses directly dependent upon the stream (including fishermen) were compensated for lost profits.[9] In deciding for Oppen, the Court paid some attention to scholarly work in economics, in particular the notion that liability should be assigned to the party in the best position to avoid the costs. However, a greater emphasis was placed upon causality:

> The injury here asserted by the plaintiff is a pecuniary loss of a particular and special nature, limited to the class of commercial fishermen which they represent. . . . [To establish injury], it must be shown that the oil spill did in fact diminish aquatic life and that this diminution reduced the profits the plaintiffs would have realized from their commercial fishing in the absence of the spill. This reduction of profits must be established with certainty and must not be remote, speculative, or conjectural.[10]

The Court specifically limited recovery rights to those whose livelihood depended directly upon the sea in the ordinary course of their businesses.

Economic Analysis

1. It is doubtful that anyone would characterize the Santa Barbara oil spill as an "efficient accident," largely because policy aimed at the deterrence of disasters is formulated well outside of the tort system. Whether Union Oil would have been found guilty of negligence is far from clear, however. Union Oil leased the mineral rights from the federal government, which bore some responsibility for oversight of drilling technology. Furthermore, Hartley's reference to the fuss over a few birds may be representative of the value judgments that underlay the pre-1969 application of the Hand Formula to environmental costs.

2. Three elements of the settlement agreement merit comment. First, the oil company's liability was, or should have been, a foregone conclusion. In retrospect, offshore drilling borders on the sort of ultra-hazardous activity that warrants the application of strict liability. Second, although there were legions of born-again environmentalists who wanted to "tar and feather" Fred Hartley, punitive damages were not warranted. The economic rationale for imposing such damages is still a matter of debate, but the two more prominent theories pertain to intentional torts and to those that are especially difficult to detect. Third, the ecological damage was compensable only to the extent that the environment was owned by someone. Conceivably, the government could have sought compensation, but private individuals or groups like the Sierra Club would not have standing to sue.

3. The narrow issue underlying this case is whether the fishermen have proprietary rights to the stock of fish in the common property ocean resources. The court seems to have found the correct answer, but its reasoning was flawed (very likely because the legal terminology is inappropriate for the fine points of the underlying economic factors). The problem confronting the court, in its words, was based on the "widely recognized principle that no cause of action lies against a defendant whose negligence prevents the plaintiff from obtaining a prospective pecuniary advantage." Unfortunately, the terminology of "loss of prospective pecuniary advantage" gets

used interchangeably with "pure economic loss" in a way that blurs the essential purpose of the rule itself.

4. In economic terms, the appropriate dividing line lies between *real* and *pecuniary* loss. To isolate the difference, suppose Oppen owned a fish that he intended to sell to you. If Hartley kills Oppen's fish, Oppen is entitled to compensatory damages. If Hartley takes your money, preventing you from buying Oppen's fish, Hartley's civil liability ends with you. The reason is simple. Oppen still has the fish, which he can sell to someone else. He may not obtain as high a price and he may have to incur some additional sales effort, but the presumption is that the market will provide satisfactory (if not perfect) compensation.

5. To apply the analogy, assume that Oppen owned exclusive fishing rights for the Santa Barbara channel. Given that premise, it follows that Hartley killed Oppen's fish and is liable for damages. In an excerpt from the *Oppen* court opinion cited above, the reference to the diminution "of aquatic life" and its link to lost profit fits the analogy perfectly. In *Rickards v. Sun Oil Company* (the major precedent underlying Union's claim), the defendant destroyed the only bridge connecting an island community to the mainland. Merchants were denied recovery for "pure economic loss," meaning the **pecuniary loss** from customers who would have bought their goods if the bridge had not been destroyed. Subject to minor market imperfections, the island merchants' losses were offset by the mainland merchants' gains.

6. Instead of labeling the fishermen's injuries "a pecuniary loss of a particular and special nature, limited to the class of commercial fishermen," the court should have indicated that the lost profit was an appropriate measure of the value of the **real resources**, to which the class of commercial fishermen had a special claim. The basis for the claim lay in their prior reliance on the use of a common property resource. The pecuniary gains were "prospective" in exactly the same sense as the merchants' prospective gains from sales to customers. In short, the fishermen collectively owned the fishing rights, but the *Rickards* merchants owned no such rights over customers.

Shrinking from Duty

Tarasoff v. Regents of University of California 17 Cal. 3d 425 (1976)

Simple Facts

After a brief romantic relationship, Prosenjit Poddar killed Tatiana Tarasoff. Two months prior to the killing, Poddar had confided in Dr. Moore, a psychologist employed by the University of California, and revealed his murderous intentions. At Moore's request, police briefly detained Poddar but released him when he appeared rational. Tarasoff's parents claimed negligence for failure to warn her of the impending danger.

Details

Prosenjit Poddar was born in Bengal, India. He arrived at the University of California at Berkeley in 1967. In the fall of 1968, he met Tatiana Tarasoff while she was attending folk dancing classes at the International House. They start seeing each other, and Poddar interpreted a New Year's Eve kiss as the commencement of a serious relationship. Tatiana told him that she was not interested in entering into an exclusive relationship.

ILLUSTRATION 11.3 A New Year's Eve kiss with bizarre consequences led to the murder of Tatiana Tarasoff by her rejected suitor.

The rejection touched off a severe emotional crisis. Poddar neglected his appearance, his studies, and his health. The depression steadily deteriorated through the fall of 1969. When Tatiana returned from a summer in Brazil, Poddar continued to pursue her. On October 27, he arrived at her home, armed with a pellet gun and a kitchen knife. When Tatiana refused to speak with him, Poddar shot her, and Tatiana ran from the house. Poddar caught up with her in the yard, where he inflicted fatal stab wounds.

A battery of psychiatrists gave testimony surrounding Poddar's insanity defense to the charge of second-degree murder. As Vitaly and Lydia Tarasoff endured the torture of the trial, they listened to Dr. Lawrence Moore testify that Poddar had revealed his intention to kill their daughter during a psychiatric therapy session!

Dr. Moore was a resident psychiatrist at the university's Cowell Memorial Hospital. With the concurrence of two of his associates, Moore had notified campus police, offering to sign a 72-hour detention order. As the story unfolded before their eyes, the Tarasoffs learned that the police had taken Poddar into custody and interrogated him, but the officers involved judged that he was rational. After Poddar promised to stay away from Tatiana, he was released from custody. Further testimony revealed the subsequent involvement of Dr. Harvey Powelson, the Director of Psychiatry at Cowell. Powelson ordered the staff to back off from their attempts to detain Poddar and to destroy all evidence of their prior actions (therapy notes and letters).

Poddar's conviction was reduced to manslaughter and remanded for retrial. Eventually, he was repatriated to India on the condition that he never return to the United States. The Tarasoffs filed a wrongful death action against the university regents, the psychiatrists, and the police. They sought punitive damages from Powelson for the malicious abandonment of a dangerous patient and targeted both the psychiatrists and the police for their failure to detain Poddar. All of these charges were essentially barred by California statutes, but the "duty to warn" issue was granted more than its "day" in court.

The Alameda County Superior Court accepted the defendants' argument that they owed no duty of care to either Tatiana or her parents. The backlash from the psychiatric and law enforcement communities from the California Supreme Court's first reversal of this decision prompted a second hearing of the same case. The Court held its ground:

> [D]efendant therapists cannot escape liability merely because Tatiana herself was not their patient. When a therapist determines, or pursuant to the standards of his profession should determine, that his patient presents a serious danger of violence to another, he incurs an obligation to use reasonable care to protect the intended victim against such danger.[11]

The Court cited a balancing of numerous considerations, including the foreseeability of harm, degree of certainty, prevention of future harm, and the extent of the burden imposed upon therapists and law enforcement officials. The overriding consideration was that a defendant owes a duty of care to all persons who are foreseeably endangered by his conduct. With regard to control of a dangerous person, the line between malfeasance and "nonfeasance" is the existence of a "special relationship" between the defendant and *either* the dangerous person or the potential victim.

In so ruling, the Court had to address an *amicus* brief filed on behalf of the American Psychiatric Association and other professional societies. Citing numerous articles indicating that therapists cannot reliably predict violent acts and that their forecasts consistently overpredict violence, the brief strenuously argued against a rule of liability based on the validity of predictions that are more often wrong than right:

> [T]he therapist need only exercise "that reasonable degree of skill, knowledge, and care ordinarily possessed and exercised by members of [that professional specialty] under similar circumstances." Within the broad range of reasonable practice and treatment in which professional opinion and judgment may differ, the therapist is free to exercise his or her own best judgment without liability; proof, aided by hindsight, that he or she judged wrongly is insufficient to establish negligence.[12]

As applied to Poddar, the psychiatric evaluation was correct and made with enough conviction as to warrant informing the police and to recommend an order of detention. In the Court's estimation, the direct social benefits of probable saving of an innocent life warranted the risks of a "Type II Error":

> The risk that unnecessary warnings may be given is a reasonable price to pay for the lives of possible victims that may be saved. We would hesitate to hold that the therapist who is aware that his patient expects to attempt to assassinate the President of the United States would not be obligated to warn the authorities because the therapist cannot predict with accuracy that his patient will commit the crime.[13]

The delicate issue of confidentiality was partly resolved by California statute. Though not required to reveal confidential communications, therapists were not bound by privilege in the face of imminent danger:

> We realize that the open and confidential character of psychotherapeutic dialogue encourages patients to express threats of violence, few of which are ever executed. Certainly a therapist should not be encouraged routinely to reveal such threats; such disclosures could seriously disrupt the patient's relationship with his therapist and with the persons threatened.[14]

In an effort to minimize the adverse impact upon patients' rights, the Court added that disclosures should be made discreetly and in a fashion that would "preserve the privacy of his patient to the fullest extent compatible with the prevention of the threatened danger." In concurring with the opinion, Justice Mosk expressed deep concern about the reference to the "standards of the profession." Mosk maintained that a duty to warn arises if a psychiatrist predicts violence but that expanding the rule "will take us from the world of reality into the wonderland of clairvoyance." [15]

Justice Clark's dissent was based in part upon his interpretation of existing statutes. Clark argued that the decision was contrary to legislative intent, but his main focus was on policy implications:

> Overwhelming policy considerations weigh against imposing a duty on psychotherapists to warn a potential victim against harm. While offering virtually no benefit to society, such a duty will frustrate psychiatric treatment, invade fundamental patient rights, and increase violence. [16]

Confidentiality encourages the mentally ill to seek treatment, to maintain trust throughout treatment, and to communicate honestly in a way that enables the therapist to apply effective treatment. Beyond its chilling effect upon the effectiveness of treatment, Clark predicted that the enforcement of a duty to warn would greatly increase the risk of involuntary civil commitments to mental institutions.

Economic Analysis

1. The American Psychiatric Association's *amicus* brief seems friendlier to itself than to the court. It is reminiscent of Helen Ackley's denial that her house was haunted after advertising in the national media that it was. The profession's low batting average ought not stop society from sending its best hitters up to the plate or from taking a swing at a fat pitch. In evaluating the profession's arguments, it is useful to draw some behavioral inference from the case. First, Moore and associates clearly believed Poddar to be a danger to Tatiana. Second, they allowed their judgment regarding the detention order to be superseded by that of campus police officers. The *amicus* brief probably did not indicate the profession's belief that police officers were better predictors of homicidal behavior than professional therapists. Third, Powelson abdicated all responsibility and engineered a cover-up. While the hypotheses with regard to the chilling effects of destroying confidentiality are worthy of consideration, they cannot be tested or evaluated under a cloak of secrecy.

2. Justice Mosk's reservations about the use of professional standards are well founded. The profession operates on rough guidelines rather than rigid standards. However, a duty to warn would be totally unenforceable without standards. As the court maintained, having standards does not imply that therapists will be rampantly second-guessed after the fact. Very likely, therapists will remain less vulnerable to frivolous lawsuits and negligence verdicts than manufacturers of ordinary consumer goods (e.g., perfume, coffee, chain-saws, and automobiles).

3. The short-run evaluation of the outcome is amenable to simple analysis through the Hand formula. The "pL" side of the equation reveals an enormous potential loss (death) combined with a more-than-negligible probability of occurrence. Multiplying probabilities and costs of death is always a slippery process, but Moore's behavior implies a belief that p was substantial. In contrast, the costs to Moore and the university hospital of warning Tatiana or her family amounted to a simple phone call.

4. However, the right-hand side of the equation must also include the costs imposed upon the patient. That dimension adds complexity to the formula. Given Poddar's social life, those costs rated to be negligible. Tatiana had already rejected him and would not even speak to him when he approached her. Poddar's actual feelings about this must be severely discounted because his thought processes were not rational. Other cases in the future might be less clear-cut on this point.

5. Applying the same standards to future cases would represent a reasonably clear efficiency gain were it not for the long-run implications. The adverse long-run consequences lie in (a) the potential loss of liberty through unwarranted commitment and (b) the compromise of treatment resulting from the dissolution of confidentiality. The "loss of liberty" argument is almost totally without merit. Therapists were already empowered to recommend detention and to encourage police involvement.

Therefore, *at the relevant margin*, the duty to warn adds nothing to that power. If anything, loss of liberty is made less likely by the involvement of those who might care about the patient's welfare. The compromise of treatment may be significant; the therapy community certainly claimed it to be. Unfortunately, the hypothesis by its very nature was unsupportable; perhaps 25 years of experience with the duty to warn will provide some enlightening evidence in this regard. A major factor in the court's decision was that this effect was wholly speculative.

Tainted Contract

General Foods v. Valley Lea Dairies 771 F. 2d 1093 (1985)

Simple Facts

General Foods and two of its business customers incurred substantial losses because a shipment of chocolate was found to be contaminated with the salmonella bacteria. General Foods had produced the chocolate from roller-dried milk supplied by Valley Lea Dairies. Because Valley Lea had failed to comply with General Food's production guidelines, General Foods claimed a breach of express warranty and sought to recover $1.2 million in damages. Valley Lea countered that General Foods incurred the risk of salmonella by not rejecting the shipment and releasing the milk for production and distribution. A jury verdict sided with Valley Lea; General Foods appealed, claiming that the jury instructions were misleading.

Details

Salmonella is a group of bacteria that cause diarrhea, fever, and abdominal cramps, with symptoms generally lasting from four to seven days. About 40 to 50 thousand cases of salmonellosis are reported annually in the United States. The bacteria may be found in all animal products, but the prime sources are raw eggs and milk products. Chocolate chip cookie dough is alleged to be a common culprit. Although the vast majority of persons inflicted with salmonella recover without treatment, the illness can be fatal for small children and the frail elderly.

The approximately 600 annual fatalities provided sufficient cause for General Foods to classify whole dried milk as a "microbiologically sensitive food ingredient." In a written policy statement distributed to all of its suppliers of dried milk, the company mandated that all of its vendors certify that their products are manufactured under conditions that conform to federal regulations. The statement explicitly specified the appropriate statistical texts to determine the levels of a variety of microbiological characteristics, including the incidence of salmonella. In addition to testing conducted by manufacturers, General Foods reserved the right to do its own testing and to accept or reject the product according to its own test results.

In November of 1978, General Foods bought 40,000 pounds of roller dried milk from the Lyons Creamery, a member of the Valley Lea Dairy Association. The milk was delivered in nine separate lots, one of which tested positive for salmonella. On that basis, General Foods tested the remaining lots at heightened levels, meaning a 95% statistical confidence level. The additional tests proved negative and the company decided to release the remaining lots for milk chocolate production. The chocolate was then subjected to additional testing, which revealed salmonella contamination. Unfortunately, General Foods had already shipped the contaminated chocolate to two customers, Elmer Candy and Frankford Candy.

Although the chocolate never reached the retail level, the customers incurred losses in excess of half a million dollars, which General Foods covered out-of-court. General Foods' own costs amounted to about $700,000 for a total of $1.2 million. After settling with its customers, General Foods brought suit against Valley Lea and Lyons for breach of express and implied warranties. In the U.S. District Court for the Northern District of Indiana, a jury delivered a verdict for the defendants, holding that General Foods incurred the risk by not rejecting the shipment, as it was entitled to do. General Foods appealed the verdict.

The appeal focused primarily upon the trial judge's very detailed jury instructions concerning "incurred risk" as a defense to a breach of warranty. In the judge's words, the defense arises "if the user, in this case General Foods, actually knew of the danger and nevertheless proceeded unreasonably to use the salmonella contaminated dry milk in the manufacture of milk chocolate and was injured by it."[17] The jury was instructed to consider whether General Foods *knew* and *understood* the risk of salmonella contamination in the lots of milk from Valley Lea and *voluntarily* released said milk into production. General Foods particularly objected to instruction #50 as excessively broad:

> If you find that General Foods Corporation discovered salmonella contamination in part of the shipment . . . and knew and understood the risk of salmonella contamination in that part of the lots being released into production . . . or in the alternative if you find that it was unreasonable for General Foods Corporation to release the milk into production knowing the possibility of salmonella contamination, then the losses sustained by General Foods Corporation may not have been proximately caused by any breach of warranty and any consequential damages may not be awarded.[18]

The company contended that the court should have been more specific as to the definition of "risk." General Foods was obviously aware of the general risk of salmonella but maintained that the defense of incurred risk should arise only in connection with a much more specialized and technical concept of risk. Essentially, Lyons' failure to comply with the mandated production and testing procedures induced General Foods to draw false inferences from its own statistical tests. This point was made more clearly in the dissenting opinion:

> Valley Lea also did not routinely clean the equipment after production of each lot, so that contamination might recur. To make matters worse, Valley Lea's equipment had been set up so that a leaky valve allowed unpasteurized milk to enter the finished product. . . . This dramatically increased the risk of contamination, and it linked the risk of one shipment with the risk of another. . . . The knowledge that whatever went wrong with lot 329 probably had gone wrong with the other lots in the shipment would have cast new light on the interpretation of the tests.[19]

Because of these flaws in the production process, the samples were not independent. General Foods contended that knowledge of these flaws was critical. Essentially, the company was taking a much higher risk than expected on the basis of its theoretical sampling model. What should have been a reasonable risk would have become an unreasonable risk in light of the additional information about Valley Lea's recklessness. Armed with that information, General Foods would not have released the milk for production and would not have incurred the $1.2 million loss.

General Foods maintained that mere awareness of the *possibility* of salmonella contamination did not constitute *understanding* of the risk that was relevant to the decision in question. In other words, the general risk depends on a variety of factors. For example, roller-dried milk makes better chocolate than spray-dried milk but requires longer exposure to air and therefore entails a greater risk of contamination. In specifying roller-dried milk, General Foods was clearly "incurring" the risk; the company understood the risk and voluntarily accepted it. With regard to the unsanitary equipment, General Foods clearly understood the risks but categorically rejected them. Ultimately, General Foods' objection to the jury instructions was that they lumped all risk into one vague generic mass rather than focusing on specific elements. Most importantly, the judge could have informed the jury that it was commercially reasonable to use the milk once the tests came out as they did—unless General Foods knew that the risks were dependent rather than independent.

Despite these considerations, the appellate court affirmed the outcome of the jury trial. In the court's view, the jury was capable of sifting through the important details and rendering an unbiased decision. The instructions may have been imperfect, but they were not prejudicial. The court emphasized that General Foods had continuous business dealings with Valley Lea and Lyons for many years prior to this particular dispute. For this reason, imputing an express warranty was far from clear-cut. Most importantly, although General Foods did not have specific information about the production flaws, it did ignore some important statistical clues:

> Assuming *arguendo* there was an express warranty here (General Foods can only assert the above statement "amounted to" an express warranty), it was waived when General Foods tested lot 329, found it was defective, and failed to return the remainder of the shipment at this point claiming violation of the warranty. . . . If salmonella contamination is an ever present risk, when does the producer's liability end concerning this risk? Certainly not after a significant lapse of time, such as when General Foods had already tested the product according to its specifications and decided to release the product into milk chocolate and sell it to customers.[20]

Reading between the lines, General Foods did not *know* that Lyons had violated established procedures but it had good reason to be *suspicious*—and acted on those suspicions by conducting heightened tests. In producing the chocolate and shipping it to its customers (instead of rejecting the entire shipment), General Foods "incurred" the risk.

Economic Analysis

1. The dissenting jurist insisted that this was a contract case, albeit a difficult one. In his view, General Foods was merely seeking damages for breach of warranty. Citing Indiana's version of the Uniform Commercial Code, he advocated awarding compensation for consequential damages. A key element of the UCC was that a buyer's acceptance of goods does not alter warranties when the defect in the goods is latent. Of course, the contract did not explicitly specify any warranty, particularly one in which Valley Lea / Lyons (henceforth, Valley Lea) assumed liability for consequential damages.

2. The economic problem faced by General Foods actually has several layers. The primary one is to organize the means of production. Although quality, reputation, and price are all relevant, the essential problem is largely technical: to implement a

set of procedures in order to minimize the cost (per unit) of producing chocolate, where costs include production, quality control, and expected cost of contamination. The key elements of the solution to this problem lay in General Foods' policy statement and testing procedures, including the division of effort and responsibility between General Foods and Valley Lea.

3. Since implementing the production involves a cooperative effort, the next layer is to address the "principal–agent" problem. The dilemma faced by General Foods (the "principal") is to induce cooperation from Valley Lea (the "agent"), which has both divergent interests and informational advantages. To put matters bluntly, General Foods knows that Valley Lea has incentives to cut costs by compromising quality control.[21] The solution to this problem lies in the structure of the contract. To enforce its policy, General Foods relied primarily on *results* (the right to reject shipments that tested positive for salmonella) rather than on *behavior* (penalties for noncompliance). The simple reason to rely on results is that behavior cannot easily be observed or supervised.

4. The structure of the actual contract lends itself to relatively simple modeling. Adopting the following notation:

   r = price received by General Foods from final buyers (net of processing costs)
   w = price paid by General Foods to Valley Lea
   q = quantity sold to final buyers
   z = quantity produced by Valley Lea
   p = probability of contamination of output shipped to final buyers
   t = expected damages if contaminated output is shipped to final buyers

   General Foods' profits are $G = (r - w - pt)q$, and Valley Lea's profits are $V = wq - cz$. Total profit is $\pi = G + V = (r - pt)q - cz$, with $q \leq z$. Valley Lea's problem is to choose a level of care (x) that trades off cost cutting with the risk of rejection. For simplicity, a higher x entails a higher acceptance rate (higher q), but at increased production costs (higher c). General Foods' problem is to set a standard (y) for its statistical testing that balances the net gains from accepting a shipment with the expected costs of accepting a tainted one.

5. While the model deals (superficially) with the problem of tainted chocolate, the next layer is the problem of the tainted contract. General Foods' claim of breach reduces to two elements: (a) Valley Lea chose $x < x^*$, a level of care below what General Foods had explicitly specified in the contract; (b) General Foods behaved reasonably ($y = y^*$) but would have employed additional caution ($y > y^*$) if it had known of Valley Lea's breach. General Foods' defense against incurred risk is that it could not have known about Valley Lea's breach. However, the very structure of the contract suggests otherwise. The contract calls for an x^* but provides incentives for Valley Lea to compromise that standard.

6. It follows that General Foods' tests should have made allowances for Valley Lea's noncompliance. Indeed, evidence suggests that the company did make such allowances. When the first incidence of contamination was discovered, every lot was subjected to "heightened" statistical testing. After releasing the milk for production, the chocolate was subjected to additional testing. The additional

testing suggested a clear awareness of the risk, but the company chose to ship the chocolate to the final buyers without waiting for the results of the tests. All things considered, General Foods' behavior suggests an understanding of not only the general risks of contamination but also of the specific risks associated with Valley Lea's noncompliance.

7. Default provisions like the ones cited in the dissent are designed to compensate for imperfect contracts. By imputing subtle terms, courts can relieve contracting parties of the burden of considering endless contingencies and thereby reduce transactions costs. In theory, courts impute terms that the contracting parties would have agreed upon if transactions costs had been negligible. In practice, it is important to question a court's ability to improve upon the contract as written. What General Foods was asking the court to do was not merely a marginal adjustment in subtle terms. Penalties other than rejection of shipments could have been written into the contract, with some reference to shared liability for consequential damages. In relying solely on rejection of shipments, General Foods incurred the risk of Valley Lea's breach.

CHAPTER 12

THE SILLY ECONOMICS OF PRODUCT LIABILITY LAW

The readers may decide for themselves whether the adjective in the chapter title applies to the economics, to the law, or to the general proposition that laws evolve in the direction of efficiency. It is certainly clear to even the most casual observer that **product liability** laws evolve. Indeed, this branch of the law was arguably the most dynamic and controversial of the twentieth century. Before engaging in theoretical speculation or critical assessment, a look at the broader picture is warranted.

In comparison with product liability law, contract law is the picture of stability. Contractual arrangements have increased in complexity to coincide with technological change, but the fundamental elements of an exchange never change. Product liability law is dynamic because it is inseparable from the technology of production and consumption. As products expand in dimension, complexity, and sheer numbers, the law has adapted. For the law to have remained static would be clear evidence against the efficiency hypothesis.

Despite the rapid change in the market environment, the fundamental objectives of product liability law have not substantially changed. The general economic goal is to minimize the total costs of injuries (including, of course, the costs of their prevention) resulting from the use of defective products. The main sources of cost to manufacturers include design, quality control, and dissemination of information. For consumers, the primary costs are injury and death, with secondary costs involving acquiring information and being diligent and cautious. Injury and death get the most attention from the media, but these are rare events for the individual consumer. In defense of the legions of apparently stupid consumers who continually injure themselves by failing to act sensibly, diligence and caution are 24 hours a day, 7 days a week, and 365 ¼ days per year jobs.

If the law is silly for awarding six- or seven-figure judgments to consumers with their heads screwed on backwards, so is economics for its unwavering dedication to the lost cause of perfect rationality. The softer view of rationality is that most people behave reasonably and responsibly most of the time, but no one behaves that way all of the time. Moreover, at least once a year, almost everyone does something that is incredibly stupid or thoughtless. Those of us who have managed to escape without serious injury after 20–80 years of iterations have done so largely independently of the product liability rules.

A Paradigm: Stella Liebeck v. McDonald's Corporation

Much of the theory of product liability may be illustrated in the context of a simple example. Every day, millions of Americans buy fast food, and a sizeable fraction of that group utilizes the drive-through window. They would not be buying fast food if they were not in a hurry, and they would not be using the drive-through window if they were not in more of a hurry. Some of the people who use the drive-through window buy coffee, and some of them spill the coffee on themselves. Most of the time, they wipe up the mess and move on, the main indices of injury being the volume and duration of the expletives. One customer was an octogenarian from Albuquerque by the name of Stella Liebeck. Stella suffered third-degree burns on her way through a McDonald's drive-through. The incident generated a widely publicized jury verdict in the neighborhood of $3 million (subsequently reduced to $160,000 for injuries and $460,000 in punitive damages). The number that went largely unnoticed was Stella's initial offer, rejected by McDonald's, to settle for $20,000 for medical expenses. The case did not produce a published opinion (it was settled before appeal), but it has become firmly entrenched in the lore of outrageous jury verdicts, annually chronicled in the "Stella Awards."

The accident in question was "produced" by a combination of apparently reasonable actions. Stella's grandson was driving the car and stopped momentarily so that she could add sugar and cream to the coffee. She placed the cup between her knees and spilled the coffee when she attempted to remove the plastic lid. McDonald's produced coffee at a temperature of 190 degrees to accommodate the average time lapse between pouring and drinking the coffee. Combined with the common expectation of cooler coffee, an accident of the type incurred by Stella was a statistical certainty.

In fact, McDonald's was evidently well aware of the problem, having settled over 700 similar claims before Stella's! In light of these considerations, holding the company responsible for Stella's injuries might not be as silly as it appears. McDonald's designed the product, knew that the design was somewhat unique, and failed to warn customers about the potential hazard. The product was not "defective" or "hazardous" in the sense that it contained poison, but the design of the product was defective (or so it was argued) in relation to the context in which it was to be used.

Economic Margins: Does Liability Matter?

The temperature of a cup of coffee is but one of millions of subtle dimensions of consumer products. More often than not, specifications of these dimensions are standardized by individual firms, but vary across firms in an industry. The extent to which a single firm might modify its product to accommodate individual consumers is also subject to variation, but individual accommodations tend to be costly. For this reason, consumer choice is exercised primarily through choice of vendor. If McDonald's coffee is too hot, have a coke or go to Burger King, Dairy Queen, or Jack-in-the-Box.

Subjecting dimensions like coffee temperature to detailed marginal analysis is a perfect example of what many people absolutely HATE about economics. However, similar considerations are routinely, if not explicitly, applied to multiple dimensions of a countless number of products. Every additional degree of heat increases direct energy costs by a miniscule amount for billions of cups of coffee per year, but improves efficiency by drawing more flavor from the ground coffee. At the margin, 190 degrees was too hot for most people to drink, but this effect was partially offset by a time lag between serving and consumption. From McDonald's perspective, the marginal gains (cost reduction) offset the marginal costs, up to the chosen temperature. The marginal costs were incurred through some customer dissatisfaction and the expected costs of consumer injury. To the extent that the law holds producers liable (*caveat vendor*) for consumer injuries, expected costs of injury enter the economic balance sheet under "lawsuits."

Assuming that actual and potential customers are fully informed about the characteristics and specifications of the products they buy, the expected cost of injury is one of the many factors that influence their choices. To the extent that the law holds consumers responsible (*caveat emptor*) for the costs of their own injuries, the lawsuits entry is removed from the producers' economic balance sheets. However, the same entry reappears under something like "loss of consumer satisfaction." Whether McDonald's actually weighed the expected costs of consumer injury of adding the last unit of heat to its coffee specifications with the marginal revenue from the net gain in sales is largely a matter of idle speculation. The record does suggest that the expected costs of serious injury were regarded as negligible. In the aftermath, McDonald's reduced the temperature of its coffee in the direction of the industry norm of 140–145 degrees. However, the industry norm was not appreciably affected.

The fact that the industry norm was not affected raises the question of whether product liability rules significantly affect production decisions. It is clear that producers incur lower costs if they are not held responsible for consumer injuries. Accordingly, a shift from a rule of *caveat emptor* to one of *caveat vendor* raises costs, as indicated by an upward shift in supply from S_1 to S_2 in Figure 12.1. However, the shift of legal responsibility does not eliminate the expected costs; the law merely *transfers* the costs from one group to the other. It follows that, at least under pristine conditions, transferring the costs from buyers to sellers increases demand from D_1 to D_2. The effect is that equilibrium moves from A to B. Output (quantity and quality) is unchanged, and the price increase merely reflects a change in how consumers are compensated for their injuries.

The foregoing conclusion is an obvious oversimplification. In particular, it ignores at least three important economic factors. First, compensating everyone who *might be injured* a few dollars for the expectation of being injured is not the same as paying compensation to the unlucky few who actually *are injured*. In other words, the allocation of risk matters. Second, it is not just the buyers who use and are injured by defective products. Expectations of injuries to third parties tend not to be included in demand conditions under *caveat emptor*, but they are included in supply conditions under *caveat vendor*. Third, there are asymmetries of information on both sides of the market. Consumers may not be aware of potential hazards, and producers may not anticipate all of the various and creative uses that consumers find for their products. Those "creative uses" lead to the fourth and final reservation. It is difficult for manufacturers to control the consumer abuse of their products. Consumer abuse is a prime reason for *caveat emptor* and a major objection to the gradual movement toward holding manufacturers more and more responsible for consumer injuries. In a milieu that does not hold consumers responsible for their mistakes, manufacturers frequently incur significant costs in an attempt to anticipate misuse and to modify product design to mitigate damages.

Is Caveat Vendor a Move in the Right Direction?

If Figure 12.1 is representative of the effects of product liability laws, a lot of court costs have been incurred to accomplish nothing. If the relevant costs and benefits of every dimension of every product are captured in demand and supply conditions, tinkering with liability rules is a shell game that provides only the illusion of effective policy. As applied to coffee served by fast-food restaurants, neither quantity nor temperature

FIGURE 12.1 Shifting liability need not appreciably affect production decisions. Under caveat emptor, consumers are compensated *ex ante* through lower prices.

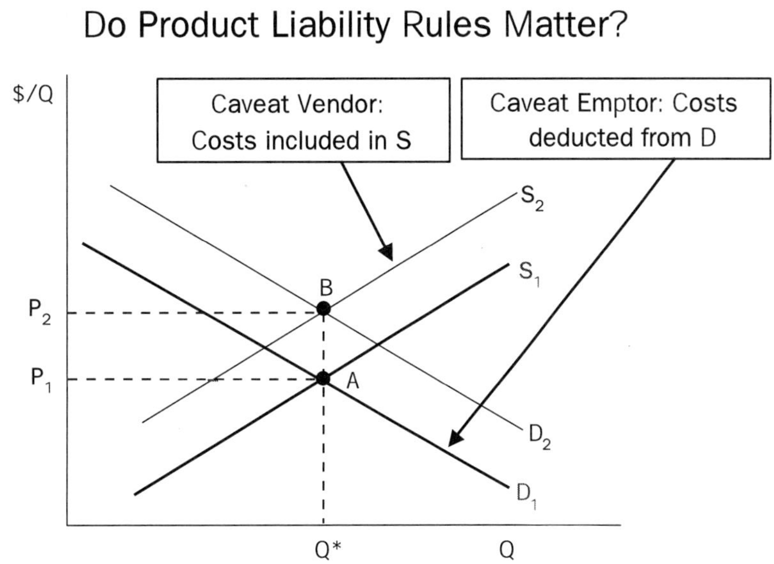

has changed significantly. Of course, *something* changed; McDonald's has turned down the heat. The key economic questions are: (1) why has McDonald's changed its policy and (2) was the change an improvement. Analyzing product liability law is largely an extension of these questions beyond this single case. Three major reasons why product liability rules matter include:

1. Buyers are not simply endowed with perfect information about product design and potential defects or hazards. Sellers are naturally more aware of the risks.
2. Producers have direct control over the manufacturing process and have choices with respect to quality control, safety features, and hazardous characteristics.
3. Consumers have direct control over the use or abuse of products.

These reasons translate into familiar economic principles about risk bearing, moral hazard, asymmetry of information, and adverse selection. By assigning duties, responsibilities, and liabilities to those who can more efficiently bear or control the costs, the law facilitates a reduction in expected real costs of accident injury and prevention. Without going into detail, these principles relate directly to identifiable trends in the product liability laws. Manufacturers have a duty to inform consumers about potential defects, hazards, and even various forms of possible consumer abuse. Manufacturers are strictly liable for defects, subject to a defense of contributory negligence (consumer abuse).

Applying the principles to *Liebeck v. McDonald's*, it is clear that McDonald's failed to satisfy a duty to inform. The coffee was 40–50 degrees above the industry norm. A printed warning on the styrofoam cup probably would have satisfied legal standards. Whether the extreme temperature constituted a "defect" is less clear. However, scientific evidence revealed that the severity of burns escalates rapidly above the normal temperatures. In context of the widespread use of drive-through service, 190 degrees seems inefficiently high. McDonald's apparently agreed and turned down the heat as soon as the temperature of the coffee came under public scrutiny. Liebeck did contribute to the accident; her small negligence did not bar recovery, but the judge reduced compensatory awards from $200,000 to $160,000. The punitive damages applied because McDonald's behavior went beyond mere failure to inform. The company pursued an active policy of suppressing information by imposing confidentiality as a condition of a multitude of out-of-court settlements.

In judging the efficiency of the law, it is important not to dwell on absolutes. In relative terms, observable changes over time in virtually all of the relevant economic factors point toward expanding manufacturer liability. The major argument against *caveat vendor* lies in the preservation of incentives for consumers to take an active interest in their own safety and incentives away from outright consumer abuse. With regard to active interest in safety, a clinical economic analysis focuses on expected costs—p multiplied by L in the Hand Formula. Aside from the fact that most people are not conditioned to think in those terms, the effects of extremely low p's and high L's are difficult to absorb and evaluate. With regard to consumer abuse, it is not entirely clear that the manufacturer should be the one to decide the meaning of "intended use." Indeed, consumer sovereignty principles argue in favor of letting the buyer use goods and services in ways that best satisfy their wants as they define them. If some of the uses are inherently dangerous, the consumer at least has the right to know that they are dangerous.

This chapter will chronicle some major milestones in the evolution of product liability law over the last century. The recognition that automobiles are more complex than stagecoaches induced the first major shift in *MacPherson v. Buick Motor Company*. The view that defective products are a matter of negligence exploded along with a very famous coke bottle in *Escola v. Coca-Cola*. The prospects of third-party injuries and consumer abuse converge with the **technology of consumption** and duties to inform in *Moran v. Faberge*. Finally, the chapter and the book conclude with the epic product liability issue of the last half-century. Personal responsibility and producer chicanery collide in *R. J. Reynolds v. Engle*.

Privity of Contract

MacPherson v. Buick Motor Company 217 N.Y. 382 (1916)

Simple Facts

A Buick automobile suddenly collapsed, injuring MacPherson, who was thrown out of the car. One of the wheels was made of defective wood. Buick did not manufacture the wheel and did not sell the automobile directly to MacPherson. No claim was made that the company knew of the defect, but there was evidence that its defects could have been discovered by reasonable inspection.

Details

Both Leonardo da Vinci and Sir Isaac Newton drew up plans for motor vehicles, and the first self-propelled road vehicle was actually invented (1769) before the American Revolution. The French Army used Nicolas Cugnot's tractor to haul artillery at a cruising speed of 2.5 miles per hour, but had to stop every 10 minutes or so to replenish its steam power. Cugnot was also the first to have an "auto accident," crashing one of his vehicles into a stone wall in 1771.

It was over a century later (1876) that Nikolaus Otto developed the internal combustion engine. The first practical automobiles were designed and built a decade later by Karl Benz (1885) and Gottfried Daimler (1886). Actually, Daimler adapted a stagecoach to house his engine. Directly or indirectly, over 100,000 patents are embodied in the modern automobile.

ILLUSTRATION 12.1 Nicolas Cugnot invented a steam-propelled motor vehicle in 1769. Cugnot was also the first to have an "auto accident," crashing one of his vehicles into a stone wall in 1771.

Public Domain

ILLUSTRATION 12.2 The 1914 Buick B-25 weighed 2,400 pounds, carried four passengers comfortably, and retailed at a price of $1,050.

© Arthur Gurmankin/2003

The 1914 Buick B-25 weighed 2,400 pounds, operated on four cylinders, and generated 22 horsepower from a 165 cubic-inch engine. Equipped with a Delco self-starter and three-speed transmission, it carried four passengers comfortably over a wheelbase of 105 inches and was offered at a retail price of $1,050. "When better automobiles are built," the company proudly proclaimed, "Buick will build them."

Lying on the ground looking up at a crumpled wheel, Donald MacPherson probably harbored doubts with regard to the efficacy of that slogan. Although MacPherson was driving at a speed of only eight miles per hour, the spokes had crumbled into fragments. When the wheel was subsequently determined to have been made of defective wood, MacPherson attempted to recover compensatory damages for his injuries. He did not claim that Buick had attempted to conceal the defect or even that the company was aware of it. Indeed, Buick had merely purchased the wheel from its manufacturer, the Imperial Wheel Company. The claim of negligence was based on evidence that Buick could have discovered the defect if it had undertaken a reasonable inspection. On that basis, the trial judge found for the plaintiff.

The claim of negligence was certainly debatable. The Imperial Wheel Company was a reputable manufacturer and had supplied Buick with more than 80,000 wheels over a period of several years. None of them had proved to be made of defective wood prior to MacPherson's accident. It would thus appear reasonable for Buick to rely upon the wheel manufacturer to perform the appropriate tests as to the strength of the material. The New York appellate court disagreed:

> We think the defendant was not absolved from a duty of inspection because it bought the wheels from a reputable manufacturer. It was not merely a dealer in automobiles.

Benjamin Cardozo: *Precedents drawn from the days of travel by stagecoach do not fit the conditions of travel today. The principle that the danger must be imminent does not change, but the things subject to the principle do change. They are whatever the needs of life in a developing civilization require them to be.*

Portrait of Justice Benjamin Cardozo by Eben Farrington Comins

> It was a manufacturer of automobiles. It was responsible for the finished product. It was not at liberty to put the finished product on the market without subjecting the component parts to ordinary and simple tests.[1]

However, the primary basis for Buick's appeal was not to contest the negligence claim *per se*. Rather, the company contended that the ruling flew in the face of legal precedents that denied recovery without "privity of contract." In short, Buick sold the car to a retailer who sold it to MacPherson. Since MacPherson had not bought the car directly from Buick, there was no contract and, therefore, no liability. The privity rule traced back to the 1842 British case of *Winterbottom* v. *Wright*,[2] an action by the driver of a stagecoach, whose employer had a contract with the postmaster general to provide and maintain the vehicle to deliver mail. The driver was denied recovery because the contract was between his employer and the postmaster general:

> If the plaintiff can sue, every passenger or even any person passing along the road, who was injured by the upsetting of the coach, might bring a similar action. Unless we confine the operation of such contracts as this to the parties who enter into them, the most absurd and outrageous consequences, to which I can see no limit, would ensue.[3]

In its attempt to escape the shackles of *Winterbottom*, the court focused on a long line of precedents. The definitive case was *Thomas* v. *Winchester,*[4] in which a vendor negligently mislabeled a poison and sold it to a pharmacist, who used the poison to fill a prescription. The vendor was liable for the customer's injuries, but the court carefully distinguished between acts of negligence that were "imminently dangerous to the lives of others" and other acts that were not so dangerous. The opinion contained a hypothetical reference to a defectively shod horse, explicitly limiting the smith's liability to the owner of the horse. Similarly, *Torgeson* v. *Schultz*[5] involved the explosion of an aerated water bottle that had not been properly tested. The servant of the purchaser was awarded damages from injury, but the court made special notice of the fact that the bottles were proved dangerous when subjected only to "customary usage." A third case, *Devlin* v. *Smith,*[6] involved the death of an employee of the purchaser of a defective scaffold. The employee's estate recovered for the wrongful death not because scaffolds were dangerous *per se*, but because the scaffold became dangerous as a consequence of negligent construction.

Writing for the majority, Justice Cardozo pieced together the three opinions to bob and weave his way around privity:

> The nature of an automobile gives warning of probable danger if its construction is defective. . . . The defendant knew the danger [and] that the car would be used by persons other than the buyer. This was apparent from . . . the fact that the buyer was a dealer in cars. . . . The maker of this car supplied it for the use of purchasers from the dealer just as plainly as the contractor in *Devlin* v. *Smith* supplied the scaffold for use by the servants of the owner.[7]

Perhaps more importantly, the court was determined to adapt the underlying common law principles to the modern world:

> The dealer was [the one person who certainty would not be using the car]. Yet the defendant would have us say that he was the one person whom it was under a legal duty to protect. The law does not lead us to so inconsequent a conclusion. Precedents drawn from the days of travel by stagecoach do not fit the conditions of travel today. The principle that the danger must be imminent does not change, but the things subject to the principle do change. They are whatever the needs of life in a developing civilization require them to be.[8]

The dissenting jurist took a much narrower view. A defective wheel on an automobile moving only eight miles an hour was no more dangerous than a similarly defective wheel on a horse-drawn carriage. Therefore, there should be no liability beyond the original sale "unless the courts have been all wrong on this question up to the present time."[9]

Economic Analysis

1. Modern economic theory is largely a nonstop bus along the vertical highway from inputs to final outputs. Ignoring transactions costs, retailers do not exist. Justice Cardozo's curt dismissal of the dealer is a clear statement of the relative unimportance of the retailer in the link between production and consumption of automobiles. The reference to the "needs of life in a developing civilization" is an explicit recognition of the complexity of the production function and the nature of "the firm."
2. Trial evidence suggests the *ex ante* probability of a defective wheel to have been negligible. The *ex post* figure lay in the neighborhood of one in 80,000. Improving upon that figure is not as simple as the court suggests. The car manufacturer would have to inspect every tire, duplicating the effort of the tire manufacturer. In the aftermath of this case, auto manufacturers might have increased their quality control efforts, but additional inspection of tires is unlikely to have been the best use of the additional effort. The larger point is that the manufacturer has superior knowledge to the customer with regard to the efficient allocation of quality control effort.
3. The modern ritual of kicking tires is a remnant of the past, when the serious purpose was to ensure that coach and wagon wheels were properly attached. It is also a symbol of *caveat emptor*. If the buyer's only concern were the functioning of the wheels, it would make economic sense to assign liability to the buyer. Those who

considered the effort worthwhile would do so, and those who did not would not. Inspection required no great expertise, and scale economies were probably insignificant. However, when Gottfried Daimler added the internal combustion engine to the stagecoach, the balance began to shift.

4. On a different scale, another balance was shifting. The *Winterbottom* court refused to assign liability outside of privity with reference to the "absurd and outrageous consequences" that would ensue without foreseeable limits. Assuming that it made sense to hold consumers responsible for inspecting their own tires, but not (say) the location of the gas tank, the collective effect of having courts allocate product parts between consumers and manufacturers is another absurd and outrageous consequence. Thus, the court held the manufacturer responsible for the finished product. Whether or not responsibility for the defective tire should be shifted back to the tire manufacturer (or the supplier of the defective wood) is a matter to be determined by contract.

5. The other prominent dimension of this case is that of "inherent danger." From a legal perspective, the undetectable mislabeling of poisonous belladonna as a harmless extract of dandelions provided the first major exception to privity. Assigning liability to the pharmacist's supplier was clearly correct because the supplier was the only person who could have feasibly prevented the accident. From an economic perspective, the question then becomes how far this margin should be extended. Ultimately, inherent danger gave way to the more subjective notion that ordinary products can become dangerous by defective construction.

Loquacious Facts

Escola v. Coca-Cola Bottling Company 24 Cal. 2d. 453 (1944)

Simple Facts

Gladys Escola, a waitress in a restaurant, was injured when a coke bottle exploded in her hand. She filed a suit against Coca-Cola Company for negligence, citing excessive pressure of gas or some defect in the bottle. Being unable to show any specific acts of negligence on the part of the defendant, the plaintiff relied on the doctrine of *res ipsa loquitur.*

Details

The coke bottle was born out of a concern that a straight-sided bottle would be confused with those of imitators of the "real thing." Representatives of Coca-Cola Company solicited ideas from glass manufacturers and, in 1916, the familiar contour bottle became one of the very few containers ever elevated to trademark status by the U.S. Patent Office. By the early 1920s, over a thousand Coca-Cola bottling companies were operating throughout the country, many under independent ownership. Six-packs hit the stores in 1923 and, with the advent of open-top coolers, bottle sales eclipsed fountain sales of the world's most popular soft drink. The open-top coolers were equipped with metal racks, from which individual bottles were suspended in ice water. These forerunners of modern vending machines came to symbolize an oasis of cool refreshment in the stifling heat of a summer day. Keeping the contents cold served another useful purpose: fewer bottles exploded from the buildup of carbonated gas within.

The climate of Merced, California, epitomizes the stifling heat of a summer day. In 1944, every gas station in town probably had an open-top cooler, but for most restaurants the rate of sales probably outpaced the capacities of their iceboxes. Gladys Escola was a waitress in a Merced restaurant that sold Coca-Cola. A few days before the accident, the local bottling company delivered several cases of Coke. The wooden cases were placed on the floor, one on top of the other, under and behind the counter, where they remained at least 36 hours. On the day of the accident, Escola picked up the top case and began taking bottles from the case with her right hand, one at a time, and putting them into the refrigerator. The fourth one exploded in her hand. The evidence revealed that the bottle broke into two jagged pieces, inflicting a five-inch cut and severing blood vessels, nerves, and muscles of the thumb and palm of the hand.

Escola testified that the bottle made a loud "pop," similar to that of an electric light bulb. Her employer testified that he heard the explosion, and a fellow employee testified that the contents of the bottle flew all over the room and covered the walls. A driver for the bottling company admitted that he had seen other bottles blow up in the past and had found broken bottles in the warehouse. In spite of the testimony, there was no direct evidence of any acts of negligence. Nonetheless, Escola filed suit against Coca-Cola Bottling Company of Fresno, relying on the doctrine of *res ipsa loquitur* (loosely translated, "the facts speak for themselves"). When the bottling company appealed the judgment of the Merced Superior Court, Melvin Belli spoke for Gladys.

Under *res ipsa*, a defendant is presumed to be negligent if an object causing injury was in his or her control. The doctrine had been applied to numerous prior cases involving exploding bottles of carbonated beverages. As a general rule, it does not apply unless the defendant had exclusive control of the object and the accident was not likely to have occurred in the absence of negligence. Inasmuch as the bottle had been out of its control for nearly 36 hours prior to the accident, the company based its appeal on the contention that the doctrine had been misapplied.

The California Supreme Court adopted a broader application of *res ipsa*. Specifically, it was sufficient for the object to have been under the defendant's control *at the time of the alleged negligent act*—provided that the plaintiff first proved that the object's condition had not been changed after it left the defendant's control. With regard to the cause of the accident, only two possibilities were considered. Either the bottle was defective or the bottle had been charged with excessive pressure (or some combination of the two). The court reasoned that *res ipsa* applied if overcharging caused the explosion and, if not, the company was negligent for failure to discover the defect in the glass bottle. The court added that it was highly unlikely that Coca-Cola bottles contain defects that are not discoverable by visual inspection. Since the defendant had exclusive control over the inspection of the bottles upon their delivery, it follows that the defendant was responsible for discovering visible defects.

In a concurring opinion, Justice Traynor implied some impatience with the court's tedious analysis of the possible causes of the accident:

> I concur in the judgment, but I believe the manufacturer's negligence should no longer be singled out as the basis of a plaintiff's right to recover in cases like the present one. In my opinion it should now be recognized that a manufacturer incurs an absolute liability when an article that he has placed on the market, knowing that it is to be used without inspection, proves to have a defect that causes injury to human beings. . . .[10]

He pointed to the presumption of negligence with regard to a variety of reasons originating out of the manufacturing process itself, inspection of the finished product, or inspection of component parts supplied by others. In Traynor's view, the issue of manufacturer negligence was irrelevant; public policy demanded that liability be assigned wherever it most effectively reduces hazards to life and health. His vision for public policy included both compensation and deterrence. With regard to social insurance:

> Those who suffer injury from defective products are unprepared to meet its consequences. The cost of an injury and the loss of time or health may be an overwhelming misfortune to the person injured, and a needless one, for the risk of injury can be insured by the manufacturer and distributed among the public as a cost of doing business.[11]

With regard to deterrence, the overriding consideration was to discourage the marketing of "products having defects that are a menace to the public." Whether manufacturers are negligent or not, they are ultimately responsible for allowing the product to reach the market.

Economic Analysis

1. The connection between this case and *MacPherson v. Buick* is more than noteworthy. There was no privity of contract between Escola and the bottling company, the

product was not inherently dangerous, and the product became dangerous as the result of negligence. The margin that is getting stretched by the majority opinion is the scope of manufacturer negligence. Under *res ipsa loquitur*, it becomes very difficult for manufacturers to exonerate themselves. Here, the only possible defense was to claim mishandling during the 36-hour interval.

2. Although Escola bore the burden of proof against the mishandling claim, that burden appears to have been slight. The court emphasized the absence of any *action* that may have contributed to the accident, the existence of extraneous harmful forces, and careful handling. It was not within her duty to attempt to eliminate every remote possibility of injury, and there was no mention of the possibility of contributory negligence by the owner or manager of the restaurant. To the extent that exposure to heat contributed to the accident (it probably did), it was up to the bottler to anticipate the problem and adjust pressure accordingly.

3. Justice Traynor's argument in behalf of social insurance has considerable popular appeal, at least among the liberal cognoscente. The general form of the argument is that of free lunches for the masses by means of price increases of a few pennies. Of course, the pennies add up when the argument is extended to all products. Moreover, not everyone wants the same level of insurance coverage, and real insurance companies may be able to underwrite consumer polices at a lower cost. In spite of these standard economic counter-arguments, however, the provision of insurance choices on a product-by-product basis would almost certainly entail significant transactions costs.

4. On the positive side, the manufacturer (or in some cases, the retailer) may be in a better position to assess the risks. Those directly involved in the vertical supply chain acquire the information through the ordinary process of operating their businesses. With regard to accident avoidance, arguments based on transactions costs invariably point to assigning liability to producers. For example, the driver testified to prior incidents of exploding bottles and to broken bottles found in the warehouse. Though hardly qualifying as scientific random sampling, such informal information gathering ought to have translated into warnings about exposing carbonated beverages to high temperatures for extended periods of time. In short, "common knowledge" tends to be more common on the supply side of the market than on the demand side.

5. In Traynor's words, the "fact" that "speaks for itself" is that "products having defects that are a menace to the public" reach the market. Put in those terms, one is hard-pressed to argue very strenuously against strict liability. Now that the "negligence margin" has been resolved, the next margin to explore is what constitutes a defect that menaces the public.

Burning Scents of Duty

Moran v. Faberge 273 Md. 538; 332 A. 2d 11 (1975)

Simple Facts

In a flight of fancy during a summertime slumber party, teenager Randy Williams poured Faberge perfume over a lighted Christmas candle in order to make it scented. The perfume burst into flames, severely burning Randy's friend, Nancy Moran, who was standing nearby. In addition to suing her friend and the homeowners, Moran filed a negligence claim against Faberge for failure to warn its customers about the flammability of its product.

Details

Perfume was developed by the Egyptians, initially for use as part of their religious rituals and burials. During the New Kingdom (about 1500 B.C.), Egyptian women began using perfumed creams and oils as tools of seduction. By the reign of Louis XV, scents were applied not just to the skin, but also to gloves, clothing, and furniture. Perfume technology changed dramatically during the nineteenth century. As alchemy was replaced by modern chemistry, natural scents extracted from such plants as rose, henna, and lily gave way to synthetics. Modern fragrances are mixtures of essential oils and numerous synthetic ingredients, the precise formulas being trade secrets.

At some point between the embalming of Tutankhamen and a 1969 slumber party at the Maryland home of Louis Grigsby, alcohol became a key ingredient of most commercial perfumes. That fact was largely common knowledge; indeed, dictionary definitions of cologne invariably refer to a composition of alcohol and aromatic oils. However, few people are fully aware of how much alcohol is contained in an ounce of scent (are you?). As Randy Williams and Nancy Moran discovered, Faberge's Tigress cologne was composed of 82% alcohol. Scientific experimental evidence revealed it to be a dangerously combustible liquid with a flash point at approximately room temperature.

Randy's "experiment" replicated the lab results. On the evening of June 8, 1969, Randy and Nancy met with a number of their friends at the Grigsby home. The group congregated in the basement, which served both as a clubroom and a laundry room. At some point, everyone except Randy and Nancy left the basement and for some reason their attentions focused on a lit Christmas-tree-shaped candle. They initially speculated as to whether it was scented. After they determined that it was not, Randy proceeded to make it scented by dousing it with a splash of Tigress. The court record indicated that Nancy suffered severe burns to her neck and breasts from the burst of flames that sprang forth from the newly scented candle.

Nancy's father filed suit in her behalf for recovery of medical and related expenses. Randy Williams and Louis Grigsby were exonerated by the trial jury, leaving Faberge with a $30,000 judgment that was taken before Maryland's Special Court of Appeals. That court noted that a manufacturer's duty to produce a safe product, *with appropriate warnings and instructions when necessary*, is subject to standard rules of negligence. The court essentially applied the Hand Formula to warnings:

> [I]n cases such as this the cost of giving an adequate warning is usually so minimal, amounting only to the expense of adding some more printing to a label, that this

> balancing process will almost always weigh in favor of an obligation to warn of latent dangers, if the manufacturer is otherwise required to do so.[12]

Given the negligible cost factor, the court focused on the question of when the responsibility to warn arises. In other words, manufacturers do not automatically have to print warnings simply because they are cheap—there must be some identifiable benefit. It did not take the court long to find one. Faberge knew of the latent danger and had no reason to believe that (all) users would be aware of the danger. This consideration had to be balanced with what normal people would call common sense and what the law calls manners of use that the manufacturer can reasonably foresee. Citing the Restatement (Second) of Torts:

> [T]he maker is entitled to assume that his product will be put to normal use, for which the product is intended or appropriate; and he is not subject to liability when it is safe for all such uses, and harm results only because it is mishandled in a way which he has no reason to expect, or is used in some unusual and unforeseeable manner. Thus a shoemaker is not liable to an obstinate lady who suffers harm because she insists on wearing a size too small for her, and the manufacturer of a bottle of cleaning fluid is not liable when the purchaser splashes it into his eye.[13]

In spite of the fact that Randy Williams' use of the cologne was a virtually perfect example of misuse, the court affirmed the $30,000 judgment! It reasoned that the potential danger existed independently of whether the product was misused. Since ordinary use is also subject to potential hazard, the manufacturer has a duty to warn. The fact that Williams misused the product did not excuse Faberge from its duty. Moreover, Moran was not guilty of any contributory negligence because she was not the one who doused the candle with flammable cologne.

The dissenting opinion concurred with the court's framing of the issues, but rejected its conclusions. As the same court had stated in prior proceedings against Randy Williams:

> There was a total absence of any evidence in this case which would tend to show or would support a rational inference that Faberge foresaw or should have foreseen that its cologne would be used in the manner which caused the injuries to Nancy Moran. Since Faberge did not foresee the use, it had no duty to warn against it.[14]

The crux of the dissent was that, while Faberge might have a duty to warn of a *general risk* because of the latent flammability of its cologne, that duty does not automatically extend to everyone, "howsoever the product might be used or abused." Precedents with regard to warnings invariably connected duty and foreseeability. A case against Revlon cosmetics illustrated the principle particularly well. A woman was burned while applying nail polish near her lighted cigarette. It is foreseeable that smokers might smoke while they apply nail polish and, therefore, Revlon owed the plaintiff a warning.[15] Since the candle incident was not reasonably foreseeable, the dissent concluded that Faberge did not owe Williams or Moran a warning.

Economic Analysis

1. Modern theories of consumer behavior have emphasized the **technology of consumption**. Market commodities are viewed as inputs, as means of producing

more fundamental characteristics or activities. Consumers' preferences are directed toward the characteristics or activities rather than the goods themselves. An example of an activity is smoking while applying nail polish. Examples of characteristics are scent and soft light. If a consumer desires those characteristics in combination, the only bizarre choice would be to produce them in ways that do not minimize cost.

2. From a strictly economic viewpoint, it is entirely outside the role of a firm to determine what constitutes normal or acceptable use of its product. Furthermore, it is a waste of time and resources for manufacturers to speculate idly about bizarre uses and their consequences. A far more productive endeavor is to inform consumers about the characteristics and the technology of consuming them. With regard to perfume manufacturers' duty to warn the public that cologne is flammable, they have a natural inclination (compounded by competitive pressures) not to do so because flammability is a negative characteristic. Beautiful women in romantic settings are more persuasive than warnings about 160-proof incendiary liquids.

3. Ignoring the flammability characteristic, the combination of a lighted candle and a splash of perfume is a creative, cost-effective way of producing the desired characteristics. Whether Randy Williams merits a patent or a Stella is a matter of opinion, but the principle of consumer sovereignty is on her side. Introducing the flammability characteristic renders her choice objectively inefficient. It is obvious that she would have behaved differently if she had been fully informed about the fire hazard. More to the point, the notion that Randy was not entitled to the warning because of the manner in which she used the product is reminiscent of President Truman's observation that banks lend money only to those who don't need it. Her unfortunate choice typifies the ultimate purpose of warnings.

4. Applying the Hand Formula to this case is not as simple as it might seem. Two probabilities are involved. One is the probability that the warning will be read. The other is the conditional probability that the warning will be heeded, if read. Given the facts of this case, the latter probability is one, but the former is zero. In other words, it is a virtual certainty that Randy would have heeded the warning if she had read it, but she acted impetuously and almost certainly would not have read the warning. This framework, if appropriate, would provide a rational foundation for acquitting Faberge of negligence. It underscores the side issue that the injured party was not the actual buyer of the product. The link between manufacturer and third-party injuries may be found in general duties regarding the provision of information.

5. All reputable manufacturers stand to benefit if their products are used responsibly and rationally. Rational consumption requires forethought and planning. Accordingly, the appropriate framework is more long-run in nature. Faberge had been marketing Tigress since 1942. Had the company started printing warnings earlier, the flammability characteristic would have been a more prominent component of individual decision making. More importantly, the information might have filtered down to more 15-year-old girls. In context of this particular case, the specific act was not foreseeable, but the occurrence of *a* senseless tragedy *of some kind* was the foreseeable result of 27 years of suppressing information.

You've Come a Long Way, Baby!

R. J. Reynolds v. Engel
672 So. 2d 39 (1996), 2003 Fla. App. LEXIS 7500

Simple Facts

On May 5, 1994, nine plaintiffs filed the class action on behalf of themselves and all of the United States citizens and residents injured by their addiction to tobacco. The primary claim was that the tobacco industry deliberately manipulated the nicotine levels in their cigarettes and concealed all information about addictive nature of cigarettes. The plaintiffs sought $200 billion in damages.

Details

As news of scientific links between cigarette smoking and cancer began to be made public in the early 1950s, the tobacco industry began a half century of stonewalling. In the decade preceding the surgeon general's 1964 report, nearly 150 lawsuits were filed without so much as a penny in damage awards. Many cases were dropped, as the tobacco companies exhausted plaintiffs' funds with an onslaught of litigation costs. In the few cases that went to trial, the defense prevailed on grounds that the injuries to the plaintiffs were not foreseeable.

By 1980, information about the risks of smoking was largely common knowledge after nearly two decades of legislation, warnings, and government ad campaigns. Moreover, strict liability for inherently dangerous or defective products was firmly entrenched in product liability law. Even though the industry was still in denial, unforeseeability was not a viable defense. As a second wave of lawsuits began, the industry's new line of defense was (a) to deny proximate causation (by attacking plaintiffs' lifestyles) and (b) to claim assumption of risk. In mandating printed warnings, the Cigarette Act of 1969 largely preempted any claim pertaining to failure to warn. The industry lost one jury verdict (out of nearly 200), but won a new trial on appeal and the plaintiffs eventually lost a war of attrition.[16]

Because of the enormous litigation costs, individual lawsuits gave way to class actions in the 1990s. Two of the first such actions provided a preview of what plaintiffs were up against. *Castano v. American Tobacco Company*[17] was filed on behalf of all nicotine-dependent persons in the United States. A Louisiana district court certified the class action, but the class was decertified on appeal—there was simply too much variance in state laws and individual circumstances (particularly with respect to addiction) to justify committing the fate of an entire industry and nearly 100 million plaintiffs to a single jury. Subsequent attempts to break the class into subgroups also failed certification. *Broin v. Phillip Morris*[18] managed to survive certification because the class was extremely narrow, limited to nonsmoking flight attendants who had been involuntarily exposed to secondary smoke.

In May 1994, Dr. Howard Engle and five other plaintiffs filed a class action against the tobacco industry. Initially, the class included all U.S. citizens and residents who had suffered or died from medical conditions caused by nicotine addiction, together with their survivors. The Third District Court affirmed class certification, but restricted the class to Florida citizens and residents. Under this modification, the class would comprise up to 500,000 Floridians. In effect, the case was permitted to go to trial and further attempts to decertify the class would be handled on appeal, if necessary. The plaintiffs sought over $200 billion in compensatory and punitive damages.

The plan devised by the trial judge entailed three phases. In Phase I, the plaintiff would have to prove that the tobacco industry caused injuries to the class by manipulating the nicotine level in its cigarettes and that the industry misled the public about the addictive nature of nicotine. The jury would also have to determine if the actions of the tobacco industry allowed for punitive damages and, if so, how they would be calculated. In Phase II, the representative class members would have to prove actual damages, and the jury would assess compensatory damages. Finally, Phase III of the trial would consist of individual trials for the other class members to determine whether they were entitled to compensatory damages.

Except for the all-important procedural matters, the verdict was virtually a foregone conclusion. One week after Engle initiated the class action, a box of internal documents of the Brown and Williamson Tobacco Corporation was delivered to a professor at the University of California, San Francisco. The documents provided conclusive evidence of 30 years of industry-wide deceit. The industry had known since the 1960s that cigarette smoking was directly correlated with cancer and that nicotine was an addictive drug. The most damning evidence was that the tobacco companies' ads targeted adolescents and that they routinely manipulated nicotine levels with the clear purpose of creating addictions. Efforts to suppress the evidence failed.

After nine months of trial, the jury returned its verdict for Phase I on July 7, 1999. The jury found the tobacco companies to have engaged in a conspiracy of false statements and suppression of information about the health effects and addictive nature of smoking. The industry's products were found to be defective, unreasonably dangerous, and not reasonably fit for the use intended. Accordingly, the tobacco industry not only failed to exercise the reasonable degree of care, but also had engaged in extreme and outrageous conduct with the intent to inflict severe emotional distress. The outrageous conduct opened up the industry to punitive damages.

After months of procedural wrangling, the jury was permitted to assess punitive damages in one lump sum and to assess compensatory damages on the basis of three "representative" plaintiffs. This procedure avoided the arduous task of evaluating damages on a case-by-case basis. On April 7, 2000, the jury found that smoking was the legal cause of the three representative class members' illnesses. The jury assessed $2,850,000 in compensatory damages to representative class member Mary Farnan; $5,831,000 in compensatory damages to Frank Amodeo; and a total of $4,023,000 in compensatory damages for the Della Vecchia family. The next step for the trial court was to proceed to the controversial assessment of punitive damages for the entire class. The trial on the assessment of punitive damages began on May 22, 2000. It took less than five hours for the jury to return an award of $144.8 billion.

For nearly three years, this outcome was a major victory against the cigarette industry. However, in May 2003, the Florida court of appeals reversed and remanded with instructions to decertify the class. The primary reason lay in the apparent inconsistency of assessing the punitive damages before determining liability for compensatory damages to individual members of the class. Although the plaintiffs contended that all class members were affected in the same way by the industry's conspiratorial behavior, the court refused to buy this argument:

> The degree of fault the jury attributed to each defendant varied significantly among each of the three plaintiffs. Thus it is apparent that evaluation of each class members' comparative fault will require experts on both sides to consider issues unique to each smoker, such as influences from friends and family members, exposure to information and/or propaganda regarding smoking, addiction issues, and actual knowledge of an injury or claim. It is impossible to determine such facts without mandating an individual inquiry into the specifics of each plaintiff class member's circumstances.[19]

With reference to racial pandering, jury nullification, and runaway jury, the court also set aside the punitive damage award as excessive. The judges expressed concern that the award would bankrupt the industry and preclude recovery of damages by other plaintiffs in the future. For example, the jury imposed punitive damages upon the Liggett Group in excess of 23 times its net worth, despite having allocated zero fault to Liggett on the nonpunitive counts.

On June 20, 1997, the tobacco industry and the states' attorneys general adopted a "global settlement," wherein the industry agreed to pay \$368.5 billion over a period of 25 years. As part of the settlement, the companies accepted expanded warnings on cigarette packages, consented to regulation by the FDA, and agreed to furnish all industry documents relating to cigarette research. In return, the industry obtained some immunity from future litigation, particularly with regard to punitive damages and class actions.

Economic Analysis

1. Without the conspiratorial evidence, it is not an easy matter to rationalize holding cigarette manufacturers liable for the health hazards of smoking. By modern standards, particularly those applied to asbestos poisoning and environmental contamination, the defense of unforeseeability would surely fail. However, that defense was compelling by 1950s legal standards and social beliefs. The economic model portrays a competitive industry providing a product that satisfies the wants and needs of consumers.

2. Producing a cigarette and offering it for sale does not cause cancer. Smoking upwards of two packs per day for 30 years causes a high probability of not only lung cancer, but also heart disease and a host of other deadly maladies. Had the industry been forthright with regard to additives, addictive properties, and health information, the assumption of risk defense would be virtually airtight—at least on economic grounds. The *Cipollone* case, briefly mentioned above, is representative. The New Jersey jury attributed 80% of Mrs. Cipollone's injuries to her voluntary and unreasonable encounter with the known danger of smoking cigarettes. The 20% attributed to the Liggett group was for failure to warn (prior to 1966) the consuming public about the health hazards of smoking.

3. Printed warnings mandated by law preempted liability for failure to warn of generic health hazards. However, those warnings did not relate to the addictive properties

of nicotine. In manipulating the nicotine content of their cigarettes, the industry became vulnerable for liability on two planes: the duty to inform and the sale of a defective product. The legitimate purpose of selling cigarettes was to provide "smoking pleasure," satisfying an individual's craving or desire. The "defect" lay in augmenting the craving—often to the point where gratifying an artificial need replaces the simple pleasures of smoking. By modern standards, the defective product triggers strict liability.

4. The suppression of information, particularly about augmenting the addictive properties of an already addictive substance, along with the targeting of adolescents, substantially compromises the defense of contributory negligence. In spite of the industry's incredible win-loss percentage, the prospect of never-ending litigation against individual and class actions evidently took its toll. Eventually, the industry would have to begin paying tort damages or, at the very least, the expected costs of avoiding and postponing payment would begin to outweigh the costs of a global settlement. For these reasons, this case is as much about public policy as it is about product liability.

5. Public policy objectives derive mainly from externality arguments, although purists would object to attaching the label of externality to costs incurred by smokers themselves. The pure externalities apply to victims of secondary smoke and to those who incur emotional distress from the loss of loved ones. Strictly speaking, the financial burden absorbed by taxpayers through social health care services does not fit the classic mold. Smokers impose costs upon themselves, the government passes the costs on to taxpayers, and then must pass them back to smokers or manufacturers.

6. From a pragmatic standpoint, this formula makes a lot of economic sense. The industry has intentionally exacerbated the adverse health effects of smoking. *Ex ante*, the risks are public, and the public is paying the tab through higher taxes to support Medicare. Administering a comprehensive program through state and federal agencies rates to be less costly than the two prominent alternatives of lawsuits and some form of Pigouvian taxation. The failure of tort law to solve the problem is evident, as billions of dollars of litigation costs have generated virtually no compensatory damages from the industry. Similarly, the taxation of cigarettes has degenerated into a noncooperative game, where state governments compete against one another for revenues and ultimately encourage tax evasion and wreak financial harm upon convenience stores.

Endnotes

CHAPTER 1

1. Milton Friedman and Leonard Savage, "The Expected Utility Hypothesis and the Measurability of Utility," 60 *Journal of Political Economy* (1952), pp. 465–467.
2. Leon Walras, *Elements of Pure Economics*, translated by William Jaffe (1954), p. 5.
3. A. C. Pigou, *The Economics of Welfare*, MacMillan, 3rd ed. (1932), Part II.
4. Ronald H. Coase, "The Nature of the Firm," NS 4 *Economica* (1937).
5. ________ "The Problem of Social Cost," 3 *Journal of Law and Economics* 1 (1960), pp. 29–39.
6. Jules E. Dupuit, "On the Measurement of the Utility of Public Works," 1844, *Annales des ponts et chaussées*. (trans., 1952, *IEP*).

CHAPTER 2

1. 1868 U.S. Dist. LEXIS, 157.
2. 8 F. 159 (1881), at p. 162.
3. 1872 U.S. Dist. LEXIS, 69.
4. 410 Mich. 616 (1981), at 633.
5. *Shizas v. Detroit*, 333 Mich. 44 (1952).
6. 410 Mich. 616 (1981), at 629.
7. Ibid., at 644.
8. 444 U.S. 51 (1979), at 52.
9. Ibid., at 58.
10. *U.S. v. Kornwolf*, 276 F.3d 1014 (2002).
11. *Mahon v. Pennsylvania Coal*, 274 Pa. 489 (1922), at 496.
12. *Penman v. Jones*, 256 Pa. St. 416 (1917).
13. 274 Pa. 489 (1922), at 507.
14. Ibid., at 510.
15. 260 U.S. 393 (1922), at 413.
16. Ibid., at 415.
17. Ibid., at 413.
18. Ibid., at 414.

CHAPTER 3

1. *Eubank v. City of Richmond*, 226 U.S. 137 (1912).
2. *Ambler v. Euclid*, 297 F. 307 (1924), at 312.
3. 272 U.S. 365 (1926), at 312.
4. Ibid., at 312–3.
5. Ibid., at 313.
6. Ibid., at 311.
7. William A. Fischel, *Regulatory Takings*, Harvard (1995), pp. 52–55.
8. 447 U.S. 255 (1980), at 261.
9. Ibid., at 262.
10. Fischel, op. cit.
11. 505 U.S. 1003, at 1025.
12. Ibid.
13. Ibid., at 1031.
14. 57 Cal. App. 3d 613 (1976).
15. 505 U.S. 1003, at 1036.
16. Ibid., at 1069.
17. Ibid., at 1070.
18. op. cit., p. 61.
19. 480 U.S. 470 (1987), at 485.
20. Ibid., at 507.

21. Ibid., at 498.
22. Ibid., at 502.
23. Ibid., at 487.
24. *Plymouth Coal v. Pennsylvania*, 232 U.S. 531 (1914).

CHAPTER 4

1. *Mugler v. Kansas*, 123 U.S. 623 (1887).
2. A. C. Pigou, *The Economics of Welfare*, MacMillan, 3rd ed. (1932), 192 ff.
3. *Ex Parte Hadacheck*, 165 California 416 (1913).
4. 239 U.S. 394 (1915), at 406.
5. 108 Ariz. 178 (1972), at 182.
6. Ibid., at 185.
7. Ibid.
8. *Miller v. State Entomologist*, 146 Va. 175 (1926), at 191.
9. 276 U.S. 272 (1928), at 279.
10. 146 Va. 175 (1926), at 179.
11. Warren J. Samuels, "Interrelations Between Legal and Economic Processes," 14 *Journal of Law and Economics*, 435 (1971); James M. Buchanan, "Politics, Property, and the Law; an Alternative Interpretation of Miller et al. v. Schoene," 15 *Journal of Law and Economics*, 439 (1972); Richard Epstein, *Takings: Private Property and the Power of Eminent Domain*, Harvard, 1985.
12. 55 Misc. 2d 1023 (1967), at 1025.
13. Ibid.
14. 26 N.Y. 2d 219 (1970), at 223.

CHAPTER 5

1. 444 U.S. 164 (1979) at 176. See also Vaughn v. Vermilion, 444 U.S. 206 (1979) for a very similar case.
2. Ibid., at 179.
3. Ibid., at 186.
4. 328 U.S. 256 (1946), at 261.
5. Ibid., at 262.
6. Ibid., at 265.
7. Ibid., at 270.
8. 483 U.S. 825 (1987).
9. 512 U.S. 687 (1994), at 386.
10. Ibid., at 384.
11. Ibid., at 405.
12. Ibid., at 400.
13. Ibid., at 403.
14. Lorraine B. Diehl, *The Late, Great Pennsylvania Station*, American Heritage Press, 1985.
15. 438 U.S. 104 (1978), at 117–118.
16. Ibid., at 136.
17. Ibid., at 137.
18. Ibid., at 140.

CHAPTER 6

1. 248 U.S. 215 (1918).
2. 35 F.2d 279 (1929), at 279.
3. Ibid., at 281.
4. 849 F.2d 460 (1988), at 463.
5. 1987 U.S. Dist. LEXIS 14367, 8.
6. 849 F.2d 460 (1988), at 462.
7. *Sinatra v. Goodyear Tire & Rubber Co.*, 435 F.2d 711 (1971).
8. *Lahr v. Adell Chemical Co.*, 300 F.2d 256 (1962).
9. *Motschenbacher v. R. J. Reynolds Tobacco Co.*, 498 F.2d 821 (9th Cir. 1974).
10. 849 F.2d 460 (1988), at 463.
11. Ibid.
12. 51 Cal. 3d 120 (1990), at 130.
13. Ibid., at 140–141.
14. 464 U.S. 417 (1984).
15. 239 F.3d 1004 (2002), at 1021.
16. Ibid., at 1021–2.
17. 284 F.3d 1091 (2002), at 1097.

CHAPTER 7

1. For a relatively nontechnical discussion of this and a wide range of game theoretic problems, see Avinash Dixit and Barry Nalebuff, *Thinking Strategically*, Norton

(1991). For a more technical approach aimed at legal problems, see Douglas Baird, Robert Gertner, and Randal Picker, *Game Theory and the Law*, Harvard (1994).

2. *Sherwood v. Walker*, 66 Mich. 568 (1887).
3. 210 Md. 352 (1956), at 361.
4. 72 N.Y.S. 2d 672 (1993), at 674.
5. Ibid., at 675.
6. Ibid.
7. 479 N.W.2d 387 (1992), at 388.
8. Ibid., at 391.
9. 350 F. 2d 445 (1965), at 448.
10. Ibid., at 449.
11. Ibid.

CHAPTER 8

1. *Stees v. Leonard*, 20 Minn. 494 (1874).
2. 678 So. 2d 378 (1996), at 380.
3. *Handicapped Children's Education Board v. Lukaszewski*, 112 Wis. 2d 197 (1983).
4. 678 So. 2d 378 (1996), at 380.
5. Ibid.
6. Richard A. Posner, *Economic Analysis of Law*, Aspen, 5th ed. (1988), p. 118.
7. *Karl Wendt Farm Equipment v. International Harvester*, 931 F.2d 1112 (1991).
8. See www.walgreens.com/about/history/hist4.jhtml.
9. 966 F.2d 273 (1992), at 275.
10. Ibid., at 276.
11. Ibid.
12. Ibid., at 277.
13. 63 F. 2d 312 (1956), at 315.
14. Ibid., at 319.
15. Ibid., at 320.
16. *Tsakiroglou & Co. Ltd. v. Noblee Thorl*, 2 QB 348 (1960).
17. *Ocean Tramp Tankers Corp. v. V/O Sovfracht*, 2 QB 226 (1964).
18. 15 F. Supp. 429 (1975), at 437.
19. Ibid.
20. Ibid., at 439.
21. 861 P.2d 531 (1993), at 536.
22. Ibid., at 544.
23. Ibid., at 548.
24. Ibid.

CHAPTER 9

1. 159 Eng. Rep. 145 (1854).
2. James B. Parsons, "A Geographer Looks at the San Joaquin Valley," http://geography.berkeley.edu/ProjectsResources/Publications/Parsons_SauerLect.html
3. 162 Cal. App. 3d 905 (1984), at 909.
4. Ibid., at 915.
5. *Sun-Maid Raisin Growers v. Victor Packing Company*, 146 Cal. App. 3d 787 (1983).
6. 251 Kan. 728 (1992), at 733.
7. 3 Cal. 3d 176 (1970), at 181.
8. Ibid., at 187.
9. Judith Maute, "Peevyhouse v. Garland Coal & Mining Co. Revisited: the Ballad of Willie and Lucille," 89 *Northwestern University Law Review* 1341 (1994).
10. *Groves v. John Wunder Co.*, 205 Minn. 163 (1939).
11. 382 P. 2d 109 (1962), at 112.
12. Ibid., at 114.
13. Ibid., at 115.
14. Ian Ayres and Robert Gertner, "Filling Gaps in Incomplete Contracts: An Economic Theory of Default Rules," 99 *Yale Law Journal* 87 (1989).
15. See Maute, op. cit., Sec. II.D.

CHAPTER 10

1. 159 F. 2d 169 (1947).
2. Ibid., at 172.
3. Ibid., at 173.
4. Ibid., at 173–174.
5. 56 N.Y.S. 2d 98 (1982), at 105.
6. Ibid., at 106.
7. Ibid., at 108.

8. 585 P. 2d 1206 (1978), at 1211.
9. Ibid.
10. Ibid., at 1212.
11. 425 N.E.2d 125 (1981).
12. 55 N.Y. 2d 571 (1982).
13. 199 P.2d 1 (1948).
14. 73 N.Y.2d 487 (1989), at 507.
15. Ibid.
16. Ibid., at 513.
17. Ibid.

CHAPTER 11

1. Richard A. Epstein, "A Theory of Strict Liability," 2 *Journal of Legal Studies* 1 (1973).
2. 232 U.S. 340 (1914), at 348.
3. Ibid., at 354.
4. Arthur C. Pigou, Wealth and Welfare, Macmillan (1912). See also The Economics of Welfare, Macmillan, 3rd ed. (1932), p. 134.
5. Ronald H. Coase , "The Problem of Social Cost," 3 *Journal of Law and Economics* 1 (1960), pp. 29–39.
6. Richard A. Posner and William M. Landes, *The Economic Structure of Tort Law*, Harvard (1987), 40.
7. http://www.geog.ucsb.edu/~jeff/sb_69oilspill/69oilspill_articles2.html
8. 23 N.J. Misc. 89, 41 A.2d 267 (1945).
9. *Fort Worth & Rio Grande Railway Company v. Hancock*, 286 S.W. 335 (1926).
10. 501 F.2d 558 (1974), at 570.
11. 51 P.2d 334 (1976), at 431.
12. Ibid., at 438.
13. Ibid., at 440.
14. Ibid., at 441.
15. Ibid., at 354.
16. Ibid., at 358.
17. 771 F.2d 1093 (1985), at 1100.
18. Ibid.
19. Ibid., at 1103.
20. Ibid., at 1099.
21. A formal setup and analysis of the underlying game may be found in Baird, Gertner, and Picker, *Game Theory and the Law*, Harvard (1994), pp. 68–87.

CHAPTER 12

1. 217 N.Y. 382 (1916), at 394.
2. 10 Meeson & Welsby, 109 (1854).
3. 217 N.Y. 382 (1916), at 397.
4. 6 N.Y. 397 (1909).
5. 192 N.Y. 156 (1908).
6. 89 N.Y. 470 (1882).
7. 217 N.Y. 382 (1916), at 391.
8. Ibid.
9. Ibid., at 400.
10. 24 Cal. 2d. 453 (1944), at 461.
11. Ibid., at 462.
12. 332 A.2d 11 (1975), at 543–544.
13. Ibid., at 545.
14. Ibid., at 564.
15. *Whitehurst v. Revlon*, 307 F. Supp. 918 (1969).
16. *Cippollone v. Liggett Group,* 693 F. Supp. 208 (1988).
17. 160 F.R.D. 544 (1995).
18. 641 So. 2d 888 (1994).
19. 853 So. 2d 434 (2002), at 447.

Index